About the author

Tim Kelsall is an associate of the Africa, Power and Politics Programme (www.institutions-africa.org) and is a resource person for the Partnership for African Social and Governance Research (www.pasgr.org). He holds a PhD from the University of London (SOAS), has taught politics at the Universities of Oxford and Newcastle, and is a former editor of the journal *African Affairs*. He is the author of *Contentious Politics, Local Governance, and the Self: A Tanzanian case study* (Nordic African Institute, Uppsala, 2005), and *Culture under Cross-Examination: International Justice and the Special Court for Sierra Leone* (Cambridge University Press, 2009) as well as articles published in journals including *Africa*, *Commonwealth and Comparative Politics*, *Human Rights Quarterly*, the *Review of International Studies* and *Development Policy Review*. He lives in Phnom Penh.

BUSINESS, POLITICS, AND THE STATE IN AFRICA
CHALLENGING THE ORTHODOXIES ON GROWTH AND TRANSFORMATION

Tim Kelsall

with *David Booth, Diana Cammack, Brian Cooksey, Mesfin Gebremichael, Fred Golooba-Mutebi, Sarah Vaughan*

Zed Books
LONDON | NEW YORK

Business, Politics and the State in Africa: Challenging the Orthodoxies on Growth and Transformation was first published in 2013 by Zed Books Ltd, 7 Cynthia Street, London N1 9JF, UK and Room 400, 175 Fifth Avenue, New York, NY 10010, USA

www.zedbooks.co.uk

FSC
www.fsc.org
MIX
Paper from
responsible sources
FSC® C013604

Set in Monotype Plantin and FFKievit by Ewan Smith, London
Index: ed.emery@thefreeuniversity.net
Cover design: www.roguefour.co.uk
Cover photo © Sven Torfinn/Panos
Printed and bound by CPI Group (UK) Ltd, Croydon CR0 4YY

Distributed in the USA exclusively by Palgrave Macmillan, a division of St Martin's Press, LLC, 175 Fifth Avenue, New York, NY 10010, USA

A catalogue record for this book is available from the British Library
Library of Congress Cataloging in Publication Data available

ISBN 978 1 78032 331 2 hb
ISBN 978 1 78032 421 0 pb

CONTENTS

ABBREVIATIONS

APPP	Africa, Power and Politics Programme
CCM	Chama cha Mapinduzi (Tanzania)
CPP	Convention People's Party (Ghana)
DfID	Department for International Development (UK)
EFFORT	Endowment Fund for the Rehabilitation of Tigray
EHPEA	Ethiopian Horticulture Producers Export Association
EPRDF	Ethiopian Peoples' Revolutionary Democratic Front
EPZA	Export Processing Zones Authority (Tanzania)
FDI	foreign direct investment
GDP	gross domestic product
GEMA	Gikuyu, Embu and Meru Association (Kenya)
HIPC	Highly Indebted Poor Country
IMF	International Monetary Fund
IPTL	Independent Power Tanzania Ltd
ISI	import substitution industrialization
KADU	Kenya African Democratic Union
KANU	Kenya African National Union
KAU	Kikuyu Central Association (Kenya)
KIA	Kilimanjaro International Airport
KTDA	Kenya Tea Development Agency
MCP	Malawi Congress Party
MDAs	ministries, departments, and agencies
MDGs	Millennium Development Goals
MKUKUTA	National Strategy for Growth and Poverty Reduction (Tanzania)
MoTI	Ministry of Trade and Industry (Ghana)
NDC	National Democratic Congress (Ghana)/National Development Corporation (Tanzania)
NGO	non-governmental organization
NPP	New Patriotic Party (Ghana)
ODA	Overseas Development Agency
OECD	Organisation for Economic Co-operation and Development
PDCI	Parti démocratique de Côte d'Ivoire

PFMRP	Public Financial Management Reform Programme (Tanzania)
PNDC	Provisional National Defence Council (Ghana)
PP	Progress Party (Ghana)
PPP	public–private partnership
PSCAP	Public Sector Capacity Building Programme (Ethiopia)
PSDS	Private Sector Development Strategy (Ghana)
PSI	President's Special Initiative (Ghana)
R&D	research and development
RDB	Rwanda Development Board
RHODA	Rwanda Horticulture Development Authority
RIG	Rwanda Investment Group
RPA	Rwandan Patriotic Army
RPF	Rwandan Patriotic Front
SAA	Syndicat agricole africaine (Côte d'Ivoire)
SOE	state-owned enterprise
TAHA	Tanzania Horticultural Association
TANU	Tanganyika African National Union
TCME	Tanzanian Chamber of Minerals and Energy
TIC	Tanzania Investment Center
TICTS	Tanzania International Container Terminal Services
TPLF	Tigrayan People's Liberation Front
TRA	Tanzania Revenue Authority
UDF	United Democratic Front (Malawi)
UGCC	United Gold Coast Convention
UMNO	United Malays National Organization
VAT	value-added tax

ACKNOWLEDGEMENTS

This book has grown out of a research stream on business and politics in Africa, led by Tim Kelsall and conducted under the auspices of the Africa, Power and Politics Programme (APPP), an international consortium funded by the UK's Department for International Development and Irish Aid, led by the Overseas Development Institute in London, with partner organizations in France, the USA, Ghana, Uganda, and Niger. The APPP was inspired by the idea that the results of the good governance agenda in Africa have been disappointing, and that it might be possible to find ways of doing development in Africa that go more 'with the grain' of existing ways of doing things, or that are better anchored in local socio-political realities. By making clear the conditions under which neo-patrimonial governance is compatible with strong economic performance, we believe the contents of this book help validate that idea, at the same time as providing important qualifications to it.

The book is a collaborative effort. The Introduction and Chapter 1 are mainly the work of Tim Kelsall, with significant contributions from David Booth, Brian Cooksey, and Diana Cammack. Chapters 2 and 4 are mainly the work of Brian Cooksey, and Sarah Vaughan and Mesfin Gebremichael, respectively, with significant contributions from Tim Kelsall. Chapter 3 is mainly the work of Tim Kelsall, and Chapter 5 of David Booth and Fred Golooba-Mutebi. Tim Kelsall wrote the Conclusion, although all of the authors contributed in effect.

It is not possible to thank all of the people who have helped in the research for this book, but deserving of special mention for either facilitating research or providing advice and encouragement on the project in general are Rhoda Acheampong, Victor Brobbey, Patrick Chabal, Richard Crook, Martin Dawson, Hazel Gray, Emmanuel Gyimah-Boadi, Jane Harrigan, Adrian Leftwich, Sue Martin, Lemayon Melyoki, Sonia Sezille, Ole Therkilsden, Richard Thomas, and Lindsay Whitfield. The usual caveats apply.

Please note also that the views expressed in this publication are those of the authors, and should not be attributed to DfID, Irish Aid, or any of the APPP's member organizations.

Tim Kelsall, David Booth, Diana Cammack, Brian Cooksey, Mesfin Gebremichael, Fred Golooba-Mutebi, Sarah Vaughan

INTRODUCTION: GROWTH, GOVERNANCE, AND ECONOMIC TRANSFORMATION IN AFRICA

In recent years Africa[1] appears to have turned a corner economically. After decades of being the world's slowest-growing region, it is now outpacing Latin America, eastern Europe, and the Middle East, posting annual growth rates of over 5 percent (Economist 2011). The IMF forecasts that African countries will occupy seven of the world's top ten growth spots over the next five years (ibid.), and a recent report by global management consultants McKinsey spoke of African 'lions' to rival Asia's celebrated 'tiger' economies (McKinsey Global Institute 2010). The slew of positive reports about Africa's economic progress has generated considerable optimism, and led to claims that conventional good governance and structural adjustment policies are finally bearing fruit.

A growing number of heterodox thinkers, however, have begun to question this interpretation. They point to the dependence of African growth on global commodity prices, investment in extractive sectors, and foreign aid, querying whether it can be sustained. African economies have yet to witness a structural transformation of the kind East Asia experienced in the latter half of the twentieth century, nor have they moved into producing higher-value commodities for export (United Nations Economic Commission for Africa 2011). In order to do so, heterodox thinkers argue, they will need to adopt more ambitious industrial policies.

Industrial policy, however, is currently out of favor in most of Africa. The explanation can be found in the conventional wisdom on African governance. In this view Africa's regimes are 'neo-patrimonial', their legitimacy tied to the distribution of economic favors to clients or cronies, meaning that industrial policies will inevitably fall prey to unproductive 'rent-seeking'. With 'government failure' such a chronic problem, economic development is best left to market forces. Unsurprisingly, heterodox thinkers disagree, arguing that market failure is a more serious problem than government failure; but in doing so they tend to understate the magnitude of governance problems in Africa.

This book is written as an intervention in this debate. For reasons that will become clear, we side with the heterodox position that Africa needs more ambitious industrial policies if it is to develop, but we accept the conventional wisdom that in many African states neo-patrimonialism is a problem. We do not think it is an insurmountable problem, however, and our main contribution is to stipulate the conditions under which neo-patrimonial governance, or else something rather different to liberal 'good governance', can be combined with sound industrial policies and strong developmental performance. We do this by revisiting the history of post-independence economic performance in a selection of Asian and African countries, and then we extend our analysis through case studies of four contemporary African states. By the end of the book, we will have a better idea of the kinds of institutional arrangements that permitted some African regimes to pursue successful industrial policies in the past, together with a deeper understanding of the relationship between governance and economic performance in Africa today.

The debate about African growth

Between 1960 and 2000, Africa was the slowest-growing region in the world. Many African countries grew respectably in the 1960s and early 1970s, but their growth was derailed after 1974, turned negative in the 1980s, and rebounded only weakly in the 1990s (Rodrik 2003: Fig. 1). Eighteen African countries recorded negative annual real per capita growth rates between 1973 and 2000, sixteen countries recorded growth rates of less than 1 percent, and six countries had growth of between 1 and 2 percent per annum. The pattern of growth was also highly volatile, with only the tiny countries of Botswana, Equatorial Guinea, and Cape Verde experiencing growth that was sustainable and steady (United Nations Economic Commission for Africa 2011: 78–80). The impact on livelihoods was severe. At the turn of the millennium social services were in chronic disrepair, nearly half the African population fell below a $1.50 a day poverty line (Ndulu and O'Connell n.d.: 2),[2] and large parts of the continent were vulnerable to lethal epidemics, famine, and war. In 2000, the *Economist* magazine ran a cover story labeling Africa 'The hopeless continent' (Economist 2000).

The next decade saw a remarkable change of fortunes. Several economies, and especially oil exporters like Angola and Equatorial

Guinea, began recording double-digit growth rates. Other, non-oil exporters like Tanzania, Uganda, Rwanda, Ethiopia, and Malawi began to grow at 6 percent a year or more. The region overall averaged per capita growth of 2.7 percent between 2000 and 2008 (World Bank 2009a).[3] In this context commentators began to point to some of the advantages of investing in Africa: a collective GDP of $1.6 trillion, combined consumer spending of $860 billion, 316 million new mobile phone subscribers, 60 percent of the world's uncultivated arable land, fifty-two cities with a population of more than a million, a bigger middle class than India, and twenty companies with a revenue of more than $3 billion (McKinsey Global Institute 2010). Others talked not just of 'lion' but of 'cheetah' economies (Radelet 2010).

This economic revival has provided support for the idea that the conventional donor approach on the continent is working. Referred to throughout this book as the 'neoliberal orthodoxy', 'conventional wisdom', or 'standard policy advice', that approach rests on the idea that African governments should limit themselves to providing macroeconomic stability, property rights security, light-touch regulation and investment facilitation, and a level playing field for economic competition (World Bank 2004). Donors have been pushing this advice for more than two decades, and there is now a broad unanimity in African governments about the importance, for example, of sound macroeconomic management. In most states, the budget deficits that fueled inflation, eroded competitiveness, and led to unmanageable debt are a thing of the past. Inflation averaged 22 percent in African economies in the 1990s, but in the 2000s this fell to 8 percent. Budget deficits shrank from 4.6 percent of GDP to 1.8 percent (McKinsey Global Institute 2010: 12).[4]

Many African countries have also taken measures to make investment easier by improving regulatory frameworks. Almost all African countries now have investment promotion centers that are supposed to cut through bureaucratic red tape by offering a one-stop shop for investors. Most have also taken significant steps to liberalize internal and external trade, and to privatize large swathes of previously moribund, state-owned industry. Nigeria, to give just one example, privatized more than 116 state-owned enterprises between 1999 and 2006 (ibid.: 12). Many countries have also made reforms in the areas of credit regulation (84 percent), labor market regulation (82 percent), business regulation (64 percent), and trade policy (50 percent) (ibid.: 13).

The World Bank's *Doing Business* annual reports and league table, which use business interviews to rank countries on criteria related to the ease of doing business, capture this progress. They are based on the belief that: 'Where business regulation is burdensome and competition limited, success depends more on whom you know than on what you can do. But where regulations are relatively easy to comply with and accessible to all who need to use them, anyone with talent and a good idea should be able to start and grow a business in the formal sector' (World Bank and International Finance Corporation 2011: 1). The reports provide a powerful index of the nature of the 'business climate' in both developed and developing countries, and thus an incentive to governments to undertake 'best-practice' economic reforms. Over the past five years, thirty-nine African countries have made progress up the table (Mitchell 2011), a result in part of donor-driven private sector development programs.

Not everyone is impressed by these statistics, however. Despite manifest progress in African growth figures over the past decade, an increasingly influential group of heterodox political economists argue that the changes are superficial and liable to be short lived. A key reason is the role of international commodity prices in driving African economic recovery. Oil and gas have been at the forefront of Africa's current growth spurt (Southall 2009: 16), with the price of oil rising from $20 a barrel in 1999 to $145 in 2008 (McKinsey Global Institute 2010: 2). Other commodities have also benefited: the price of coffee tripled between 2000 and 2010, and cocoa and cotton have more than doubled (World Bank 2011b: 8). These rises have been fueled primarily by increased market demand in other developing countries, especially in Asia. Between 1995 and 2008 China, for example, increased its share of African oil exports from 1 percent to 13 percent (McKinsey Global Institute 2010: 45), and trade between China and Africa overall leapt from less than $10 billion a year in 2000 to over $50 billion by the end of 2006 (Alden 2007: 8).

Emerging economies in Asia and Latin America have also been at the forefront of foreign direct investment (FDI) in Africa, supplementing increased investment from Africa's traditional trading partners. Heterodox economists point out, however, that much of this investment has been focused in 'capital-intensive extractive sectors that have few forward and backward linkages with the rest of the economy' (United Nations Economic Commission for Africa 2011: 3). Over the period 2002–07, for example, the resources sector expanded by 24 percent, twice the rate of agriculture and more than two and a half times that of manufacturing (McKinsey Global Institute 2010: 2). In fact, manufacturing growth was near the bottom of twelve growth sectors, with only public administration growing more slowly (ibid.: 2). These factors find reflection in the balance of Africa's external trade. Sixteen countries still rely heavily on just a single commodity, and the share of manufactures in African exports has barely increased, rising from 30 percent to just 33 percent in fifteen years (World Bank 2011b: 14). Over the past thirty years, the structure of African economies has remained virtually unchanged. South Africa and Mauritius aside, no country has an internationally competitive manufacturing sector, or an internationally competitive services sector (Amoako 2011: 24).[5] Fundamentally, Africa remains an exporter of raw materials and an importer of consumer and capital goods (Southall 2009: 27). To make matters worse, although FDI has been growing, it is still the lowest of any region, and the rate of private investment generally is about half that of Asia's (World Bank 2011a: 4).

Partly as a result, improved economic performance has not translated into commensurate reductions in unemployment and poverty, nor significant progress toward the Millennium Development Goals (MDGs). In the words of the United Nations Economic Commission for Africa, 'The continent is experiencing a jobless recovery' (United Nations Economic Commission for Africa 2011: 3; see also World Bank 2011a: 4). According to one of Africa's most distinguished economists, Africa needs to grow at about 7 percent a year for the next twenty or thirty years to make a serious dent in poverty, but 'growth induced by commodity price increases, static efficiency gains from better allocation of resources through economic liberalization, new discoveries of natural resources, or increases in foreign financial assistance – is simply not sustainable' (Amoako 2011: 24). Current policies, which focus on strengthening macroeconomic management, reducing official corruption, and providing a friendly business environment, have their uses, but according to Amoako, what Africa really needs is a structural transformation. Governments must work more proactively with the private sector to remove market failures and structural distortions, boost productivity growth, diversify production and exports, upgrade technology in all sectors, and increase global shares of, in particular, high technology exports (ibid.: 27).

The role of industrial policy in development

Heterodox thinkers believe that Africa can only sustain high growth and poverty reduction if it adopts a more ambitious form of industrial policy, sometimes referred to as 'learning, industrial, and technology' policy (LIT). According to Noman and Stiglitz,

> LIT policies focus on learning, especially by infant industries and economies; they focus on externalities and knowledge spillovers; they typically (especially in Asia) consist of promoting exports and the private sector. They apply not only to manufacturing, but also to other sectors, such as agriculture, and to modern services, such as information technology or finance. (Noman and Stiglitz 2011: 24)

The idea is that because growth and wealth rest ultimately on the productivity of labor, successful developers need to move out of low-productivity activities and into higher ones. Typically this begins with a productivity revolution in agriculture, proceeds with an increased role in the economy for industry and in particular manufacturing, and continues with movement into more sophisticated, high-tech or knowledge-intensive areas of production and services (Breisinger and Diao 2008; Whitfield 2011a). Although neoliberal economists have a faith that entrepreneurs in competitive markets will be led down this path as though by an invisible hand, heterodox authors identify a number of reasons why this may not be so.

The first set of reasons concern what are called 'knowledge externalities' or 'knowledge spillovers'. Consider a developing-country entrepreneur with an idea for a new type of investment. To determine its potential profitability, considerable market research may be necessary, and the costs incurred in setting up a new operation significant. However, if the said investment proves to be profitable, the initial investor may experience a flood of competitors, find his profit margins quickly eroded, and not even recoup his initial research costs. It is for these reasons that developing-country entrepreneurs tend to stick to tried and tested sectors, such as transport, haulage, or real estate, instead of moving into new sectors with potentially greater social benefits. In cases like this there is a case for government industrial policy to subsidize initial discovery costs, or to protect an initial investor from undue competition (Rodrik 2003, 2004; Whitfield 2011a).

Another sort of market failure is bound up with coordination or collective action problems. Consider an investor who knows that a horticultural operation in a developing country will be profitable, but only if he has access to freight services, input suppliers, etc. In the absence of these investments he cannot proceed; but in the absence of a horticultural sector, there are unlikely to be any suitable services or suppliers. In a case like this, there is a rationale for government to underwrite simultaneous investments across a sector, perhaps by providing credit guarantees (Rodrik 2004).

A final, and arguably most important, source of market failure is associated with learning costs. Even if there exists a potential comparative advantage in a new economic activity, novel technologies and industrial processes take time to learn and adapt. Entrepreneurs in developing countries will usually struggle to make profits initially, and many will fail. Extending capital to such ventures is therefore a risky business. In a context of perfect information, strong contract enforcement mechanisms, and functioning credit recovery systems, the market should be able to supply credit at an appropriate cost. But these phenomena are invariably absent in developing countries, meaning that private capital is likely to be undersupplied. Here is another example, then, of where subsidized credit, credit guarantees, or limited forms of market protection may be desirable (Khan 2011b: 58–61).

Economic development, in the heterodox view, is a dynamic process. As a country's endowments of physical and human capital evolve, so does its comparative advantage in different industries (Lin 2011b). Governments need to follow this advantage at each stage of their economic development by coordinating industrial policy and supporting the private sector: 'Economic development is a process, it involves the private sector entering new industries, learning new skills, building new infrastructure, establishing new financial systems and enjoying access to capital. But individual companies cannot coordinate these changes – and this is where the state steps in' (Lin 2011a: 16). In particular, 'first movers' who step into 'unknown territory' need special incentives such as tax breaks, co-financing arrangements, and help identifying markets: 'Without first movers there is no dynamic growth' (ibid.: 16). The state also plays a key role in supplying or facilitating the upgrades to 'hard' and 'soft' infrastructure that permit the realization of new comparative advantages (Lin 2011b).[6]

This is demonstrated by the history of today's developed states.

Virtually all successful developers have at one time or another employed industrial policies that have helped first to raise productivity in agriculture, then to increase the share of manufacturing and services in GDP, and then to move into higher-value areas of manufacturing and services (Breisinger and Diao 2008; Noman and Stiglitz 2011; United Nations Economic Commission for Africa 2011; Whitfield 2011a).[7] In fifteenth-century Britain, for example, the government imposed tariffs on unprocessed wool products, with the aim of developing a textiles industry (Whitfield 2011a). Sweden in the eighteenth and nineteenth centuries developed a number of strategic industries such as iron and steel, railways, telegraph and telephone, and hydroelectric power through public–private partnerships. It also provided some protection for heavy industry (Chang 2010). Nineteenth-century France and Germany both used the power of the state to create and protect investments in the period during which they were catching up with Britain (Gerschenkron 1965). Until the early twentieth century, the US state was one of the most protectionist countries in the world, and its government invested heavily in railways, higher education, and research and development (R&D) (Chang 2010). Japan's post-World War II industrial policy, which saw the country transition from light manufactures to heavy industry to information technology, sought to steer the economy into the highest-value areas of the world economy, *and* identified the most efficient methods Japanese firms employed, before propagating them industry-wide (Johnson 1982). South Korea used an even more extreme form of market-defying industrial policy, while Taiwan used both state and party to create strategic industries and to push and prod the private sector into doing the same (Wade 1990). The most recent group of successful developers, Southeast Asian states, poured resources into agricultural R&D and rural development, lifting millions out of poverty in the process (Van Donge et al. 2012).[8]

Rents and economic development

We noted in the introduction to this chapter that industrial policy is currently out of vogue in Africa. To understand this we need to grasp the role played in industrial policy by 'economic rents'. In economic theory, 'rents' are windfall gains or excess incomes that accrue to agents who operate in imperfect markets. They are often, although not always, created by government intervention: for example, when the government awards a monopoly over trade or production of a certain good to a particular business, where it restricts import trade through a licensing or tariff scheme, or when it provides subsidized credit to an entrepreneur, it permits the holders of these privileges to earn rents. In neoclassical theory government intervention and the rents it creates have long been regarded as economically damaging. By granting an infant industry a monopoly over the production of some good, for example, the monopolist will tend to produce a smaller amount at a higher cost than could have been provided by a competitive market. The monopolist's rent is society's loss. In addition, the possibility of earning these lucrative rents stimulates a process of rent-seeking, as agents compete with each other to gain access to them (Khan 2000a; Krueger 1974). Sometimes rent-seeking takes the form of legitimate lobbying activities; but often it takes the form of bribery and corruption. In either case, because rent-seeking activity doesn't actually produce anything, it is socially wasteful. An economy that has a lot of rent-seeking will consequently operate inside its transformation curve, with growth and incomes less than they could have been (Khan 2000a; Krueger 1974).

In the neoliberal interpretation, industrial policies shoulder much of the blame for Africa's dismal economic performance up until the beginning of the last decade. The story is that African governments introduced a range of market distortions into their economies with the aim of promoting industrialization, and that these distortions undermined the economy. For example, granting monopoly licenses to industrial producers led to low production at high cost, and little innovation. Overvaluing exchange rates with a view to importing cheap technology lowered the real price paid to export crop producers, leading them to smuggle their goods or stop producing altogether. Artificially low prices for food, designed to keep down the cost of the urban wage, deterred food production by small farmers. These distortions combined eventually to produce a generalized economic crisis, as exports dried up, industrial inputs could not be imported, and only parallel markets could supply the cities with food (Bates 1981, 1988; World Bank 1981). We will see in the cases of Tanzania and Ghana in Chapters 2 and 3 that there was substantial empirical support for this interpretation (see also Williams 1994).[9]

Another part of the neoliberal analysis is the role of rents in preventing policy reform. The story is that even when it was clear to African governments that industrial policies were failing, they resisted reforms primarily because of the rent streams those policies created. Specifically, large farmers benefited from subsidized inputs, urban workers from cheap food, traders from import licenses, industrialists from an absence of competition, and politicians and bureaucrats from the opportunities for kickbacks furnished by the entire architecture of economic controls. Together, these groups constituted a powerful 'urban coalition' that forestalled the adoption of better economic policies (Bates 1981, 1988; for a critique, see World Bank 1981; Leys 1996).

Consequently, the standard policy advice to African governments today is to avoid trying to promote industrialization through selective interventions in the market, nurturing infant industries or 'picking winners'. Such interventions are said to lead not to the kinds of industries that innovate, expand, and provide good-quality employment, but to the creation of a class of privileged business cronies or clients (World Bank 2004). Instead, African governments are enjoined to reduce opportunities for rent-seeking, first by reducing the scope of their industrial interventions, and secondly by reducing instances of red tape and bureaucratic discretion. The aim is not to promote specific businesses or business sectors, but to make the investment climate easier for business across the board. As Moore and Schmitz argue, standard investment climate advice 'embodies an excessive distrust of governments insofar as they have any direct role in undertaking or shaping economic activity' (Moore and Schmitz 2008: 9). Today, these principles are operationalized all over the continent in private sector development programs, which focus on implementing 'best practice' reforms, and 'light touch' industrial policy such as investment centers and export processing zones.[10]

Heterodox thinkers, however, have a different interpretation of the role of rents in development. Mushtaq Khan (2000a), for example, agrees with neoliberal economists that rents are 'excess incomes' which in perfectly efficient markets should not exist. But in the real world, he argues, and especially in developing economies where markets are far from perfect, rents are pervasive (ibid.: 21). Some rents, as the neoliberals argue, are inefficient and growth retarding; but for other rents, the opposite can be true. For example, the process of development and structural transformation often involves the transfer of assets such as land and mineral resources into the hands of new owners with the ability to use them more productively, a process Marx referred to as 'primitive accumulation'. By conferring new property rights, the state provides an opportunity for the new owners to earn rents. Another example is the subsidies that protect firms from competition while they are learning new techniques and production methods, which, as we saw in the previous section, may be a necessary incentive to induce investments in new areas. A further example is income transfers designed to placate political groups with the potential to disrupt the growth process (ibid.).

The creation of rents like this does not guarantee growth, thinks Khan. Indeed, it is likely to be associated with wasteful and sometimes corrupt 'rent-seeking'. But if rents are well managed, being quickly withdrawn from unproductive users, or from users who can survive without their support, their creation may have net positive effects. As Khan says, 'Managing development may, in fact, require the continuous discrimination of efficient from inefficient rents by policy-makers and analysts' (ibid.: 21–2). History furnishes examples in the shape of developmental states like Japan, South Korea, and Taiwan. According to Robert Wade, in each of these countries 'creating "rents" (above normal market returns) by "distorting" markets through industrial policies' was essential, first to stimulate high levels of investment in activities deemed important for economic transformation, and secondly, 'to sustain a political coalition in support of these policies' (Wade 1990: xviii).

But what about Africa's dismal experience with industrial policy? Generally speaking, heterodox thinkers can admit that there were problems with Africa's previous industrial policies: in most cases they were too ambitious and too undiscriminating, aiming for the creation of industries in which a latent comparative advantage did not exist. To give just one example, Ghana in the 1960s constructed mango-processing factories with a capacity greater than the entire world trade in mangoes (Killick 2010: 255). In addition, the state often lacked the resources to discipline the recipients of industrial policy rents, meaning that there were few incentives to innovation or efficient production (Khan 1996, 2011a; Noman and Stiglitz 2011). However, heterodox thinkers offer a different solution to the standard policy advice. Whereas the standard package focuses on rolling back the state, using private sector development programs to try to create textbook functioning markets, heterodox advice is to build state capability for smarter industrial policy (Khan 2011a).

Neo-patrimonialism and the problem of African governance

Even if one accepts the heterodox argument for smarter industrial policy, there remains a stumbling block that comes in the shape of African politics. For many years now the conventional wisdom, backed by a large volume of political science, is that Africa suffers from a pathological form of governance known as 'neo-patrimonialism'. The term grows out of Max Weber's notion of 'patrimonialism', an 'ideal-type' of traditional rule in which authority is based on ties of *personal* loyalty between a leader and his administrative staff (Weber 1947). In Weber's schema patrimonialism has various subtypes, including 'sultanism' and 'prebendalism', but the details need not concern us here. The important point is that in all its variants, the system is held together by the personal distribution of material resources and perks (many of which are 'rents' in modern economic terminology), distributed and consumed as though they were the private property of the ruler and/or his staff. 'Neo-patrimonialism' refers to a political economy in which this basic authority system is combined with, or exists behind, some formal, impersonal elements of governance, such as a legal system that demarcates the public and private domain, or an administrative code with formal criteria for staff hiring and promotion (Chabal and Daloz 1999; Médard 1982; Zolberg 1966).

No one is quite sure where neo-patrimonialism comes from. Some authors emphasize its links to pre-colonial political cultures, others see it as a transmogrification of the bureaucratic colonial state, others as a rational response to economic scarcity. But whatever the origin, contemporary neo-patrimonialism is said to exhibit a variety of common characteristics, which include: power concentration, often expressed as an extreme form of presidentialism or 'big man' politics; power informalization, in which informal practices are more important than formal rules, and in which power is often exercised clandestinely; a blurring of the boundaries between public and private spheres; and a pre-eminent role for patronage and clientelism in cementing the legitimacy of the political system (Bratton and Van de Walle 1997; Chabal and Daloz 1999; Jackson and Rosberg 1982; Médard 1982; Sandbrook 1985; Van de Walle 2001).

In the standard political science analysis, neo-patrimonialism is almost always bad for economic development. Power concentration is thought to increase the risk of extra-constitutional challenges to power, and consequently the prevalence of plots, coups, purges, insurrections, ethnic strife, and civil wars. The informalization of power is said to encourage arbitrariness and unpredictability, which is at cross-purposes with the calculability nexus required for the development of modern, rational capitalism. The blurring of public and private roles leads to high levels of corruption that deprive the state of resources that might otherwise be spent on public goods like roads, or education. Finally, patronage and clientelism run counter to the creation of autonomous, competent bureaucracies, and to the impartial administration of investor-friendly economic regulations (Bratton and Van de Walle 1997; Callaghy 1988; Chabal and Daloz 1999; Jackson and Rosberg 1982; Médard 1982; Sandbrook 1985; Van de Walle 2001). Because of this, African governments cannot be trusted with industrial policy.

Certainly, there is no shortage of evidence that neo-patrimonialism, or at least its associated phenomena of big-man politics, clientelism, corruption, and rent-seeking, is widespread on the continent. After independence many African leaders overturned democratic constitutions and arrogated an increased number of powers to themselves. They used the state as a source of patronage for their followers, often turning a blind eye to the illegal appropriation of state revenues by their ministers and senior officials, while using the wider civil service as a reservoir of 'jobs for the boys'. In addition, they distributed rent-earning economic assets such as state farms, businesses, or import licenses as benefices to their clients. In some cases – for example, General Mobutu's Zaire, Idi Amin's Uganda, or, more recently, Robert Mugabe's Zimbabwe – the results were disastrous. Even in less extreme examples, such as Zambia or Senegal, economic performance was less than impressive. These trends have persisted even in the face of economic and political liberalization. Privatizations, for example, have often been used as a source of political patronage, while political liberalization has put a premium on the ability to attract large political clienteles via the promise of cash, jobs, or tangible goods such as roads or schools. This often puts established big men, with their long-standing access to state resources, at a considerable advantage (Tangri 1999; Berman 1998; Van de Walle 2007).

Donors are consequently anxious to eradicate or overcome neo-patrimonialism in Africa, and the way they do this is by trying to make African states more like Western states. This is the nub of what is called the 'good governance' agenda. Donors have encouraged civil service reform, multiparty elections, support for parliaments, civil society strengthening, judicial capacity-building, and assistance to watchdog institutions like the media, anti-corruption commissions, and ombudsmen. The aim is to create the kinds of institutions that underpin liberal market economies in the West (Mkandawire 2011; Moore 1993; Williams and Young 1994; World Bank 1992).

Heterodox thinkers, by contrast, tend to regard the entire discourse surrounding neo-patrimonialism and good governance as a red herring. For Adebayo Olukoshi, director of the UN Institute for Economic Development and Planning in Africa, 'neo-patrimonialism' is little more than an ideological prop for structural adjustment policy (Olukoshi 2003) and an analytical dead end (Olukoshi 2011; see also Mustapha 2002). The United Nations Economic Commission for Africa, in an otherwise very useful report, does not even refer to the concept, and appears somewhat naive about the political challenges of building developmental states in Africa (United Nations Economic Commission for Africa 2011). Other critics acknowledge the concept, but suggest that it is being used in a way unfaithful to Weber (Pitcher et al. 2009), or else argue that other modes of governance may be equally or more important (Therkilsden 2005). In a recent example of this viewpoint, Whitfield and Therkilsden claim that:

> neo-patrimonialism cannot explain cases of successful state intervention in the economy (only failures), and it cannot explain variation across countries, or across sectors within the same country. In particular, it cannot explain why industrial policies are formulated in some sectors and not others, and why they are implemented with more or less success. (Whitfield and Therkilsden 2011: 9)

A structuralist perspective comes from Mushtaq Khan. Khan sees neo-patrimonialism – or, to be more precise, the patronage, corruption, and rent-seeking with which it is associated – as a transitional phenomenon related to developing-country governments' weak fiscal capacities. Developing-country governments find it difficult to secure political legitimacy via the provision of universal public goods in the way that developed countries do, because they lack strong revenue streams and sophisticated bureaucracies. This leads them to fall back on informal, clientelistic relationships, frequently using off-budget resources (Khan 2005, 2011a, 2011b). Clientelism and associated phenomena are unlikely to disappear until the economy has grown enough to support bureaucracies that can deliver universal public services, a claim supported by comparative historical analysis, which shows that in almost all cases, good governance has been institutionalized only *after* an economy has reached middle-income status (Khan 2011a, 2011b).[11]

For Khan, developmental success rests less on attempts to create good governance across the board, and more on incremental approaches to enhancing industrial policy capabilities (Khan 2011a). A plausible inference is that states can begin the process of economic transformation even under neo-patrimonial conditions. As we will see in the next chapter, Khan has provided some clues in his analyses of South Korea and Malaysia to show how this might work, but he does not take the analysis very far.

More generally, the issue remains under-theorized in the heterodox literature. Most heterodox thinkers, as noted above, appear to be in denial about the seriousness of governance challenges in Africa, and have little way of discriminating between countries in which industrial policy may be viable and those in which it is presently a lost cause. The current fashion is for promoting 'pockets of efficiency' or 'islands of effectiveness' in African bureaucracies (Crook 2010; Whitfield and Therkilsden 2011: 29–30). But as we shall see when we study Tanzania in Chapter 2, in some countries islands of effectiveness are at risk of being swamped in a neo-patrimonial sea.

Developmental patrimonialism?

Our own view is that even though the neo-patrimonial concept is not without problems, to discard it would be premature. This does not mean we think that neo-patrimonialism explains 'everything', is uniquely African, or is the same everywhere. All it means is that we believe the concept captures important aspects of governance in many African states, namely the combination of more or less concentrated forms of personalized rule with significant levels of informality and high levels of rent-seeking, clientelism and corruption. There are good reasons to think that in many African countries, these phenomena are deeply rooted, and that they will change only slowly. For example, donors have been promoting good governance policies in Africa now for two decades, yet most countries still seem a long way from operating according to liberal-democratic ideals. In 2012 Freedom House adjudged only six out of fifty sub-Saharan African countries to be 'free', with the rest either 'partly free' or 'unfree'. Meanwhile twenty-two out of the bottom fifty countries in Transparency International's 2011 Corruption Perception Index are in sub-Saharan Africa.[12] The *only* country that approached the 'cleanliness' levels of western European and North American countries was Botswana.[13] Given the obstinate persistence of neo-patrimonialism, there is arguably a need to find development solutions that work more with its grain than current good governance policies do. This is not to say that all conventional good governance policies are useless – only that by themselves, they are unlikely to facilitate the economic take-off that Africa needs.

Encouraging evidence that sustained development can be anchored in existing African realities comes from Asia, where several countries have made rapid economic progress in spite of having governance arrangements very far from the good governance ideal, and similar in many ways to those in African states. Further encouragement comes from a reinterpretation of the African record of state-building and development itself. In an important 1995 article, Chris Allen rejected the idea that all African countries had been equally dysfunctional, arguing that the more stable and successful economies had endured by introducing forms of 'centralized bureaucracy', which, while retaining clientelism, were by and large able to prevent competition for rents or spoils from assuming its most damaging form (Allen 1995). Sandbrook (1985) recognized that rulers of exceptional skill, such as Côte d'Ivoire's Félix Houphouët-Boigny, had been able to prevent the personalized state's characteristic downward slide. Richard Crook (1989) went so far as to coin the term 'developmental patrimonialism' in that connection. Even Jackson and Rosberg (1982) recognized that personal rule had brought political stability to large parts of Africa for significant periods of time. All of which is to say that we disagree with the conventional wisdom on the relationship between neo-patrimonialism and economic development. In fact, a major aim of this book is to illuminate the conditions in which neo-patrimonialism does not derail development, and may even assist it.

In the next chapter we pick up these themes through a review of politics, clientelism, industrial policy, and rent-seeking in six Asian and six African states. We argue that key to explaining why some of these states performed better than others was the way in which clientelism and rent-seeking *were organized*. Specifically, almost all of the better-performing states had been able to centralize the management of economic rents and orient it to the long term, a feat they achieved with the help of strong, visionary leaders, constrained democracy, top-down patron–client relations, and confident and competent economic technocracies. We proceed to model these relationships, generating four different types of rent-management regime, which we believe go a long way to explaining differences in economic outcomes in Africa and Asia. Our model is then illustrated in more depth by providing case study narratives of more and less successful periods of development in Kenya, Malawi, and Côte d'Ivoire. We argue that at different points in their history, all have demonstrated that neo-patrimonialism can be compatible with workable industrial policy, economic transformation, and growth. At the same time, they demonstrate some of the limitations of developmental patrimonialism, as well as the problems that occur when rents are not centralized, not oriented to the long term, or both.

In Chapters 2–5 we use this theoretical and historical discussion as a launch pad for four contemporary case studies, encompassing Tanzania, Ghana, Ethiopia, and Rwanda. Our rent-management model helps illuminate the strengths and weaknesses of industrial policy and development in these countries, arguing, with certain caveats, that Ethiopia and Rwanda come closer to the centralized-long-horizon ideal than do Ghana and Tanzania, and are more likely to realize their transformative potential as a result. The book concludes by reflecting on the model and its usefulness for understanding the relationship between politics, rent-seeking, and economic performance in contemporary Africa, touching also on a small number of intriguing issues that lie outside the model's scope.

1 | DEVELOPMENTAL PATRIMONIALISM?

We began our investigation into the circumstances in which neo-patrimonialism may be conducive to economic growth and transformation by picking a sample of six East Asian and six African countries.[1] These twelve states evidenced a considerable diversity of economic performance, necessary, we thought, to provide some comparative leverage over the institutions and processes that matter for development. Some were consistently strong performers, others displayed considerable internal diversity, while others were more or less consistently weak. Malaysia, South Korea, and Botswana, for example, all grew strongly and consistently from before the 1960s until the late 1990s, when growth in the former two briefly dipped before recovering again. Indonesia had a disastrous start to independence, but grew strongly from 1967 to 1997, although growth collapsed thereafter, would not recover for several years, and would never again attain the same levels. Kenya and Côte d'Ivoire also grew strongly in the 1960s and early 1970s, but then growth began to falter. Vietnam and Cambodia both went backwards during long post-colonial wars, but rebounded strongly in the context of peace and economic reforms in the mid-1980s and late 1990s respectively. By contrast, Nigeria, Congo-Zaire, and Sierra Leone have all been more or less consistently disappointing performers, never managing to sustain growth in per capita GDP for more than a few years at a time.[2]

We conducted a review of the literature on politics and development in these countries to get a better understanding of the relationship between types of neo-patrimonialism or clientelism, rent-seeking, and development. Our key finding was that in the successful developers rent management almost always took a centralized form, by which we mean that in each country there was an individual or group at the apex of the state with the ability to control the major rents created and distribute them at will.[3] For example, in the case of South Korea, the political leadership was in a dominant position vis-à-vis business actors, and was able to establish a network of top-down patron–client relations, distributing rents on its own terms – that is, in the interests of realizing long-term development goals (Khan 2000b: 95–8). Similarly in Malaysia, the United Malays National Organization (UMNO), the dominant party in the ruling coalition, was able to effect a centralized redistribution of rents from Chinese businessmen to indigenous Malays, thereby securing support for a capitalist development strategy (ibid.: 98–101). In Indonesia after 1967, General Suharto and his family stood at the apex of a network of relations linking army officers with Chinese businessmen and foreign capitalists, many of whom profited from initiatives in import substitution and later export-oriented industrialization (Crouch 1979). After the end of civil war in Cambodia in 1997, Prime Minister Hun Sen was able to establish a greater degree of rent centralization, and turn his attention to creating the conditions for capitalist investment (Un 2005, 2010). Even in squeaky-clean Botswana, there is evidence that the leadership channeled diamond rents through the Botswana Meat Commission, which it used as a vehicle for centralized patronage in its relations with the countryside (Samatar 1999).

By contrast, where rent management was not centralized, economic performance tended to be very poor. In the First Republics in Nigeria and Congo-Zaire, in Sierra Leone between 1961 and 1967, in Indonesia between 1949 and 1966, and in Cambodia between 1991 and 1997, the leadership found it impossible to control rent-seeking (Clapham 1976; Forrest 1993; Hall 1981; Hughes and Conway 2003; Le Billon 2000; MacGaffey 1987; Migdal 1988). Almost every area of economic policy was invaded by unrestrained corruption, leading to economic crisis, lack of political mediation, and the collapse of authority. Most of these countries teetered on the brink of collapse until armed interventions or authoritarian rule restored order and recentralized rent management to some degree.[4] As we have seen, in Suharto's Indonesia and Hun Sen's Cambodia, this initiated a period of prolonged economic growth. However, for reasons to be explained, the improvements in Sierra Leone, Nigeria, and Congo-Zaire were modest and short lived.

In his discussion of rent-seeking as a process, Mushtaq Khan explains that a government is more likely to be able to use rents for development if its clientelist politics has a top-down structure. It can then set the terms of rent creation, distributing and reallocating rents to favored clients in line with its development goals. By contrast, where clientelist systems are bottom-up, the government is beholden to social groups which set the terms of rent creation and distribution (Khan 2000b: 135). Top-down or centralized rent management doesn't guarantee developmental rent utilization, but bottom-up or decentralized rent-seeking certainly seems to make it more difficult.[5] If there are numerous low-level actors all seeking rents for themselves, it is difficult to coordinate their actions so that rent-seeking works to the benefit of the economy overall.

This can be illustrated by taking a closer look at Indonesia. Indonesia is an archipelago of more than six thousand islands and numerous ethnic and religious groups. It gained independence from the Netherlands in 1949 under the flamboyant leadership of President Sukarno. The latter was a committed nationalist with ambitious plans for nationalization and creation of an indigenous business class. Almost immediately, however, the regime confronted ethnic and regional secessionist claims, together with intense ideological conflict, in what Clifford Geertz described as 'a classic case of integrative failure' (cited in Berger 1997: 323). In 1957 Sukarno began to rule by decree under the 'strident anti-Western nationalism and idiosyncratic socialism' of 'Guided Democracy', introducing even more radical plans for industrialization. These were consistently undermined, however, by 'the President's preoccupation with balancing rival factions' (Crouch 1979: 573). The economy entered a period of profound macro-imbalance: budget deficits exceeded total revenues, inflation turned into hyperinflation, and investment in industry ground to a halt. Just as in the worst-performing post-colonial African states: 'The predictability that Weber believed to be necessary for modern economic development was almost entirely lacking' (ibid.: 581). With the economy in disarray and political tension mounting daily, the army intervened in 1965 to crush a communist plot to take power. In the process, Sukarno was eased out of office and communist supporters up and down the country massacred.

The man who ultimately replaced Sukarno was army general Suharto. Immediately the latter began to fashion a state based not on Weberian legal-rational bureaucracy, but on personal exchanges of rent-seeking opportunities between himself, the military, and business. Military officers, their wives, brothers and cousins, together with the Suharto family itself, entered private business in conjunction with commercially skilled Indo-Chinese immigrants (ibid.: 577). On the basis of credits from state banks, monopolies in trade, and large infrastructure and supply projects issued by government ministries and state agencies, new politico-business families and Chinese business conglomerates built huge commercial empires (Hadiz and Robison 2005: 224). Banks, including the central bank, were directed to provide subsidies and bailouts to ailing firms, money was skimmed from oil receipts, donor funds were subject to creative accounting processes, and private firms and businessmen were tapped for contributions that might reach hundreds of millions of dollars. All of this provided individuals in the state apparatus, most notably Suharto himself, huge discretionary funds to finance political operations, fund industrial projects, and finance counter-cyclical macroeconomic smoothing (MacIntyre 2000).[6]

Surprisingly, firms prospered in spite of all this rent-seeking, waste, and corruption, and the economy grew. Take, for instance, the Salim Group. Its founder, Liem Sioe Liong, began life as a merchant and trader, moving into cotton spinning, weaving, and flour milling with encouragement from the government's import substitution industrialization (ISI) policies. During the second phase of ISI he diversified into cement and steel. When the government began to promote export-oriented industrialization in the 1980s, Liong reduced or liquidated investments in cement and steel, and moved instead into exporting sports shoes, toys, garments, leather goods, and agro-exports (Rock 1999: 698). A similar story could be told for William Soeryadjaya, another merchant, whose Astra Group got into auto-assembly during first-phase ISI, then moved into component parts, and then, via partnerships with Japanese multinationals, began exporting batteries, spark plugs, Toyota engines, and forklift frames (ibid.: 698). The paper industry provides another example. It developed rapidly in the 1970s behind high tariffs and subsidized energy costs, operating at this stage inside the global technological frontier. By the mid-1980s, however, large tracts of tropical hardwood were made available to investors, and, with the help of political connections and state subsidies, the large conglomerates then invested in the most technologically advanced machinery, making Indonesia by the mid-1990s one of the largest paper manufacturers in the world (Van Dijk and Szirmai 2006: 2139).

The Indonesian economic model was far from ideal: it was wasteful, politically repressive, and environmentally destructive, but its growth potential was extraordinary. Between 1967 and 1997, Indonesia was one of the fastest-growing economies in the world. In the 1970s mining, agriculture, oil and timber all boomed. Between 1967 and 1975, the manufacturing sector provided over eight million jobs, growing at more than 16 percent per year (Berger 1997: 342, 350). Between 1965 and 1990, the country achieved self-sufficiency in rice, there were dramatic advances in basic education and literacy, and income per capita grew at 4.5 percent per year (Rock 1999: 691). Poverty (using a $1-a-day indicator) declined from 64.3 percent in 1975 to 11.4 percent in 1995 (Dowling and Chin-Fang 2008: 474). Agriculture's share in total production declined from 51 percent to 22 percent and the share of manufactures in GDP more than doubled; manufactured exports were worth $21 billion in 1993 (Rock 1999: 691). Indonesia thus appears to confirm the idea that 'In the early stages, a patrimonial political structure need not be an obstacle to capitalist economic development' (Crouch 1979: 579).

According to Peter Lewis, the Suharto state succeeded because it provided 'credible commitments' to investors and producers (Lewis 2007: 4). At its core was a team known as the 'Berkeley mafia', a group of US-educated technocrats responsible for the implementation of orthodox macroeconomic policies. They kept the economy in balance despite the massive influx of oil revenues, and the subsequent decline in revenues when world prices fell. Investor confidence was buttressed by liberalization of the capital account, which allowed businessmen to transfer assets out of the country in the event of anything economically untoward. As far as secure property rights went, Suharto came to personal arrangements with key producers, while Cukongism, the practice of linking Indonesian elites with Chinese capitalists through informal networks, supplied the coordination needed for rapid growth (Berger 1997; Dowling and Chin-Fang 2008; Hadiz and Robison 2005: 67; Lewis 2007).[7]

But this is not the whole story. We still need to understand how it was that bribery, corruption, and personalized distribution of favors didn't degenerate into the kind of downwardly spiraling free-for-all that characterized several African regimes, or indeed Indonesia under Sukarno. There are several reasons, important among which is *the way that rent-seeking and corruption were organized*. Andrew MacIntyre suggests that we think of regulatory agencies and relevant state sections under Suharto as a unified or centrally coordinated monopoly for bribe-collecting. Monitoring and enforcement from the top was sufficiently strong that the center was able to prevent regulatory agencies from acting independently, ensuring that a healthy share of bribes flowed upwards, with the remainder distributed proportionately at the coalface. Officials were unable to operate independently to maximize their own take. Thus, a firm seeking permits to open a factory, for example, could acquire secure property rights to the package of 'regulatory goods' it purchased, as soon as it had paid the requisite bribe (see also the discussion in Khan 2000a: 118–39; MacIntyre 2000: 265).

Compare this to a more decentralized situation where there are lots of competing agents, each trying to extract the maximum revenue possible. In this context political control is weaker and less centralized. There is a multitude of actors selling complementary regulatory goods. Because the political leadership is unable to exercise effective control, officials look to maximize their own take without regard for the effect on the economy overall. In this situation 'the firm purchasing all these government goods can never be sure it has secure property rights as any agency might subsequently seek to extract further bribes. The weaker the political leadership's control, the greater the scope for independent and un-coordinated extraction by officials pursuing their own individual interests' (MacIntyre 2000: 265). MacIntyre concludes that this framework not only helps explain differences between the Sukarno and Suharto periods, but might also explain the economic successes of other centralized, corrupt, but high-growth regimes.

A highly centralized political framework is an 'enabling set of conditions, creating incentives for a political leader to promote a pattern of rent-seeking which is not too costly to national economic efficiency' (ibid.: 270). It does not guarantee effective rent management, however. Rather, for the economy to be successful, rent management must also be oriented *to the long term*.[8] This is for reasons similar to the ones that make countries that forgo consumption in the present for investment in the future faster growing over the long run. Long-horizon rent management means directing a substantial portion of rent-earning opportunities to activities that involve increases in value-added, or transformations in the productive forces over time – as when subsidies are provided to an infant industry that in the long run will compete internationally. This does not mean, it must be stressed, either that the motivations for creating this rent structure are public spirited, or that all the rents earned in this system are productive or clean – even a purely selfish leader may calculate that he stands to maximize his take (i.e. his parasitic rents) from the economy if it is allowed to grow over time (see Olson 1993). The point, however, is that some parasitic rent collection will have to be forgone in the present if it is to be maximized in the future, otherwise businesses will be so burdened with parasitic demands that they lose their ability to grow.[9]

Rent management and development – a model

With the discussion of the above section in mind, we can think about categorizing regimes according to two different dimensions of rent management: the degree of centralization, and the length of time horizon to which rent management is oriented. Definitionally speaking, we take it that *rents are centrally managed when there is a structure in place that allows an individual or group at the apex of the state to determine the major rents that are created and to distribute them at will. It is long-horizon when leaders have a vision that inspires them to create rents and discipline rent-seeking with a view to expanding income through productive investment over the long term.* These distinctions indicate four regime types from a rent management perspective, as illustrated by the model in Figure 1.1.

In the top left quadrant of our model rent centralization is low, and the leadership has little interest in disciplining rent management with a view to the long term. We have glossed this as 'competitive clientelism', a competitive free-for-all in which anyone with the ability to extract rents takes the maximum they can in the short term, grasping as much as they can today for fear that tomorrow there will be nothing worth taking. Economic growth is likely to be well below potential in this scenario, since there is no limit to the shakedowns potential investors can expect. Competitive clientelism, if left unchecked, has a tendency to degenerate into 'spoils politics',

CENTRALIZATION

		Low	High
TIME HORIZON	**Short**	Competitive clientelism	Non-developmental kleptocracy
	Long	Ineffective developmental state	Developmental patrimonialism

1.1 A typology of rent management

characterized by 'winner takes all', corruption/looting of the economy, economic crises, lack of political mediation, repression and violence, communalism, endemic instability and erosion of authority (Allen 1995: 308). As the preceding discussion has shown, the clearest example from Asia might be Sukarno's Indonesia, and from Africa, the Nigerian First Republic, the First Republic in Congo-Zaire, or Sierra Leone prior to the first military coup.

The bottom left quadrant represents a different type. Here, the leadership desires to take the long view, limiting rents so as to maximize its own take or to serve what it views as the interests of society as a whole. However, because it lacks the machinery to centralize rents, its ability actually to implement the long-term view is strictly limited. The result is likely to be an ineffective developmental state. An example from our literature review might be Cambodia between 1979 and 1991. The leadership had a vision influenced by Vietnamese socialism, but could keep the country's various political factions together only by permitting rampant rent-seeking at local level (Gottesman 2004). Another contender is Nigeria under General Gowon (see Forrest 1993).

The upper right quadrant, by contrast, describes the situation where the leadership has had considerable success in centralizing the rent process. Few big rents are generated or allocated without the knowledge of the leadership. In theory, the president and his inner circle would have the power to limit rent-taking, but for one reason or another, perhaps because of feelings of political insecurity, or a lack of knowledge of or interest in economics, they do not take the long-term view. Consequently, the regime takes on a kleptocratic aspect, and those with connections to the top leadership are allowed to enrich themselves almost without limit. Mobutu's Zaire and Siaka Stevens's Sierra Leone fit this type (Reno 1995; Schatzberg 1988), as perhaps does Nigeria under General Abacha (Lewis 2007).

The bottom right quadrant of Figure 1.1 is the most interesting from our point of view. Here, the leadership has succeeded in centralizing control over rents, and also takes a long-term approach to rent maximization. It is 'developmental patrimonial' in the sense that the regime retains a neo-patrimonial character, with a more or less systematic blurring of the boundaries between public resources and the private property of the ruler(s).[10] It is not necessarily free of illegality or 'corruption'; in fact, these may reach quite high levels and may well be the major source of finance for the political activities of the ruling groups. However, the rent process is organized in such a way that it does not hurt the climate for investment in the ways that typify the other regimes. Indeed, if it finances domestic investment, including public works and other industrial policy initiatives with positive externalities for other investors, the net effects may be quite favorable. Corruption, too, may be less harmful than under the other types of regime because it is more predictable and moderated by concerns to grow the economy. As we have argued, South Korea between 1961 and 1987, Malaysia from 1957 to 1997, Indonesia from 1967 to 1997, Botswana from 1966 to 1998, Kenya from 1965 to 1975, and Côte d'Ivoire from 1960 to 1975 all fit this type.

If, as our model proposes, long-horizon rent centralization is crucial to strong economic performance, we need to understand how some regimes achieve it while others fail. Four factors stand out. The first is the presence of a strong and visionary leader. We see this with Park Chung-hee in South Korea, Suharto in Indonesia, Abdul Razak in Malaysia,[11] and Seretse Khama in Botswana. The second is the creation of a single or dominant party system – a constrained yet inclusive form of political democracy. South Korea and Indonesia were dictatorships during their most rapid growth periods; Vietnam is a single-party state; and while Malaysia and Cambodia are formally multiparty democracies, their ruling parties have been highly dominant and competition is constrained. Even in multiparty Botswana, the political playing field has been far from level (Holm 1988).[12] This often goes hand in hand with the third enabling factor: a top-down patron–client network. We have already touched on this in the cases of South Korea and Indonesia, and we can infer it for the cases of Botswana, Malaysia, and Cambodia too.

A final factor is the maintenance of a competent and confident, vertically disciplined economic technocracy, free from the most damaging clientelist pressures. We have already discussed the role of the Berkeley mafia in Indonesia. In South Korea, the Economic Planning Board had a high degree of competence and has been called 'the brain and engine of the Korean economic miracle' (Castells, cited in United Nations Economic Commission for Africa 2011: 99). In Malaysia, the creation of a Ministry for Rural Development, the Economic Planning Unit and the Ministry of Finance formed a powerful nexus for economic planning and management (ibid.: 108). In Botswana, economic planning was centralized in the Ministry of Finance and Development Planning, an institutional nerve center which acted rather like a Botswanan version of Japan's MITI (Samatar 1999: 30–41).[13] Countries where the economic technocracy was permeated by clientelist demands, by contrast, tended to perform poorly. For example, in the Nigerian First Republic, regional governments commissioned a wave of uneconomic contractor-financed turnkey projects partly because of the opportunities for kickbacks they afforded, while regional development boards commissioned many non-commercially viable projects on patronage grounds, a trend that weakened federal control over external debt and undermined the attempt to plan (Forrest 1993: 37). In the First Republic in Congo-Zaire, around 75 percent of Belgian civil servants left the country, while government employment swelled in response to strong patrimonial pressures (MacGaffey 1987).

Rent management and economic performance in Côte d'Ivoire, Kenya, and Malawi

We can illustrate these relationships further by means of a comparison of different rent management regimes in Côte d'Ivoire, Kenya, and Malawi. All of these countries are moderately sized, resource poor,[14] and fall within Africa's tropical belt. They also share certain politico-cultural features, belonging to what Michael Schatzberg has termed 'Middle Africa' (Schatzberg 2002).[15] Aside from being broadly comparable in these ways, they also have the virtue of having generated a considerable body of secondary literature, which has allowed us to provide detailed causal narratives to strengthen our findings. Originally, these case studies were part of a larger study, the results of which we have presented elsewhere.[16]

A word about our classificatory schema is in order. We have defined and selected regimes by reference to our independent variable, viz. type of rent management. When we see a new type of rent relationship take hold, we inaugurate a new regime. Thus some regimes change with rulers – Kenya pre- and post-Kenyatta, for example – whereas other rulers preside over different regimes, like early and late Houphouët in Côte d'Ivoire. Most of the regimes in the sample, including these ones, are clear cut, but two are 'fuzzy', displaying rent centralization in some areas but not in others. Specifically, in Mwai Kibaki's Kenya (2002–10), we find that rents are quite successfully centralized at a macro-level by the Ministry of Finance, but at a micro-level, members of the high political leadership are permitted to indulge in non-productive rent creation and rent-seeking with the tacit if not direct knowledge of the president (who may or may not profit personally). Some of the proceeds are used to fund election expenses, and some are pocketed privately. In addition, ruling party candidates are permitted to engage in various types of rent-seeking in order to fund their own constituency campaigns. This is coupled with a certain permissiveness toward petty rent-seeking at lower levels of the administration (Wrong 2009).

Another slightly fuzzy case is the first-term government of Dr Bingu wa Mutharika's Malawi (2004–09). Although there are signs that Mutharika made efforts to centralize rent management, neutralizing democratic organs, reawarding lucrative contracts from political opponents to his own allies, fighting corruption at a number of levels, and providing some space for long-term technocratic decision-making, there are also signs that these measures were not entirely successful (Cammack et al. 2010; Cammack and Kelsall 2011). Certainly, in Mutharika's second term, rent management became increasingly oriented to the short term, dominated by the question of political succession (Cammack 2011).

Despite the ambiguities, we have placed these regimes in the categories to which we think they best approximate.

The dependent variable also bears some discussion. In our view, relying on quantitative indicators alone to make assessments of economic performance in Africa is highly problematic, mainly because of the compromised nature of economic data and statistics (Jerven 2010). At best, these data might give an idea of trends in the relative performance of economies over time, but they need to be supplemented by more qualitative indicators. Consequently we have based our categorizations on evaluations from the best academic literature available for the period concerned, examining in both quantitative and qualitative fashion factors such as economic growth, structural transformation, diversification, macroeconomic balance, growth in per capita incomes, poverty reduction, and also *whether or not performance has surpassed expectations* given a country's history, resource endowments and the global economic conditions of the time.

Obviously, this involves an element of judgment, and doubtless some readers will take issue with ours. Some might argue that performance in Kenyatta's Kenya was not 'strong', given the inequalities

TABLE 1.1 Regimes, rent management, and economic performance

Type of rent management	Regime	Economic performance
Long-horizon centralized	Côte d'Ivoire, 1960–75	Strong
	Kenya, 1965–75	Strong
	Malawi, 1964–78	Quite strong
	Malawi, 2004–09	Quite strong
Short-horizon centralized	Côte d'Ivoire, 1981–93	Quite weak
	Kenya, 1982–2002	Weak
	Malawi, 1980–94	Weak
Long-horizon decentralized	Côte d'Ivoire, 1975–80	Weak
Short-horizon decentralized	Côte d'Ivoire, 1993–2010	Weak
	Malawi, 1994–2004	Weak
	Kenya, 2002–10	Mixed

of wealth and the structural imbalance it created. We would agree that Kenya's growth model had definite problems. Nevertheless, we believe that the beginnings of structural transformation and growth that it generated were not dissimilar to some of the experiences of import-substituting Asia, and could have laid the foundations for more sustained growth had the right choices subsequently been made. Finally, there are a few gaps in Table 1.1, in which our findings are tabulated, such as Malawi between 1978 and 1982, when one regime appears to be transitioning to another, making it difficult to classify the rent process.

Clear patterns are revealed in Table 1.1. Looking at the top quadrant, all of the centralized long-horizon regimes are strong or quite strong performers. Indeed, there are no strong performers to be found in any other category. In this sample, long-horizon rent centralization was a *necessary* condition for steady, transformative, poverty-reducing growth.[17] By contrast, all of the centralized, short-horizon regimes are weak or quite weak performers. The other two categories, short-horizon decentralized and long-horizon decentralized, contain mostly weakly performing regimes. The exception is Kibaki's Kenya between 2002 and 2010, which we have categorized as 'mixed'. As noted earlier, rent-centralization in this regime has something of an interstitial character, and this perhaps explains its inconsistent economic performance.

In the following sections we provide historical narratives from Côte d'Ivoire, Malawi, and Kenya, to show how economic performance was affected by changes in types of rent management regime. We also show how the latter was bound up with changes in leadership, political institutions, patron–client relations, and technocratic discipline.

Centralized, long-horizon rent management We begin by discussing three regimes that fall under the category that interests us most: centralized, long-horizon rent management. Like the Asian countries in our review, all the regimes in our sample that displayed this pattern were associated with better economic performance. We begin with Félix Houphouët-Boigny's Côte d'Ivoire.

CÔTE D'IVOIRE, 1960–75 Pre-colonial Côte d'Ivoire was a thinly populated territory home to about sixty ethnic groups, inhabiting a savannah zone in the north, and a forest zone in the south. The colonial period created an economic infrastructure to extract agricultural resources from the country, deploying coerced labor on European-owned coffee and cocoa estates. Alongside this expatriate development there emerged an indigenous planter class with roots in the traditional elite that resented these European privileges, and out of this resentment was born the Syndicat agricole africaine (SAA) (Campbell 1987). In time, the SAA became the base for the Parti démocratique de Côte d'Ivoire (PDCI), the political party that led the country to independence, co-opting the other, minor parties, and securing a monopoly on popular support (Crook 1990a: 221; Médard 1991: 190).[18]

The PDCI was led by the redoubtable Félix Houphouët-Boigny. Houphouët was from one of the richest plantation families in the country, had worked as a doctor, led the SAA, and also been a member of parliament in France. After rumors of plots against the regime in 1963 and 1964, he took the opportunity to concentrate power around his own person, imprisoning some of his rivals and establishing a one-party state (Crook 1990a: 223; Médard 1991: 191). The party itself was then rendered dependent: nominations for section secretaries were controlled by central party organs, national elections were non-competitive, and once elected, MPs represented not a particular constituency, but rather the whole of Côte d'Ivoire (which meant to say they represented Houphouët) (Médard 1991: 198). Local party notables, meanwhile, became 'a client class totally dependent upon the ruler for their position and perquisites' (Jackson and Rosberg 1982: 150).

With the polity tightly constrained, Houphouët stood at the apex of a top-down clientelist system. Everyone knew that they owed their position to the president: 'The domination Houphouët-Boigny exercised upon his country, his political system, and more directly upon the elite reached a point where the members of the elite are perceived and perceive themselves as his men and the access to power as his' (Bakary 1984: 34). It was an inclusive system none the less, based on a skillful system of 'quotas' that allowed a certain balance between ethnic groups (ibid.: 35). The outcome was a 'multi-ethnic, con-fraternity of power' (ibid.: 27), characterized by a series of 'inter-connected family compacts' or pyramids, at the top of which stood the country's most powerful families, both in economic and political terms (see also Médard 1991: 194; Rapley 1993: 108).

With no plausible challengers, Houphouët was able to take a long view and devolve considerable power to a competent economic techno-cracy (Crook 1990a: 235). Up until 1965, the finance minister was a Frenchman, and it was not uncommon to find up to fifteen French advisors in a ministry (Rapley 1993: 67). With their help, Houphouët presided over a sophisticated system of French-style indicative plan-ning, which quantified economic goals, assured consistency between objectives, and provided regional and local breakdowns, together with financial plans (Tuinder 1978: 26). These plans were then im-plemented, using a combination of expatriate technical expertise and a socially embedded political class. The implementation of orders from a minister in Abidjan could be supervised 'by his or her family members or close colleagues who controlled mayoralties or prefectures in the cities or towns' (Rapley 1993: 67).

Industrial policy was to expand and diversify the agricultural economy in order to fuel industrialization. The Caisse de Stabilisa-tion set an efficient price for cocoa growers for many years, while the Ministry of Agriculture, provincial administration, and extension services supervised the expansion of the cocoa industry into virgin lands (Crook 1990b; Tuinder 1978). In addition, new investments were made in bananas, pineapple, rubber, coconut, and palm oil (Tuinder

1978: 17). Industrial growth was largely based around the processing of agricultural raw materials, and included canned goods, coffee and cocoa processing, edible oils and fats, tobacco, textiles, rubber, and wood products (ibid.: 50).

The results were impressive, with Côte d'Ivoire frequently referred to as an 'economic miracle' during these years. In the first fifteen years after independence, coffee and banana production almost doubled, cocoa expanded sixfold, while pineapple increased by over 4,600 percent. By the early 1980s, the country was the world's largest producer of coconuts, the largest exporter of tinned pineapple, the third-largest exporter of palm oil, and Africa's second-largest producer of cotton (Rapley 1993: 78). Between 1965 and 1980, the manufacturing sector in Côte d'Ivoire grew at 9.1 percent per year, and GDP at 6.8 percent (Riddell 1990: 152). On the back of this kind of growth, GDP per capita far outstripped that of the country's neighbors: at independence, Côte d'Ivoire's per capita income was barely a third of Ghana's; by the early 1980s, that ratio had reversed (Riboud 1987).

MALAWI, 1964–78 A less celebrated but perhaps equally valid example of developmental patrimonialism can be found in Malawi between the years of 1964 and 1978. In many respects Malawi presents an environment unfavorable to economic growth. It has few exploitable natural resources, is landlocked, has but a single rainy season, is subject to unpredictable weather, and is poorly connected to the outside world. In the colonial period, development policy focused on developing the agricultural sector, carving out estates for white settlers, and later promoting an African 'yeoman farmer' class. None of these efforts was particularly successful, and in 1964, when Malawi obtained independence, the country was under-resourced, exceedingly poor, lacking in capacity and indebted (Chanock 1977; Vail 1976, 1977).

The country's first prime minister, and later 'President for Life', was Dr Hastings Kamuzu Banda, a sixty-eight-year-old medical doctor who was to dominate the country's politics for the next thirty years. Banda was a dictator by nature, and his authoritarian tendencies were given free rein following the Cabinet Crisis of 1964, in which disagreements with younger colleagues led to a coup attempt, expulsions, and the banning of all political opposition. Thereafter, Banda's Malawi Congress Party (MCP), representatives of which were handpicked by the president, became the only permitted political party.

Local governance, chiefs' authority, the courts and parliament were all subordinated to his authority. So too were women, the media, and youth groups; independent trades unions and cooperatives were muscled aside. Political detention was used frequently, and the population cowed into submission by the security services and Banda's Malawi Young Pioneers (Baker 2001; Short 1974). The human rights record of the regime was notoriously poor.

As in Côte d'Ivoire, this downgrading of politics permitted Banda to rule largely through his civil service. Many Europeans were retained in high positions, helping create a dedicated, disciplined bureaucracy that was largely corruption free. Ministers – junior men whom Banda routinely referred to as 'my boys' – were powerless by comparison. Their primary role was to win support for Banda's policies in the regions (Williams 1978: 200–1).

Development policy emphasized infrastructural, agricultural, and industrial development. In agriculture, the main emphasis was on drawing privileged Africans into an expanding commercial estate sector. Termed *achikumbe* by extension workers, these favored farmers were eligible to grow high-value crops and received a range of credits, inputs, and advice, not to mention favorable prices, to help them boost production. Commercial estates, especially tobacco estates, provided a return on investment that ranged between 22 percent and 67 percent in the 1970s. Many of the *achikumbe* taking advantage of this favored treatment were politicians and civil servants (Chipeta and Mkandawire 2008; Harrigan 2001; Mhone 1992; Mtewa 1986; Pryor 1990).

Small business was also a font of patronage. From 1969 onwards, legal restrictions were placed on white and Asian rural business and many of their enterprises were abandoned. Africans filled the gap with the help of lending institutions created to advance credit without the usual collateral guarantees. Mhone reports that 'local entrepreneurs ... were deliberately promoted and protected by government in accordance with ... patronage and client imperatives' (Mhone 1992) as well as national development policies. The most successful farmers-bureaucrats-businessmen went on to invest in small-scale secondary industries, such as food processing.

Industrial policy was geared toward processing agricultural products for domestic use and export. It focused on attracting private investors, including foreign firms, via a range of incentives. The 1966 Industrial

Development Act, for example, provided generous investment and depreciation allowances, plus tariff barriers and protection from competition (Chipeta and Mkandawire 2008: 157). Banda was 'very successful in obtaining investable resources both from external and internal sources, particularly for the public sector' (Pryor 1990: 47–8). Funds came from aid, foreign companies (e.g., Lonhro, Carlsberg), and from the public sector itself (parastatals' profits averaged about 1 percent of GDP). In partnership with foreign capital, three entities – the Malawi Development Corporation (MDC), ADMARC (the state agricultural marketing corporation), and Press Holdings (see below) – dominated industrial development, forming a highly monopolistic and oligopolistic market structure (Kaluwa et al. 1992).

The biggest beneficiary was Banda himself, whose ownership of Press Corporation plays a key role in any story of Malawi's economic development. In 1961 he had founded Press to handle the printing of the party newspaper. After independence Press Holdings, in which he was the majority shareholder, rapidly diversified into tobacco farming and trading; food processing, wholesaling, and retailing; financial services; textiles and manufacturing; and distilling and bottling. Press, and thus Banda, controlled

> the largest chain of retail supermarkets and shops in Malawi (Press Trading Ltd.), a major chain of hardware stores (Hardware and General Dealers Ltd.), a major share in the flue-cured tobacco industry (Press Farming Ltd.), a stake in the burly tobacco industry (General Farming Ltd.), and a haulage firm (Press Transport Ltd.). There [were] also Press Properties, Press Industries, Press Produce and others. (Thomas 1975: 48)

Before its restructuring in the early 1980s, Press had interests in seventeen subsidiary companies and twenty-three associated companies (Press Corporation 2009). Described by van Donge as 'an African *chaebol*', it contributed to economic growth, paid hefty state taxes, and became something of a model for African entrepreneurship (Van Donge 2002). Doubtless it was also a source of employment and income for individuals Banda wished to reward, though evidence suggests that merit weighed heavily in hiring decisions (Cammack et al. 2010).

In these various ways, Banda used the power of the state to direct assets into the hands of those he thought would use them most productively (politicians and civil servants with capitalist ambitions), and/or those whose political support was useful (smaller African businessmen, in particular MCP members, and investors). By contrast, other forms of rent-seeking – corruption, predation, or theft – were not much tolerated. Banda felt his 'main business' was the maintenance of a stable government, an efficient, honest, and incorruptible administration. '"People must come here when they have money to invest, get a license without putting so many pounds in the pocket of a certain Minister first"' (Baker 2001: 162).

Performance-wise, the early years of Banda's government were marked by rapid national-level economic growth, averaging 5.9 percent annually between 1964 and 1979. In 1972 the World Bank described Malawi's record of economic development as 'remarkable' and 'impressive', attributing it to the 'prudent management of the economy in which both the public and private sectors have played an important part' (Thomas 1975: 32). Government's policy of setting aside part of its revenues and public enterprise profits had helped raise gross national savings in this period (to 11 percent during 1970–74 and 13 percent in 1975–79). Growth in real GDP per worker was about 3 percent per annum in the period 1960–79. The manufacturing sector increased its share of GDP from 7 percent at independence to 13 percent in 1980. Employment in the manufacturing sector, in turn, increased by a high average rate of 6.8 percent per year (Chipeta and Mkandawire 2008). Harrigan calls the fifteen years' growth 'healthy' and notes that it compared favorably with that of sub-Saharan Africa as a whole, not to mention that of other resource-poor, landlocked countries (Harrigan 2001). More troublingly, the impact on poverty was marginal (Mhone 1992), leading us to classify Malawi's economic performance as only 'quite strong'.

KENYA, 1965–75 Kenya under the presidency of Jomo Kenyatta also fits the developmental patrimonialism model, although the process of centralizing rents was more of a struggle there. Pre-colonial Kenya was inhabited by about forty ethnic groups, with seven groups (Kikuyu, Luo, Luhya, Maasai, Kamba, Kalenjin, and coastal tribes) accounting for about 70 percent of the population. In the colonial period, a significant number of Europeans settled. Large tracts of land were set aside in the central highlands for white settlement, with Africans confined to native reserves. Nevertheless, some economic development occurred among Africans, especially the Kikuyu, the group most affected by white settlement. By the 1930s, these more prosperous Kikuyu began to become politically active, forming the Kikuyu Central Association and later, together with other ethnic groups, the Kenyan African Union (KAU). In the 1950s the KAU split into radical and moderate wings, with the radicals becoming part of an underground movement, Mau Mau, which fought a guerrilla war against the settler state (Berman and Lonsdale 1992; Berman 1997).[19]

By the late 1950s Mau Mau had been squashed and the British began to plan for a handover of power. A massive land-titling program (the Swynnerton Plan) was instituted for the Kikuyu highlands, and provisions were made to transfer white farmland to Africans through the Million Acre Scheme. KAU leader Jomo Kenyatta was released from prison and political competition was legalized. Two political parties emerged: KANU, led by Kenyatta, which drew on mainly Kikuyu and Luo support, and KADU, a collection of the smaller tribes, co-founded by Ronald Ngala and Daniel arap Moi. KANU won the elections and in 1963 the country entered independence with a multiparty constitution and strong regionalist government. Kenyatta quickly sought to change this, and his efforts bore fruit in 1964 when KADU members of parliament crossed the floor, enticed partly by grants of land in the Rift Valley (Bates 1989). A republic was created, in which Moi was made vice-president and Kenyatta, as president, granted sweeping powers. The next few years saw a struggle against KANU's left wing, leading to the emasculation of the trade unions and formation of the breakaway Kenyan People's Union (KPU). In 1969 the KPU was banned, making Kenya a de facto one-party state (Anyang' Nyong'o 1989; Goldsworthy 1982; Leys 1975; Tamarkin 1978).

Much like Houphouët in Côte d'Ivoire, Kenyatta proceeded to neuter the power of KANU itself. Soon it existed merely as a network of local and regional bosses that he held together (Barkan 1994: 16). It continued to play a role loosely screening candidates for multi-member elections in parliamentary seats, which was just about the only source of political competition in the country. The latter contests were intimately linked to the practice of *harambee*, under which local people would part-supply social services through self-help, expecting their MP to act as an intermediary with central ministries to secure matching government support. MPs who failed in this respect tended to be rejected by the electorate, while those who succeeded could expect to be made junior ministers. This ensured an increased supply of patronage resources to the constituency, and cemented the MP's loyalty to the president (ibid.: 19). The majority of funds, projects, and coercive powers, meanwhile, flowed through the strong provincial administration created by the British and responsible to the chief executive.

Kenyatta had succeeded in creating a top-down patron–client system, in which the lion's share of the rents went to the 'Gatundu clique', also known as 'The Family', that innermost circle of Kenyatta's Kiambu court. Beyond these close courtiers Kikuyu more generally could be expected to 'eat', and then the ethnic leaders of the smaller tribes that had formerly comprised KADU. Allegedly Kenyatta told non-Kikuyu ministers that: 'My people have the milk in the morning, your tribes the milk in the afternoon' (Wrong 2009: 51). There was nothing like an equal division of spoils under the Kenyatta regime, but only the Luo, after 1969, and more radical elements such as former Mau Mau, were thoroughly marginalized. The lower classes were not well organized, although some of their concerns were articulated by figures like political tycoon J. M. Kariuki; when the latter could not be co-opted by the regime, he was assassinated (Tamarkin 1978). A consequence was a level of political stability in the ruling elite and more generally, which commentators of the period have described as 'remarkable' (Goldsworthy 1982), a 'rare blessing', and Kenya's 'main economic asset' (Tamarkin 1978: 297).

With stability assured, a competent bureaucracy could be maintained. The top ranks of the civil service were Africanized more rapidly than in Côte d'Ivoire or Malawi, but as in those countries, expatriates remained well represented in the technical cadres for quite some time (Goldsworthy 1982: 250). Leys described the civil service as 'an autonomous administrative apparatus' (Leys 1975: 122), while Barkan observed that it functioned in much the same way as the colonial state had done (Barkan 1994: 17). Within this apparatus Kenyatta delegated responsibility for growth-enhancing performance to his ministers and civil servants. According to Leonard: 'Kenyatta gave his attention more to personnel than to the details of public policy' (Leonard 1991: 143). He had 'a decision-maker in whom he had confidence in virtually every public organization that was important to him' (ibid.: 170), intervening only when economically necessary and politically desirable. A good example is the way in which he supported Charles Karanja of the Kenya Tea Development Agency (KTDA), in his efforts to ensure that tea growing did not expand into uneconomic areas (ibid.).

The agricultural sector was a key political-economic arena (Heyer 1981: 92). We have already seen how land in the Rift Valley was made available to KADU leaders in the process of creating a one-party state (Bates 1989). Settlement schemes which redistributed land in the White Highlands were another resource. Through access to state credit, politicians and civil servants acquired stakes in the large-farm sector, while yeomen, peasants, and the landless got land in the high- or low-density schemes (Leo 1984). The bulk of the peasantry had already been given a conservative cast thanks to 1950s land consolidation, carried out under the Swynnerton Plan (Heyer 1981: 102). More generally, smallholders in many areas were for the first time permitted to grow high-value export crops, notably pyrethrum and tea (ibid.: 105), and encouraged to do so by a combination of competitive prices and relatively effective agricultural development agencies (Bates 1981, 1989; Leonard 1991).

When it came to industry, government policy was to be simultaneously open to foreign investment, while encouraging Africanization of the economy. Firms such as Union Carbide, Firestone, United Steel, Del Monte, Mitsui, Nomura, Schweppes, Inchcape, Lonrho and many more came to Kenya (Leys 1975: 118). New industries developed in plastics, pharmaceuticals, steel rolling and galvanizing, electrical cables, welding rods, paper, vehicle assembly, industrial gases, rubber, ceramics, batteries, refractory bricks, oil recycling, and so on. Others in textiles and garment manufacturing, food processing, leather tanning, and footwear greatly expanded in scale (Coughlin 1990).

Through a clutch of state agencies, including the Industrial and Commercial Development Corporation, the Development Finance Company of Kenya, the Kenya Tourist Development Corporation and the State Reinsurance Corporation, government acquired equity in these firms, and through it encouraged the promotion of African management. Other Africans used their political connections to help them invest directly in enterprise. Entrepreneurial Kikuyu, for example, employed state power to displace Asian retail trade (Swainson 1987: 143–7). Bigger Kikuyu operators bought equity, even controlling shares, in foreign firms through cooperatives or consortia (ibid.:

153). One of the most significant indigenous conglomerations in this respect was the Gikuyu, Embu and Meru Association (GEMA), which included some of the country's most prominent politicians, and invested in land, property, and manufacturing projects through its holding company, Gema Holdings (ibid.: 155–8).

Economic performance was accordingly strong, evidencing growth, structural transformation, and poverty reduction. Between 1964 and 1973, agriculture grew at 4.6 percent per year, manufacturing at 9.1 percent, and GDP at 6.6 percent (Mwega and Ndung'u 2008: 359), rates that were around twice the sub-Saharan average (Sharpley and Lewis 1990: 206–7). Although growth was not experienced equally and some were actually impoverished, the incomes of very large sections of the population substantially increased (Heyer 1981: 90).

Centralized, short-horizon rent management Neither the Kenyatta regime, nor our two other 'developmental patrimonial' regimes, proved sustainable, however, and it is important that we grasp the reasons why. In the case we discuss next – Kenya between 1980 and 1992 – centralized rent management was retained, but rents were increasingly oriented to short-term objectives.

KENYA, 1980–92 By the mid-1970s the development model established by Kenyatta was ripe for restructuring. Insufficient incentives had been provided to encourage a serious move into exporting, and the individual operators seemed focused on political lobbying to protect their access to protected markets. With a high import content to production and falling productivity, the manufacturing sector could be sustained only by means of increased subsidy from the agricultural sector, and foreign loans. Both options appear to have been tried, and both appear to have forced the economy into greater external imbalance, with the manufacturing sector acting as a drag on the entire economy. The failure to reform the model while export prices were high was a major missed opportunity (Sharpley and Lewis 1990). Instead, observers noticed a relaxation of discipline and an increase in corruption.[20]

It is difficult to know how far this paralysis was generated by problems inherent to the model, and how far by a looming crisis of political succession. In 1978 Kenyatta died and, as per the constitution, former KADU leader Daniel arap Moi, ethnically a Kalenjin, acceded to power. He did so in the teeth of opposition from Kikuyu heavyweights, especially the GEMA group. The next few years were spent trying to disorganize them. First he used the police to launch an assault against corruption at high level in government ministries, thereby undermining their patronage base (Widner 1992: 137). Then he set his two main Kikuyu backers, Mwai Kibaki and Charles Njonjo, against one another. Simultaneously, the president intervened repeatedly in *harambee* activities and factional disputes throughout Central Province, promoting his own men to challenge more established players, but then pulling the rug from the former if they proved too independent. In this way he succeeded in keeping the Kikuyu seriously fractionalized, but at the cost of wasteful expenditure (ibid.).

The civil service was also under suspicion. Readers will recall that Jomo Kenyatta's approach to administration was to delegate responsibilities to trusted managers, often kinsmen, intervening when necessary in policy disputes on their behalf. Moi, however, had little affinity with the men who served under him: 'Moi frequently had to rely on men with whom he had no strong ties and some of whom he distrusted' (Leonard 1991: 171). Civil servants did not dare voice opposition to the president, but they did sometimes fail to take initiative or dragged their feet implementing his policies (ibid.).

Moi began to shuffle ministers and civil servants, systematically replacing Kenyatta's Kikuyu supporters with representatives from his own and allied ethnic groups. Soon he had removed all but one of Kenyatta's eight provincial commissioners, and retired or moved on many other prominent Kikuyu civil servants. Mostly they were replaced by members of ethnic groups who had made up the old KADU alliance, especially Moi's own Kalenjin people. A similar process afflicted marketing boards, state-owned enterprises, and regulatory agencies. Charles Karanja at the KTDA, for example, lost his job when he enquired too deeply into a tea-smuggling operation almost certainly linked to the president's allies (ibid.). The frequency of civil service shuffling also increased: 'Whereas under Kenyatta senior members of the civil service would remain in their posts for five years or more, Moi rotated personnel every two to three years, often less' (Barkan 1994: 24). Understandably, competence and efficiency frequently declined.

While Kenyatta had used the administration as his main patronage vehicle, Moi chose KANU, which was reconstituted as 'a well financed machine of personal rule' (ibid.: 25). The president surrounded himself with an inner circle of old-KADU loyalists 'with little understanding of the macroeconomic issues facing Kenya and a proclivity to use the financial instruments of the state for patronage needs' (ibid.: 26). Corruption in this context reached kleptocratic proportions, a phenomenon caused partly, Barkan thinks, by an oblivious attitude to Kenya's economic future, and partly by the more rapid circulation of administrative and political elites, inducing a mentality of steal as much as you can while you can (ibid.: 27–8). Moi thus succeeded in replacing Kenyatta's centralized rent management structure with one of his own. But while Kenyatta's was geared to a considerable extent to long-term development goals, Moi's was focused more on short-term self-enrichment and political survival (ibid.: 27).

Contemporaneously, political competition was constrained and the coercive arms of the state strengthened. Ethnic welfare societies, including GEMA, were banned. Following a coup attempt in 1982, Kenya became a *de jure* one-party state. Queue voting was introduced in both party and national elections, expenditures on the police and security services grew, while the economy stagnated, with per capita income falling by as much as 2.75 percent a year between 1980 and 1984, then growing by the same amount between 1985 and 1989 (Mwega and Ndung'u 2008: 328, Table 10.1). Popular opposition to the regime became more vocal, and with the threat of increased unrest and a suspension of donor aid, multiparty elections were held in 1992. Moi demonstrated remarkable skill in dividing and ruling the opposition each time, and was returned to office both in 1992 and 1997 (Ajulu 1998; Throup and Hornsby 1998). The cost, however, was election-related ethnic violence, even more anti-developmental rent management, and a chilling of the investment climate. In the early 1990s, per capita income grew by just 0.08 percent a year (Mwega and Ndung'u 2008: 328, Table 10.1).

In 2002 Moi stepped down, and his great rival Mwai Kibaki won the ensuing presidential election. Economic management improved on the basis of the kind of interstitial rent management we outlined earlier in this chapter. Nevertheless, continuing instances of grand corruption, associated in particular with Kibaki's Kikuyu ethnic group, generated serious grievances against the regime. Manipulated by politicians on both sides of the political divide, resentments erupted in election-related violence in 2007, with deleterious consequences for the investment climate (Economist Intelligence Unit 2008c: 2009).

Decentralized, long-horizon rent management Just as Kenya slid from a successful rent management system in the mid-1970s to a less successful one, so did Côte d'Ivoire. But the details are different. In the previous section we saw that Kenya managed to retain a centralized structure of rent management, even though rents became increasingly oriented to the short term. In Côte d'Ivoire, the opposite was true. The desire and vision for long-term development remained, but the system for centralizing rents had fallen into disrepair.

CÔTE D'IVOIRE, 1975–80 Commentators do not quite agree on when the Ivorian model began to go wrong, but it is clear that by the mid-1970s, not all was well. In 1970, Houphouët had announced a new direction in development strategy, declaring that Côte d'Ivoire was aiming to be the next South Korea (Alemayehu Dereje 1997). Henceforth, the focus would be on industrial diversification, in particular the promotion of agro-processing export industry. The aim, among other things, was to absorb into the labor force a new generation of school leavers, many of them scions of the elite, as well as to try to ameliorate growing regional disparities (Rapley 1993; Riboud 1987; Tuinder 1978). A panoply of organizations was created to fund new business and industrial ventures in the private sector, and the state's own role in industry increased (Alemayehu Dereje 1997: 145; Rapley 1993).

In retrospect it is clear that these plans were overambitious. By the mid-1970s, the number of parastatal projects was mushrooming. The planning process had become less detailed, consisting in the adumbration of some broad objectives, and a cascade of investment proposals (Tuinder 1978: 28). Many investments also took place outside the planning process, and financing decisions became decentralized, so that parastatal agencies ran up large debts without the knowledge of the central bank (Alemayehu Dereje 1997: 155). Investment increased by 50 percent in 1975 and 1976, and by 70 percent in 1977 (Riboud 1987: 13). Alemayehu speaks of an 'almost uncontrolled expansion of public spending' (Alemayehu Dereje 1997: 150). Making matters worse, the parastatal sector did not operate with the same norms of efficiency and probity as the private sector, summed up by Houphouët's injunction to not 'look too closely at a peanut-roaster's mouth' (Akindes 2004: 11–12).[21] The incremental capital-output ratio and domestic resource costs rose, returns on investment began to shrink, and private investment began to dry up (Alemayehu Dereje 1997: 150). And yet the state continued to fund the expansion, draining resources from agriculture and running up huge external debts.

The impact on economic performance was notable. Growth slowed from 8 percent a year in the 1960s to between 5 and 6 percent in the 1970s. Inflation jumped from 12 percent in 1975 to 27 percent in 1977 (Riboud 1987: 15). The debt/GNP ratio reached 43.4 percent in 1980, and the debt service ratio 23.9 percent. The current account imbalance, which had begun only in the 1970s and had reached 9.8 percent in 1975, was 17.4 percent by 1980 (ibid.: 16). The result was a serious financial crisis (ibid.: 3).

Commentators agree that underlying the loss of macroeconomic control was a change in the structure of patronage, which shifted from a centralized to a 'segmentary' system. At the beginning of the post-independence period, the president himself decided the amount and form of patronage distribution. But in the 1970s, smaller centers of power were building their own patronage networks. According to Fauré, 'The decision-making process was decentralized in the sense that the peripheral networks were also gaining power, leading to the emergence of a "*gagne-qui-peut*" mode of behavior among competing network centers' (discussed in Alemayehu Dereje 1997: 153). Médard agrees: 'Although we have seen how Houphouët centralized his management of patronage, it seems that he lost control of it to the benefit of his "barons" towards the second half of the 1970s' (Médard 1991: 202).[22]

In the early 1980s, Houphouët restored a degree of centralization, reining in some of the excesses of the parastatal sector (ibid.: 202–4). But given the challenges in the external environment, these measures proved insufficient to halt the economic slide. The government was weakened, and proved politically incapable of taking measures to protect the health of the economy in the long run, such as reducing the price of cocoa. A youthful population became more and more restive, while land pressure in the countryside began to put a premium on the question of 'autochthony'. Increasing political tension, not helped by the uncertainty surrounding Houphouët's succession, led in the early 1990s to a democratic transition, which the ruling party initially survived. However, following Houphouët's death in 1993, the PDCI fractured further, and the polity became increasingly divided along ethno-linguistic lines. This set the scene for winner-takes-all multiparty politics, the 1999 coup, civil war, and disputed elections in 2010 – events from which the country has yet to recover.

Decentralized, short-horizon rent management Finally, we present our fourth regime type. If Kenya between 1980 and 1992 experienced centralized but short-horizon rent management, and Côte d'Ivoire between 1975 and 1980 suffered long-horizon decentralized rent management, in Malawi between 1994 and 2004, evidence suggests that rent management was both decentralized and oriented to the short term.

MALAWI, 1994–2004 By the end of the 1970s the economic model established by Banda was in trouble. A series of external shocks put the highly leveraged estate and parastatal sector under pressure, but instead of making necessary adjustments the regime gambled on an upturn in the external environment that failed to arrive (Pryor 1990). By this stage Banda was already in his eighties and there are signs that he was losing his grip on the administration. 'Advisors' including his nurse and mistress, Cecilia Kadmazira, and her uncle John Tembo, became more influential, but there is little sign that they had the nation's development at heart. As Banda became more erratic, and as rumors of political succession loomed, the civil service became paralyzed, and policy-making passed into the hands of the IMF and the World Bank, who presided over halting and ineffective reform programs. Dissatisfaction with the regime grew, and by the early 1990s the momentum for political transition was unstoppable (Cammack et al. 2010).

Banda and the MCP were removed from power following a referendum and multiparty elections in 1994. The new president was Bakili Muluzi, a former businessman and senior member of the Malawi Chamber of Commerce and Industry. Unfortunately his party, the United Democratic Front (UDF), failed to win an outright majority in parliament, initiating a period in which lower-level political actors and factions set the terms of rent distribution. Muluzi attempted to hold his minority government together by manipulating a series of shifting coalitions, whose members were always vulnerable to being bought by opposition leaders (Englund 2001). At the same time local UDF activists clamored for deliverables, trying to fulfill the expectations of a demanding electorate. Muluzi began to expand his cabinet and fill parastatal positions with cronies, and to promise expenditures that bore no relation to the budget. These trends accelerated around 1998 as pressure to win the election intensified, and became even worse subsequently as the president sought to change the constitution and run for a third term.[23]

Rent-seeking at all levels became rampant. It is clear that Muluzi and his close associates were the biggest culprits. Rumors and scandals surfaced regularly, especially after his first term, and there is evidence that the president profited personally from scams in sugar distribution and vehicle procurement. Money was illicitly earned and used to fund political careers, pay off supporters, hire youth, and crush opponents. But at the same time, benefits were 'scattered': you 'could not point to one person who was in charge of spoils'.[24] At one point there was talk of creating a UDF-linked company, but apparently this was shelved when Muluzi and close associates realized they would not be able to control its flow of funds. Instead they deliberately used outsiders to win government contracts and took kickbacks;[25] even national food reserves were sold. Many politicians bought farms, transport companies, buses, guest houses, hotels, bars, and private schools, as did bureaucrats. Government jobs were used as a 'stepping stone' to business opportunities, which civil servants prioritized over their official duties. Corruption with impunity spread, and public service provision declined (Anders 2006; Global Integrity Report 2007; Khembo 2004). Meanwhile Press Corporation was broken up, partly to undermine the economic base of the opposition (Van Donge 2002).

Patronage considerations also came to dominate the bureaucracy. The UDF perceived many civil servants to be MCP loyalists, and in a single day during the first term, thirteen principal secretaries were retired. They were replaced or augmented by 'personal advisors' whose main qualification was that they were loyal (Cammack et al. 2010). Apparently development planning continued along more or less rational lines in the first years of Muluzi's tenure, but as the 1999 election approached, political imperatives became paramount (Cammack 1998, 2000).[26] Matters were not helped by the prevailing climate of 'rights talk', which encouraged civil servants to protest and strike over issues like restructuring and inflation, and to take cases of dismissal to the ombudsman or courts. Senior officials' willingness to manage staff, already weakened during the late Banda era, declined still more (Cammack et al. 2010).

The impact on economic performance was damaging. The Muluzi regime came to office during an acute economic downturn, characterized by strikes, political unrest, low levels of aid, and drought-induced hunger, and initially its bold new liberalization policies met a favorable response. Between 1995 and 1997 investment and public finances recovered, growth reached 10 percent, the smallholder sector expanded and there were early signs of economic diversification (Harrigan 2001). But the gains were short lived. Thereafter growth declined year on year until 2001, when it turned sharply negative, the economy sinking under the weight of what Harrigan calls 'election pressures'. In almost every sector problems increased: food insecurity resulted periodically in famine, environmental degradation worsened, deindustrialization proceeded, as did joblessness, infrastructural deterioration, and fiscal instability (Fenkenberger et al. 2003). Malawi's GDP per capita hovered at around US$160, while the Human Development Index stagnated (Government of Malawi 2006; International Monetary Fund 1998, 2003).

Conclusions

In the previous four sections we have used the historical experience of political and economic development in Côte d'Ivoire, Kenya, and Malawi to illustrate the rent management relationships identified by the model we presented earlier in this chapter. Together with our wider Asia–Africa literature review, these historical cases confirm that successful developers centralized economic rents, orienting them to the long term through reasonably successful industrial policies that provided incentives for transformative investments in agriculture and industry. In all three of the cases we considered, strong post-independence leaders did this by limiting political competition (while ensuring that the polity remained relatively inclusive), building top-down patron–client networks, and creating space for competent technocratic management and industrial planning.

The model and supporting case studies confirm the conditions under which neo-patrimonialism is compatible with strong economic performance. The conventional wisdom that development is impossible under neo-patrimonial arrangements is thereby shown to be wrong. Provided the right conditions hold, neo-patrimonialism is a 'good enough' form of governance for economic development, and one that may go more with the grain, and make a 'better fit' with socio-political realities in many African states, than good governance.[27]

Some words of caution are in order, however, and here the hetero-dox intimation that governance challenges in Africa are insignificant is also shown to be wrong. Even the successful neo-patrimonial states we studied were not without problems, and all eventually succumbed to more damaging forms of clientelism and rent-seeking. What were the reasons? A first set of reasons might be called 'policy mistakes'. There is growing evidence, especially from Southeast Asia, that successful developers invariably place increasing productivity in agriculture, and in particular in smallholder agriculture, ahead of industrial expansion, with the former providing a secure foundation for the latter (Henley 2010a; Van Donge 2002; Van Donge et al. 2012). While Kenya, Malawi, and Côte d'Ivoire all had serious agricultural development policies, and avoided the most egregious forms of urban bias that we touched on in the last chapter, none devoted as many resources to agriculture, or to smallholders, as did Indonesia, Vietnam or Malaysia (Henley 2010b). This was particularly the case in Malawi, where smallholders were sometimes impoverished by the expansion of the estate sector. Further, with the possible exception of Côte d'Ivoire, none of the countries we studied made a serious effort to convert gains in import substitution industrialization (ISI) into export-oriented industrializa-tion, in the way that successful East Asian states did.

A second set of reasons relate to what we call 'succession issues'. All three of our cases saw performance deteriorate either when the post-independence leader died, as in Kenya, or when their abilities began to decline, as in Malawi and Côte d'Ivoire. It is difficult to know whether this was an inevitable consequence of economies becoming too large and diversified for a personalistic structure to manage, or whether it was because these states had the misfortune of being led by aging leaders, whose faculties were on the wane. It is probably a combination of both, but political succession is clearly a major problem for developmental patrimonial regimes (see also Crouch 1979; Olson 1993).

A different sort of caution relates to the human rights record of developmental patrimonial states. All had more or less constrained forms of democracy, imperfect judicial institutions, and a tendency to flout civil liberties, sometimes, as in the case of Malawi, to a drastic extent. We spend more time elaborating on the pitfalls of competitive multiparty democracy for long-horizon rent management in subsequent chapters. At this point we merely note that there may be a trade-off between human rights in the form of political civil liberties, and human rights in the form of social and economic rights. In this book we try to avoid taking a normative position on which is more important, and focus instead on elucidating processes and relationships.

In the following chapters we develop these points, using our model to illuminate patterns of development in contemporary Tanzania, Ghana, Ethiopia, and Rwanda. We were drawn to these countries in part because of their recent economic success, which gave us cause to think that they might be modern-day examples of 'developmental patrimonialism'. As we will see, the story is actually more complex than that. Nevertheless, the extent to which these regimes have succeeded in centralizing rent management and gearing it to the long term plays a key role in our analysis of their developmental strengths and weaknesses.

2 | TANZANIA: GROWTH WITHOUT POVERTY REDUCTION

Our first case study is Tanzania, an East African country of more than forty million people, rich in land and natural resources, with a long coastline that provides a gateway to the sea for a regional market of six landlocked countries. Tanzania has a dominant ruling party that has governed the country since independence, presiding over a remarkable degree of political stability. In the past decade this has been combined with quite strong economic growth, and very recently with some signs of structural transformation. When we began our research for this project, we thought that Tanzania might be a modern-day example of developmental patrimonialism. However, closer scrutiny reveals that there are problems with its system of rent management, and that although sharing some of the features of regimes in the bottom right quadrant of the model outlined in Chapter 1, it also has elements from the top left quadrant. In other words, it is a mixed type, and probably closer to the short-run decentralized ideal type than to the centralized long-horizon one.

Historical context

Tanganyika, one of Britain's least-developed colonial possessions, gained independence in 1961.[1] It had been led there by the young Julius Nyerere, leader of the territory's only significant nationalist party, the Tanganyika African National Union (TANU). TANU had won all but one of the seats in the first non-racial elections, its domination assisted by the fact that Tanganyika was and remains an extremely diverse nation, with around 127 ethnic groups, none of them providing a suitable vehicle for political mobilization. Despite this already unusual degree of political control, Nyerere felt that further centralization was necessary for his political and developmental vision to be realized. Between 1962 and 1965, a number of measures were taken to further strengthen his grip, including the creation of a republican constitution, a one-party state, and the co-optation of trade unions. The party's supremacy over the parliament, and Nyerere's supremacy over the party, were confirmed in 1967, first with the expulsion of several Lake Zone MPs, and then with the flight into exile of party secretary and populist organizer Oscar Kambona (Coulson 1982; Pratt 1972, 1976; Sterkenburg and Thoden van Velzen 1973). Thus was cemented a political architecture which provided Nyerere and the inner circle around him with considerable discretion over the direction of economic policy and the creation and utilization of rents.

Nyerere's economic vision was one of *ujamaa* or African socialism, which posited that socialism could be built on traditional African work practices and ways of living (Nyerere 1962). Nevertheless, for the first six years of independence, economic policy remained broadly neo-colonial. The country's economic plans were written largely by Europeans, and they emphasized expanding cash crop production through the progressive farmer or 'focal point approach', and attracting foreign capital by means of appropriate investment guarantees and incentives in industry. Nyerere's influence was clearest in the rapid expansion of the rural cooperative movement, which was seen as a suitable vehicle for the transition to rural socialism, and in isolated, largely unsuccessful experiments in communal farming (Coulson 1982).

Economic performance under these arrangements was quite good overall. With the exception of sisal, the country's main export crops all expanded at a fairly rapid rate, and food crops were also in surplus. In the industrial sphere, a mini-investment boom that began around 1955 continued until the mid-1960s, the main investors being East African Asians, settlers, traders, and multinationals. Between 1960 and 1966, value added in manufacturing grew by two and a half times (ibid.: 168–75), the balance of payments was healthy (ibid.: 145–67), and per capita incomes grew at 2 percent a year (Bigsten and Danielson 2001: 15). Even though there were signs that some rents were being squandered in the cooperatives and in petty acts of predation by TANU officials, it was clear that rent management was much tighter than in countries like Congo or Nigeria, with their extremely destabilizing contests for spoils. Moreover, policy, while unambitious, was reasonably well aligned with Tanzania's resource base and governance capabilities.

Nyerere, however, worried that this pattern of development was leading to inequalities that would ultimately undermine the new nation. With the Arusha Declaration of 1967, the government made a turn to the left. The Declaration contained two major components:

nationalization of the economy's commanding heights, including the banks, major industries, and retail trade; and a leadership code that prohibited TANU officials from owning private businesses. It was the Leadership Code, according to Cranford Pratt, that was the key aspect of the Declaration, and it was motivated by Nyerere's concern over the degree of personal acquisitiveness and corruption in the party (Pratt 1976) – an attempt to restrain rent-seeking, in other words. The nationalizations, meanwhile, were promulgated, apparently, in order to get the party on board.[2]

Unfortunately, the increased control over rents that the Arusha Declaration afforded did not lead to faster or more sustainable economic growth. The main problem was an economic policy that was anti-capitalist and anti-smallholder. To begin with, private investors were now discouraged from investing in Tanzania, except in joint ventures with the state. Foreign management was often brought in to manage state projects, but often it proved unsatisfactory. Tanzanian managers, meanwhile, were often chosen on political rather than economic grounds, and worker discipline also slackened under the prevailing anti-colonial, anti-capitalist ideology (Bryceson 1990; Coulson 1982; Hyden 1983). The result was that many investments were non-performing and wasteful, and while industry grew initially, this was not sustained (Coulson 1982). In agriculture, the policy became one of forcibly moving peasant farmers into communal villages, where they were supposed to spend part of their time working on their own farms, and part on a communal or 'bloc' farm. However, work on communal farms was often of poor quality, and there were other problems caused by pests and soil erosion. At the same time the state, via marketing boards and an appreciating exchange rate, was taking an increasing share of the world price for Tanzania's cash crops, which acted as an incentive to smuggling and a disincentive to production. Further problems were caused by inefficient marketing arrangements for cash crops, and, even more seriously, for food. By the late 1970s the economy was heading toward a profound macroeconomic imbalance; the 1978 war with Idi Amin's Uganda tipped it over the edge (Bryceson 1990; Coulson 1982; Ellis 1983; Havnevik 1993; Raikes 1986; Shao 1986; Svendsen 1986).

With the economy in crisis, the system for managing rents collapsed. Smuggling and black-marketeering became rife, and parastatal agencies became little more than vehicles for peculation. In the early

1980s most Tanzanians lived by their wits, while a small minority became rich through illicit activities. The leadership attempted to get its long-term vision back on track via a succession of unrealistic policy initiatives combined with crackdowns on so-called 'economic saboteurs' (Bryceson 1990; Campbell and Stein 1992; Maliyamkono and Bagachwa 1990; Tripp 1997). But it was not until 1985, when Nyerere stepped down and was replaced as president by Ali Hassan Mwinyi, that the tide began to turn. The new regime rapidly came to an agreement with the IMF, which signaled a new policy direction. In the agricultural sector, some aspects of trade were liberalized (Havnevik 1993: 298), while in the industrial sector some parastatals were privatized, and others wound up. Other companies saw management or employee buyouts, but many remained under state control (Tripp 1997: 91). Trade was freed, importers and exporters made large profits, and, while most of the gains were secured by Asians and Arabs, a small African business class began to emerge (Havnevik 1993; Tripp 1997).

With an increasing amount of economic activity reoriented to formal channels, the state regained some control over rents. In addition, the deal with the IMF saw the resumption of large foreign aid transfers to Tanzania. But the desire or ability to discipline rent-seeking never reattained the levels of the 1960s or early 1970s. The Mwinyi era witnessed unprecedented scandals. In the most notorious instance, improper discretionary tax exemptions originating in the Ministry of Finance in 1993/94 led to a large fiscal deficit and the freezing of much foreign aid (Bigsten and Danielson 2001: 20). There were equally massive abuses of a government import-financing 'counterpart funds' scheme. If *ruksa*, or laissez-faire, was one of the era's watchwords, another was '*rushwa*', or 'economic corruption'. Many leaders had been running private businesses on the sly for years, and in 1991 this was legitimized by the Zanzibar Declaration, which overturned the Arusha Declaration's Leadership Code. Those with political connections rushed to acquire land, the assets of former parastatals, and directorships in private companies (Gibbon 1995: 14; Havnevik 1993: 308–9).

By the late 1980s Tanzania had embarked on a period of modest economic growth. Per capita incomes grew at 0.6 percent a year between 1986 and 1997 (Bigsten and Danielson 2001: 20). However, improvements to the investment and business climate left much to be desired. In spite of the National Investment (Promotion and Protection) Act of 1990, which offered safeguards against nationalization without compensation, an Investment Promotion Center, and a package of incentives (Tripp 1997: 89), economic volatility, poor infrastructure, red tape, and governance problems, including high levels of corruption, remained major concerns (Bigsten and Danielson 2001: 102).

In 1992, Tanzania made a transition to multiparty democracy. The first elections were held in 1995, returning the *Chama cha Mapinduzi*'s (CCM's) Benjamin Mkapa with a large majority. Mkapa was widely regarded as being sympathetic to the good governance agenda, and the pace of reform quickened. Privatizations accelerated, a tough line was promised on corruption, and the government began running cash budgets. This last policy was an attempt to get the macroeconomic situation under control and thereby qualify for HIPC debt relief, which became something of an obsession for the regime (Kelsall 2002). More generally, the government seemed keen to court donors and investors, a trend which led, as we shall see, to some sizable investments in the mining sector. According to *The Economist*, 'This period of concord between the Government and the Bretton Woods institutions led to Tanzania becoming a star reformer in the eyes of many donors: foreign loans and grants have accounted for around 40 per cent of the Government's budget revenue since then' (Economist Intelligence Unit 2008b: 17).

Today, Tanzania's broad economic goals are embodied in three main documents. Vision 2025, which was adopted in 1999 and envisages Tanzania becoming a middle-income, industrialized country over the next twenty-five years; the Medium Term Plan, adopted in 2004, which sets out sector strategies to achieve that goal; and the National Strategy for Growth and Poverty Reduction (MKUKUTA), adopted in 2005, which provides a further framework for attaining 'high and shared growth, high quality livelihoods, peace, stability and unity, good governance, high quality education and international competitiveness' (United Republic of Tanzania 2005: 1).[3] Among the targets are accelerating GDP growth to 6–8 percent per annum, increasing growth in manufacturing from 8.6 percent to 15 percent, increasing agricultural growth from 5 percent to 10 per cent (ibid.: 37), reducing rural poverty from 38 percent to 24 percent and urban poverty from 26 percent to 13 percent (ibid.: 37).

As we shall see in the next section, the government is not on course to meet all these goals, and we shall argue that this is because rent management is subject to serious short-term pressures and is only partially centralized. This could already be seen by the time of Benjamin Mkapa's second term in office, when old corrupt elements in the party were invited back into his cabinet, and there were signs that the president himself was feathering his own nest. Since then, public discontent with government policy and practice, articulated mainly through the media and civil society, has grown more vocal (Kelsall 2002, 2003). Criticisms of the ruling party notwithstanding, its presidential candidate, Jakaya Kikwete, swept to victory with 80 percent of the vote in 2000 (Kelsall 2007). Corruption scandals and controversy have continued, however, and when Kikwete was again returned to office in 2010, it was with a much smaller margin of victory.

Rents, industrial policy, and investment

The pattern of rent management in Tanzania today is a mixed one. On the one hand, rents are a virtual monopoly of ruling party members, and there has been some success in centralizing rents at a macro level, primarily through new financial management systems. Combined with some modest initiatives in industrial policy, these have furnished sufficient macroeconomic stability for some significant foreign investments in Tanzania. But on the other hand, significant areas of rent management, at the level of ministries, departments, and agencies (MDAs), remain short-termist and decentralized. This to some extent undermines current industrial policy, while constraining more ambitious initiatives.

Rent centralization Turning to the successes first, Tanzania since 1995 has made considerable progress in strengthening macroeconomic management and balancing its budget. This is partly due to a raft of reforms, including the Civil Service Reform Programme, the Accountability, Transparency and Integrity Programme, and most importantly, the Public Financial Management Reform Programme (PFMRP) (Gray 2012). The latter aims to improve budgeting, public accounting, auditing, and procurement. It uses sophisticated computer software to strengthen budget preparation and implementation, while an integrated financial management system known as EPICOR is used to provide better financial controls by forcing government departments, ministries and agencies to justify their estimates with evidence from past performance. The initiative also enables civil society and development partners to monitor public expenditure management through the Public Expenditure Review, and to evaluate performance annually through the Public Expenditure and Financial Accountability Review (PEFAR) (HakiElimu and Policy Forum 2010: 49).

While the success of PFMRP in attaining its most ambitious goals is debatable, one relatively simple and powerful mechanism for resource centralization, as mentioned earlier, has been the introduction of a cash budget system for budget execution. The Ministry of Finance and Economic Affairs (MoFEA), which is pivotal in this process, limits aggregate expenditure in any given month to average revenue collection in the previous three months, plus program aid (ibid.: 20–1). By controlling resource disbursements in this way, MoFEA is able to keep the budget broadly in balance, with the happy effect, at least until recently, of a generally low inflation rate, a phenomenon that has undoubtedly helped the investment climate.[4]

The investment climate has also been helped by some specialized investment promotion institutions. Probably the key agency stimulating Tanzania's economic growth is the Tanzania Investment Center. The TIC was set up under the Tanzania Investment Act of 1997 with the aim of promoting and facilitating investment in Tanzania. Consistent with the kind of 'light-touch' investment facilitation favored by Western donors, it is a one-stop shop for investors that brings various government departments, including the Ministry of Lands, the Tanzania Revenue Authority, the Ministry of Industry, and the Business Registration and Licensing Agency, together to streamline investment processes (Corporate Guides International Ltd 2010: 57). The TIC also offers a package of incentives to investors who meet a minimum investment threshold, including duty exemption on capital goods, capital allowances on industrial plant, buildings and machinery, VAT exemption on inputs, investment guarantees, repatriation of profits, and import duty drawback.

The TIC has won various African and international awards, including 'Best Investment Promotion Agency in the World' in 2007. Since 2000, when it became operational, investment inflows have increased from 178 projects worth $870 million per year to 871 projects worth $6.68 billion per year in 2008 (ibid.: 58).

The government has also introduced other institutions in line with international best practice. In 2001 it established the Tanzania National Business Council, chaired by the president, to provide a forum for consultation between government and business (ibid.: 57). There are also 'round tables' for domestic and international investors, and for chief executive officers. All provide an opportunity for private investors to dialogue with the president (ibid.: 57). In 2004, the government set up the Business Environment Strengthening for Tanzania (BEST), and in 2006 Tanzania was rated as one of the top ten business reformers by the World Bank. Recently, according to the Doing Business survey, improvements seem to have run into a wall, prompting the creation of a government task force to address these problems (ibid.: 59–60).

Another key agency is the Export Processing Zones Authority (EPZA). EPZA is an autonomous agency acting under the Ministry of Industry, Trade, and Marketing, established as part of the Tanzania Mini-Tiger Plan 2020 (2004), which is an attempt to emulate some of the methods of successful Asian countries. The idea is to attract FDI 'migrating birds' by means of special economic zones, or 'ponds'. The Plan targets GDP growth at 8–10 percent per annum by 2020, exports to expand from $1.1 billion to $40 billion, and per capita income to be increased from $280 to at least $1,000 (Mbelle 2007).

Under this plan, EPZA 'coordinates, facilitates, promotes and licenses export-led manufacturing investments' in Tanzania (Corporate Guides International Ltd 2010: 99), in part by administering thirteen Economic Processing Zones, with five industrial parks currently functioning. EPZ investors need to export 80 percent of their production, which makes them eligible for a range of incentives, including exemption from corporate tax for ten years; unconditional transferability of profits, dividends, royalties, etc.; exemption from taxes levied by local government authorities; and exemption from VAT on utility and wharfage charges. EPZ investors also get lower port charges, access to an export credit guarantee scheme, and rapid project approvals (ibid.: 99). A recent report stated that some eighty-five companies have been registered to work under EPZA, about half of which were infrastructure developers, and half manufacturers. The latter included diamond and gemstone cutters, and manufacturers of mosquito nets and steel rods.[5] Since its creation, EPZA has apparently facilitated over $300 million worth of exports, and created thousands of jobs (EPZA 2010). In 2008 the Chinese and Tanzanian governments discussed the possibility of Chinese investment in a $2 billion special economic zone south of Bagamoyo, scheduled to include an international airport, a deep seaport, and satellite communications equipment (Various Authors 2011b).

Setting up economic zones under specialized agencies is a type of industrial policy that both orthodox and heterodox development thinkers agree upon. Tanzania has had some success, it seems, in creating these agencies as 'islands of excellence' in a sea of less developmental rent-seeking. As we will see, however, these islands are under threat of being submerged. In addition, it is not clear that EPZA pays much attention to fostering the kinds of backward and forward linkages to the rest of the economy, or other types of spillover effects, that heterodox thinkers recommend (see Stein 2011).

The government is also preparing a more ambitious Integrated Industrial Development Strategy and Master Plan, which aims to develop the industrial sector by looking at the entire supply chain (Corporate Guides International Ltd 2010: 88). Among other things, the Strategy aims to develop large-scale economic zones at the waterfronts of each of Tanzania's four 'development corridors' (ibid.: 88), and to develop agro-processing industries (ibid.: 91).

One example is the Mtwara Development Corridor, under discussion since 1992, which aims to boost development in a zone encompassing parts of southern Tanzania, northern Malawi, and Mozambique. The strategy, which is overseen by Tanzania's National Development Corporation (NDC), includes upgrading transport links, developing port facilities, and energy infrastructure. The NDC has identified mining, petrochemicals, agriculture, and tourism as potential growth areas (National Development Corporation n.d.). In January 2011, the strategy finally began to show signs of bearing serious fruit, as the government and Chinese firm Sichuan Hongda Corporation finalized a $3.5 billion deal that would see production of coal, electricity, and iron ore at Mchuchuma and Liganga, both located in the corridor. It was hoped that the deal would be the key to solving Tanzania's chronic electricity shortages (Felix 2011).

Short-horizon, decentralized rent management But this is only one side of the rent management story. The other side is that rent and resource centralization appear to be much less successful at the level of individual ministries, departments, and agencies (MDAs). In other words, although the center is broadly successful in disciplining the amount that MDAs spend, it has much less influence over what that money is spent on. In several institutions critical to economic performance, incompetence, corruption, and waste are rife. For example, rent-seeking in the Ministry of Agriculture means that fertilizers do not reach the farmers they are supposed to; cronyism in the Department of Education prevents schoolchildren receiving sufficient schoolbooks with which to learn; incompetence in the health service means that Tanzanians suffer chronically poor health; venality in the national roads agency means that Tanzania pays over the odds for its roads; corruption in the forestry service means that the nation's natural resources are being plundered, and so on (Cooksey and Kelsall 2011; Cooksey 2011b).

Perhaps the most damning indictment of Tanzania's overall development strategy is that unproductive rent-seeking has been allowed to intrude into the strategic and essential areas of power generation, Dar es Salaam port management, and agriculture. Two major scandals have affected the Ministry of Energy and Minerals and TANESCO, the state-owned electricity supply company, in recent years. Numerous surveys have identified energy supply as the single biggest obstacle in the business environment in Tanzania, and thus a binding constraint on investment (see Confederation of Tanzania Industries 2011; Cooksey 2011b).

The first scandal involved Independent Power Tanzania Ltd (IPTL), and the government purchase in June 1995 of a diesel power plant from a Malaysian company, with a view to addressing an acute seasonal power shortage (Cooksey 2002). At $160 million, the project was vastly overpriced and advised against by Ministry of Energy and World Bank officials. High-level members of the government were rumored, however, to be profiting from the deal, and it received approval in record time, in the process further postponing a natural gas power project designed to reduce dependence on hydro and oil-fueled power plants. When details surfaced, there was a public outcry and President Mkapa referred the contract to international arbitration. However, allegations of corruption that could have invalidated the contract were withheld from the tribunal, which ruled that the value of the investment had been seriously inflated. Though the final power purchasing agreement was considerably less than that originally proposed, Tanzania was still saddled with a project that depended on imported fuel, did not figure in the country's long-term power strategy, and was commissioned too late to avoid the power crisis that it was designed to avoid (ibid.; Khan and Gray 2006).

The next scam also occurred at a time of seasonal power shortage, but was even more brazen. In 2006 an American company called Richmond-Dowans Ltd won a tender to supply electricity with a low-priced bid that was deemed suspicious by TANESCO officials. Particularly worrying was the fact that the contract contained a clause that forced TANESCO to pay the company money, whether or not it was successful in supplying power. According to a parliamentary probe into the matter, the Richmond bid was steamrollered through by the prime minister, Edward Lowassa, assumed to be acting in concert with CCM treasurer Rostam Aziz. The probe also found that Richmond-Dowans had no previous experience in supplying electricity, and was in fact a fictitious company registered at the premises of a small print company in Houston. Not surprisingly, the new power supply failed to materialize, and yet Tanzania was still paying $100,000 dollars a day to the company, in the context of an acute power shortage (Gray 2012; Parliamentary Select Committee 2008). Subsequently Lowassa resigned as prime minister, thus beginning a long factional struggle within the CCM that culminated, in 2011, with Aziz resigning his seat.

It is difficult to know how much Presidents Mkapa and Kikwete knew or wanted to know about the IPTL and Richmond scams. Khan and Gray interpret the fact that Mkapa referred the case to arbitration, but then failed to ensure that documents alleging corruption reached the tribunal, as evidence of his being unable to discipline rent-seeking networks within his own party (Khan and Gray 2006: 51–4). If they are right, it is evidence for the decentralization of rent management in Tanzania. But even if they are wrong, it is clear that these deals were made with a view to short-term profiteering.[6]

Another major constraint on Tanzanian economic performance is its ports system. Dar es Salaam is an inefficient overburdened port. In 2008 goods took an average twenty-three days to clear, compared to 3.5 days in India and ten hours in Hong Kong (Economist Intelligence Unit 2008b: 15). The concession for the terminal is held by a Far Eastern company operating under the name Tanzania International Container Terminal Services (TICTS). Initially the company had great success improving efficiency at the port, and even began to attract traffic from Mombasa and Mozambique. However, the terminal rapidly reached full capacity (a situation not helped by problems with the Tanzania Harbour Authority, and with the fact that some importers use the port as a cheap storage location), and traffic slowed.[7] The company was then granted approval for expansion plans and an extension to its lease by the cabinet, in non-transparent circumstances. The fact that TICTS' local business partner was Nazir Karamagi, a former minister for energy forced to resign over the Richmond scandal, fueled fears that there was something untoward about the contract (Tarimo 2008).

A further example of a short-horizon approach to rent manage-ment comes from the agricultural sector. In 2005 President Kikwete, without consulting his technical advisors, announced that by 2010 Tanzania would plant one million additional hectares of irrigated rice. This overambitious plan subsequently failed to secure the backing of most donors, but it has proceeded using the government's own funds and soft loans from the World Bank worth $155 million. Initial research into the schemes suggests that although there has been a rapid increase in irrigation infrastructure in certain areas, and some corresponding rice production gains, the infrastructure is already falling into disrepair. One theory is that the increase in local public goods provision has been aimed less at a sustainable increase in rice production, and more at creating opportunities for rent-seeking by local-level bureaucrats, through the control they have over procure-ments and construction contracts (Therkilsden 2011).

Tolerance of damaging rent-seeking deals like IPTL and Rich-mond can be partly explained by electoral pressures. The CCM has now triumphed in four multiparty elections, but its victories can be attributed more to the regime's broad social base and organizational power than to the popularity of its policies or the performance of the government.[8] CCM has a large network of party officials extending from the center to village level. The bureaucracy is also generally sympathetic to the ruling party, and many are party members, even though party and state are supposed to be delinked. The armed forces and security forces also have intimate links to the ruling party, and taken together they make a formidable organizational structure. The mere presence of an opposition, however, offers an exit option for lower-level CCM cadres, and increases their bargaining power within the party, as did the post-1992 democratization of internal party structures, which made the presidential nomination a matter for the national conference. Because of these changes the party roots and branches must be generously fed and watered, which creates huge pressures for politicians to engage in corruption and other income-generating projects (Kelsall 2002, 2003).[9]

In recent years both CCM and the opposition have tried to mobilize support from private businessmen, and the CCM has been the more successful at this. Prominent private businessmen like Iddi Simba and Rostam Aziz have acted as campaign managers for Presidents Mkapa and Kikwete respectively, and Aziz became CCM's treasurer (he subsequently resigned, as we have seen). In fact, many MPs have business interests themselves, and the links between politicians and business in Tanzania are the subject of much public disapproval.

As political competition within the ruling party and between the ruling and opposition parties increases, so short-term considerations come to dominate. CCM candidates need the resources of men like Lowassa and Aziz, especially when it comes to buying the support of local activists in primary elections. These determine the composition of the national conference that selects the presidential candidate. One interviewee stated: '[These days] nobody is thinking longer-term … the political apex cannot stop a dubious deal because nobody is asking and nobody knows what is dubious.'[10]

A variety of institutions exist to try to stop such scams, and to reduce corruption and waste. Most have received donor support in recent years. For example, the parliament and its committee system, the Office of the Auditor and Controller General, the Prevention and Combating of Corruption Bureau (PCCB), and the media and civil society (HakiElimu and Policy Forum 2010: 20–1). 'Capacity-building' in these institutions is supposed to improve governance, and with it the investment climate. However, progress has been slow. In spite of vociferous criticism of rent-seeking deals from opposition (and some ruling-party) politicians and civil society, the incentives for long-term development provided by these horizontal and bottom-up accountability mechanisms appear to be outweighed by the incentives Tanzania's party system and political culture provide to engage in short-term corruption. Partly as a result, Tanzania has been trending downwards in the World Competitiveness Report and Doing Business surveys since 2006 (Various Authors 2011b).

Sectoral examples

We can get a better understanding of these processes by looking in more detail at some of Tanzania's more productive economic
sectors, namely gold and horticulture. These sectors were chosen
because they have experienced growth in recent years, and have a
high potential, either directly or indirectly, to alleviate poverty. We
expected, then, that they would provide an illuminating window on
how the Tanzanian regime manages rents, and the likely implications
for long-term development. We find that in both cases the government
has provided only mixed support, occasionally doing things that have
helped the sectors and occasionally harming them.

Gold Gold has been mined commercially in Tanzania since the 1920s
and was an important commodity for the country prior to World
War II. After independence, however, private mining companies were
nationalized, investment dried up, and production reverted largely to
artisanal methods (Holloway 2000). This was to change in the late
1980s, after gold was identified by the government and its donors
as a potentially lucrative sector to develop. When President Mkapa
formally opened the first large mine at Bulyanhulu in July 2001,
Randall Oliphant, president and chief executive officer of Barrick
Gold, the world's largest gold mining company, said, 'When we came
to look at Africa for mining investment, our destination of choice was
Tanzania. Why? Because Tanzania has become a role model for Africa
and the world in terms of creating a progressive economic, investment
and legal climate for mining companies' (Cooksey 2011a). The story,
however, is actually much more complicated than this. While the
government has taken various measures, some of them probably not
legal, to support the growth of the gold sector, in other ways it has
hindered it. Here we outline these different faces of the government's
mineral policy, and explain the furore that surrounds it.

The first investors in gold mining in Tanzania were junior exploration companies, attracted by the government's new attitude
of openness to foreign investment, and the promise of a favorable
incentives regime. Exploration yielded promising finds, and between
1998 and 2003, six major mines, some of them involving the world's
biggest mining companies, were commissioned. These investments
took place under the auspices of what are called Mineral Develop-

ment Agreements, in other words a concession or a contract for a company to develop a mine.

Some of these Agreements' terms and conditions were consistent with international best practice in investment promotion. They were designed to facilitate mining operations as well as to protect large mining investments against risks that could undermine long-term profitability. They protected the companies against changes in tax rates, made provisions for profit repatriation, hiring of foreign staff, arbitration and so on. They also included various investment incentives, including tax waivers on imported capital equipment and fuel imports, VAT exemption on local and imported supplies, and provisions for standard-rate income and payroll tax. The royalty rate on mining company profits was set at 3 percent, and although this has been controversial, it is not out of line with international practice.

There were other aspects of the Agreements, however, that were internationally unusual. Particularly glaring was a tax write-off for capital (investment) costs plus an additional 15 percent in capital allowances for 'unredeemed capital expenditure'. If these were not claimed in a given year they could roll over to future years, meaning that the mining companies could put off the payment of company tax for a number of additional years, if not indefinitely. Given that these are worth millions of dollars a year to the big mining companies, a suspicion of corruption has inevitably arisen (although we have been unable to find any hard evidence of this). These commitments were later consolidated with the 1997 Financial Laws Act and the 1998 Mining Act (Cooksey and Kelsall 2011).

The next stage in developing the mining industry was the physical clearance of mine sites. Over the years, hundreds of thousands of artisanal miners had drifted into mining sites, and they had now to be removed. The problem was that the legal situation was complex, and many of the miners claimed legal title to the land they mined. At Bulyanhulu, the site of the first major clearance, miners entered a dispute with Sutton Resources – the Canadian company that originally signed the agreement to develop the mine – that dragged on for two years.[11] Throughout this process the authorities vacillated, appearing sometimes to support the small miners, and sometimes the company. The tide began to turn some time in 1995. Shortly after coming to power, new president Benjamin Mkapa began to be lobbied by a pro-Sutton Resources team that included the Canadian high commissioner.

Mkapa was desperate to win donor confidence and present Tanzania as a destination favorable to foreign investment, and was himself a former high commissioner to Canada, so it is little surprise that the team got a favorable hearing. In July 1996 the small miners were ordered by the government to leave, and the Field Force Unit began evicting them. The miners secured a High Court injunction ordering the evictions to cease, but nevertheless, in August 1996, regional authorities gave the green light for the company's bulldozers to clear the site. There are reports from miners and NGOs that fifty-four miners were buried alive during this operation. The mining company and the government have contested this claim and it has never been proved. Nevertheless, it has haunted the mining industry ever since (Cooksey 2011a; Cooksey and Kelsall 2011).

Although these actions helped to get commercial gold mining off the ground in Tanzania, subsequent high-level political support for the sector has been uneven. In 1994 the World Bank financed a $14.5 million Mineral Sector Development Technical Assistance Project to build capacity and strengthen regulatory authority in the Ministry of Energy and Minerals. However, the program never gained much traction, and the Mining Division continues to suffer from widespread petty rent-scraping. In the words of one of our informants, 'Everybody is on the take.'[12] Among the problems mentioned are the demanding of bribes to issue mining or prospecting licenses, the purchase by officials themselves of mining rights, the pre-emptive issuing of rights to speculative investors upon learning of genuine mining company interest, the leaking of inside information to speculative parties, and the issuing of multiple titles by different offices. Problems like this have acted as deterrents to exploration, which in turn have constrained the development of a more mature, and pro-poor, mining sector (Cooksey 2011a; Cooksey and Kelsall 2011).

Another way in which government support for the mining industry has been uneven is in the honoring of incentives extended to the mining companies. The Mineral Development Agreements, as we have seen, came bundled with some highly attractive tax incentives. However, in practice mining companies have not always been able to realize these incentives, and this is because of problems at the Tanzania Revenue Authority (TRA).[13] The TRA's performance was widely criticized by our respondents. They argued that TRA officials ignore the tax conditions contained in different Agreements,[14] routinely ignore responses and challenges to tax assessments, and use their authority to make illegal demands.[15] One respondent described receiving 'ridiculous' assessments.[16] The process of taking disputes to the Tax Revenue Appeals Board, the Tax Tribunal, and the Appeal Court is lengthy and unpredictable (the latter can take 'years' to make a decision), and a favorable decision by the Appeals Board may be reversed by the Tax Tribunal if TRA appeals.

The government, especially under the leadership of Jakaya Kikwete, has also failed consistently to defend commercial mining against a rising tide of negative public opinion. Revolted by the nature of mine clearances and the scale of the incentives gifted to mining companies, a number of prominent national and international NGOs, backed by sections of the media and the opposition parties, have maintained a steady stream of criticism. By 2010, an election year, the pressure on government had grown so strong that a new, more populist, mining law was drafted. This was opposed by the Tanzanian Chamber of Minerals and Energy (TCME), the mining companies' business association, but to no avail.

The Act, according to industry insiders, meant that Tanzania can no longer expect to attract significant investments in exploration and mining. On the contrary, it is likely to accelerate the exodus of exploration and mining companies. In a press release, the TCME stated that the new Mining Act 'carries fundamental weaknesses and concerns that are bound to hold back the growth and development of a sustainable and competitive mining industry in Tanzania'. The Bill 'fails to appreciate' that to 'become the preferred destination for mineral exploration and investment', Tanzania needs to become 'significantly competitive vis-à-vis other countries' mining jurisdictions'.[17] Barrick has criticized the 2010 Mining Act for the way it grants the minister discretionary powers to make or interfere with commercial decisions, together with its potentially negative impact on 'transparency and room for abuse of power', the combined effect being additional 'insecurity and unpredictability in the investment regime' with 'negative impacts on [the] ability of investors to finance projects'.[18]

Although the mining industry has been Tanzania's biggest source of foreign investment and furnishes large amounts of foreign exchange, its development has to be regarded as something of a failure. Arguably, Tanzania would be best served either by a flourishing artisanal mining sector, or a dynamic commercial sector, but currently it has neither. The way in which the commercial industry was established deprived tens of thousands of small miners of their livelihoods, while making overgenerous concessions to mining company interests. This constrained the potential for mining to contribute in a meaningful way to public finances. Between 1998 and 2005, Tanzania exported $3 billion in gold but received only $90 million in revenue, 3 percent of the export value (Economist Intelligence Unit 2008b: 21). At the same time, lack of strong political support in enforcing the regulatory regime has retarded the growth of the sector. According to some industry experts there could be two hundred or more junior explorers in Tanzania when in fact there are only thirty; and there could be up to two hundred medium-sized gold mines, when instead Tanzania has none (Spencer 2008). The recent populist turn in mining policy makes the continued expansion of the sector even more unlikely, despite unprecedented gold prices.

Horticulture Tanzania, having the soils and climatic conditions to suit a variety of flowers, cuttings, and seeds, has a high potential for export horticulture. Today, it has a small horticultural sector. Its first firms began to arrive in the late 1980s, attracted over the border from Kenya by Tanzania's comparative political stability. While most of the early experimenters failed, some survived, and the industry continued to grow throughout the 1990s. The value of horticultural exports from Tanzania increased from $5.2 million in 1997 to $26.7 million in 1999 (ESRF 1999), and in 2008 exports were worth an estimated $146 million.[19] By mid-2010 there were fifteen or so companies growing flowers, flower cuttings, and seeds for export. In addition, five companies export vegetables, vegetable seeds, and fruit.

The government has supported the sector in a variety of ways. We have already mentioned the country's famed political stability, which was a key consideration for several investors. Divestitures from the government's non-performing estate sector also permitted investors to acquire land. Several grew their businesses with the help of concessional finance from the Tanzania Investment Bank, and horticulturalists are eligible for the standard package of incentives offered by the TIC. In addition to this, the government has helped support a farmers' association, the Tanzania Horticultural Association (TAHA), also funded by the Dutch and American governments. Finally, there is a good road linking the main horticultural export areas (Arusha and Kilimanjaro) with Kilimanjaro International Airport, although it was not built specifically with horticulturalists in mind.

However, in a number of other ways the Tanzanian government is falling short of what we might expect from a state serious about supporting development in this sector. The subsequent paragraphs will discuss land and water rights, taxation, air transport, and credit.

Most of Tanzania's horticultural exporters acquired land, as we have seen, by purchasing farms in Tanzania's state-owned estate sector. The history of land rights in this sector is a complex one, dating to the early years of the last century when German, and subsequently Greek and British, settlers carved out farms around the base of Mount Meru and Mount Kilimanjaro. These land acquisitions were highly controversial, since they limited the local population's access to grazing land and their scope for agricultural expansion (Spear 1997). After independence, most of the settlers left. The estates were handed over to parastatals, villages, and cooperatives, but when these were unable to farm them economically, informal occupation or squatting of the land ensued (Cooksey and Kelsall 2011).

When Tanzania began liberalizing its economy in the 1980s, some of this land found its way back into the hands of former owners, and some into the hands of politicians, officials, and other private individuals, including the flower farmers mentioned above. The process appears to have been fairly haphazard and not part of a deliberate policy to develop the horticulture sector. Perhaps as a consequence, local authorities have often been equivocal in their support of investors. Most have had to fight ongoing battles, legal and physical, with squatters and other hostile members of the community to clear land and prevent farm reinvasions, a task that has constrained their investment decisions and the size of their businesses. Moreover, victory in the courts is not always translated into success on the ground, since, in the words of one investor, 'What matters is local politics, not the law.'[20] Although state support for investor interests grew throughout the 1990s, most investors still spend considerable time and energy cajoling local officials or going over their heads in defense of their property rights (although as of 2010 most felt those property rights were quite secure). Most also spend considerable sums on private security. A similar situation sometimes obtains with respect to water rights.[21]

There are also problems with taxation. During the early 2000s, the TIC offered a package of incentives to horticulture investors, which doubtless helped attract some of them to the country. Unfortunately, implementation of these measures has tended to be poor. Several respondents reported that VAT and import duty exemptions granted by the Ministry of Finance through the TIC are not honored by the TRA or the Director of Customs respectively. According to some respondents, TRA officials routinely inflate tax liabilities as a ploy to negotiate unofficial deals. Claims for VAT refunds can take up to two years to complete.[22] In addition, businesses frequently have their imported inputs held up at the border point until duty is paid, despite the fact that they should be duty free. Claiming back duty is a 'long and often futile task' (World Bank 2005). One respondent told us that 'bureaucracy' and lack of coordination between government departments costs his business hundreds of thousands of dollars. These and other weaknesses in the business environment add an estimated 20 percent to the cost of doing business.[23] In the words of another investor, the tax authorities 'try to make your life as miserable as they can'.[24]

Nor has the government been particularly constructive with regard to taxation during the recent global financial crisis. Many governments around the world reduced taxes on key productive sectors in response to the crisis. The government of Tanzania did not reduce taxes on the horticulture sector. Worse, the 2009/10 budget abolished exemptions on 'deemed capital goods'. This came as a rude shock to the horticultural investors since most of their agro-inputs came into this category (Tanzania Horticulture Association 2009). In the 2009 budget, the government of Tanzania also announced the imposition of VAT of 18 percent on airfreight exports, a provision rescinded only after sustained lobbying by TAHA.[25]

We saw in an earlier chapter that one of the most useful things a government can do to stimulate investment is to use its convening power to correct coordination failures. For example, at nearby Kilimanjaro International Airport (KIA), small exporters rely on sending cargo with commercial airlines, but by doing so they run the risk of flight cancellation or being told there is no free cargo space on any particular day.[26] Risks would be reduced if there were a dedicated horticultural freight handler. To make freight handling commercially viable, each consignment needs to be about forty tonnes, but Tanzanian horticulture producers are still below this critical mass. In 2008, TAHA temporarily solved this problem by entering into an agreement on behalf of its members with British freight handlers MK Airlines. The deal involved MK collecting a consignment of fish from Entebbe, then horticulture products from KIA, and finally other freight from South Africa. However, MK failed to survive the global credit crunch, and there is no longer a dedicated freight carrier at KIA. In mid-2010, exporters were using Nairobi and Dar es Salaam for their exports, pending a second attempt at securing a dedicated freight service into KIA. A government with a more proactive industrial policy might have done more, it seems, to ensure either that the industry had critical mass, or that a freight handler was temporarily subsidized during an expansion phase, or both.

Aside from the problem of not having a dedicated freighter for horticultural products, Kilimanjaro International Airport is comparatively expensive. This is in part because freight handling in Tanzania is a monopoly of Swissport. In contrast to Swissport's monopoly in Dar es Salaam and KIA, in Nairobi there are five companies vying for customers. In addition, landing fees and fuel taxes are much higher in Kilimanjaro than in Kenya. For example, in 2008/09, fuel taxes alone added $23,000 to a typical consignment exported from Tanzania (although intensive lobbying by TAHA has succeeded in reducing freight costs by an estimated 30 percent).[27] Because of these problems, most exporters prefer to transport their produce 250 kilometers to Nairobi. However, the road to the border at Nairobi is poorly maintained, and the border itself does not operate efficiently.[28]

The past few years have been a challenging period for farmers. Many small Dutch flower and seed companies were bankrupted by the 2008 financial crisis, which saw a 15 percent decline in flower sales. Flower auction prices fell, and demand for some varieties ceased completely. As we have seen, a government-guaranteed financial facility for flower companies helped the industry get off the ground in its early years, and following the 2008 credit crunch the Tanzania Investment Bank agreed to reschedule growers' loan repayments. But it has not supplied sufficient overdraft facilities for the sector to finance running costs, and most farms are therefore permanently cash strapped. Investors in Tanzanian horticulture are yet to see a return on their investments, and the credit crunch has put the break-even point back perhaps by years.

Economic performance

What has been the effect of this system for managing rents on economic performance? According to the Economist Intelligence Unit, 'Tanzania's economic performance over the past 10 years has been one of the best in sub-Saharan Africa' (Economist Intelligence Unit 2008b: 19). A report by the OECD and other partners states that 'Economic prospects for the medium term continue to look bright' (Various Authors 2011b: 3). GDP growth has been strong, averaging 7 percent a year from 2001 to 2009, and rebounding to 6.8 percent in 2010, following a dip in 2009 (ibid.). It is forecast to remain around this level into 2012 and 2013 (Economist Intelligence Unit 2011d: 3). Growth has been combined with one of the lowest inflation rates in the region and a manageable external deficit (Economist Intelligence Unit 2008b). There have been high inflows of FDI (mainly in the mining sector, where inflows peaked at $516 million in 1999) (ibid.) and aid. As discussed in a previous section, strong management in the Ministry of Finance takes much of the credit for this.

Unfortunately, this economic growth has had a negligible impact on poverty. In the sixteen-year period 1991–2007, poverty fell by about 5 percent, but most of the change resulted from progress in Dar es Salaam. While the percentage of people living in poverty declined slightly, population growth meant that the total number of people living in poverty increased by about 1.3 million (Various Authors 2011b). Meanwhile the gap between rich and poor increased also, with the poorest 10 percent of the population experiencing falling consumption. Poverty in rural areas remained a stubborn 37.6 percent, down only 1.2 percent from 2001 (ibid.).

When it comes to meeting the poverty reduction targets of the MKUKUTA, or the Millennium Development Goals, Tanzania is consequently well off track. In fact, Tanzania performs much worse in this respect than comparator countries in Africa and Asia, such as Ghana, Uganda, India, and Vietnam (Policy Forum 2010). It is not doing much better on other social indicators, and is likely to reach only about half of the MDGs overall (Various Authors 2011b).

These trends are partly explained by the composition of growth. Most has come from the construction, tourism, mining, and telecoms sectors (Department for International Development 2011). Agriculture and manufacturing, sectors with a typically high impact on employment and poverty, grew less quickly. In the decade to 2009, agriculture grew at 4 percent a year, but with population growth at 3 percent a year, the impact on livelihoods was marginal (Policy Forum 2009). The manufacturing sector grew at 6.5 percent per year between 1996 and 2006 (Mwaigomole 2009: 32), with its share of value added to GDP remaining constant at around 7–8 percent. Moreover, diversification remained poor, with industry highly concentrated in food, beverages, tobacco, and textiles, putting Tanzania virtually at the bottom of the trade diversification index (103 out of 110) (UNIDO n.d.).

This is beginning to change. Recently the Tanzanian economy has shown progress in attracting new, lumpy investments, such as the Mchuchuma/Liganga coal and iron plant discussed above, and also in developing relatively new industries like steel, driven in part by the rise in construction. As we have seen, Tanzania's export processing zones are also attracting increased levels of investment, manufacturing exports within the region are increasing, and it is not impossible that these investments will boost employment and income in a significant way. Figures released since we began writing this book show a rather dramatic surge in manufacturing production and, even more surprisingly, in manufacturing exports (Various Authors 2011b). Manufacturing exports hit $808 million in 2010, an increase of 55 percent on the previous year (ibid.), and continued to rise thereafter. According to the Bank of Tanzania, manufactured goods were destined mainly for the region, and included cement, textile apparels (including mosquito nets), edible oil, plastic items, and iron and steel products as well as wheat flour (Kamndaya 2011).

Yet at the same time, the government has allowed fiscal discipline to slip, and in 2010 its budget deficit reached 6.9 percent of GDP (Economist Intelligence Unit 2011d).[29] Inflation has risen sharply and is now in double digits, the shilling has hit new lows against the dollar, and the external deficit is forecast to reach 10.9 per cent of GDP (ibid.). The government is taking measures to support the shilling as a result, but this is perhaps attacking the symptom of the problem and not the cause (ibid.). In fact, the government is facing a major financial squeeze, hit by rising food and energy prices, and reduced tax collection. Donors, disappointed with the progress of good governance reforms, have also contributed, scaling back their funding pledges for 2010/11 by about $250 million (Various Authors 2011b). It is not clear, then, that recent gains in manufacturing and exports will be sustained, while the outlook for agriculture appears gloomy.

Conclusions

Tanzania has certainly made progress since the early 1980s, when the socialist economy was mired in crisis and people returned to subsistence production and black markets just to survive. Growth has been steady and macroeconomic management, with a few blips, has generally been sound. However, the country seems stuck in a state of moderately high growth without entering take-off, while poverty reduction remains poor. Recently there has been some progress in manufacturing, but it is too soon to say whether or not this will be sustained. We are inclined to be skeptical.

The main reason is that although Tanzania has succeeded to a large extent in centralizing rent management through the Ministry of Finance, the mechanisms that would permit Tanzania to really maximize its growth and poverty reduction potential are underdeveloped. This manifests in a number of forms: first, in the failure of policies intended to raise productivity in agriculture; secondly, in the decentralized, opportunistic rent-seeking that has been allowed to infect areas of crucial strategic importance to the Tanzanian economy, notably energy; thirdly, in the comparative lack of drive behind the country's industrial policy, meaning that investments in sectors like gold and horticulture lack the kinds of coordination that would maximize their contribution to sustainable growth; fourthly, in endemic and unproductive corruption in the country's ministries, departments, and agencies that diverts resources from the production of public goods essential to long-term investment; and finally, in corruption endemic to Tanzania's regulatory agencies, especially the taxation service, that increases the nuisance and unpredictability of doing business in the country, and undermines some of the incentives to investors provided by Tanzania's better development agencies.

Because of its favorable location, natural resource abundance, and easy-to-manage ethnic politics, it is possible that Tanzania will continue to attract investment and to grow, and that some of that growth will trickle down. But we still believe that Tanzania is underperforming by some margin. To accelerate growth, and more importantly poverty reduction, the leadership must transcend its focus on short-term rent-seeking for factional and electoral gain, and focus instead on tightening rent-seeking within the ruling party. It needs to stop anti-developmental rent-seeking from undermining strategically important sectors, such as power generation, ports and roads, while building the capability to undertake smarter industrial policy for areas like agriculture and manufacturing industry. Whether this is possible in Tanzania's prevailing political system, where both ruling party factions and the political opposition are growing in strength, remains to be seen (compare the discussion in Khan 2010).

3 | GHANA: A STAR BUT STATIC PERFORMER

Our second contemporary case is Ghana, a country of some twenty-five million people, lying on the West African coast. Although not a 'mineral-dominated economy', it is relatively rich in natural resources, with significant deposits of gold and recently developed oil reserves. The south of the country is well watered and fertile, suitable for the production of cash crops, in particular cocoa, which has traditionally formed the mainstay of the economy alongside gold. After years of political turmoil it made a democratic transition in 1992, and now has one of the most lively democracies on the continent. It has been growing quite rapidly over the past decade, poverty reduction has been strong, and in 2011 the Overseas Development Institute hailed it as a developmental 'star performer' (Overseas Development Institute 2011). If anywhere on the continent proves the idea that the good governance agenda is working, it is Ghana, and in this chapter we take a critical look at this view. Behind the impressive figures for growth and poverty reduction, we show there are rather few signs of structural transformation, or of the kinds of technological upgrading required for transition to sustained growth. The reason, we argue, is that a pattern of decentralized, short-horizon rent management means that long-term strategic objectives, such as might be served by a credible industrial policy, tend to be subordinated to short-term goals.

Historical context

The territory today known as Ghana was home in the pre-colonial period to several centralized polities, including the kingdom of Asante, which had risen to become Africa's greatest empire on account of its trade in slaves and gold. With the introduction of colonial rule, the structure of the economy changed, with gold production passing largely into European hands, and cocoa coming to dominate the domestic cash economy. Colonial development brought education and class differentiation, which gave birth to Ghana's nationalist movement (Austin 2005; Crook 1990a; Rathbone 1978).

Ghana's first nationalist party, the United Gold Coast Convention

(UGCC), was formed in 1949 (Whitfield 2009). From the beginning, it had two wings, a conservative wing associated with chiefs and higher-level professionals, and represented by J. B. Danquah, the party's founder; and a more radical wing associated with blue-collar workers, junior civil servants, ex-servicemen, and the unemployed, which looked for inspiration to Kwame Nkrumah, the party's general secretary. When it came to business interests, the conservative wing tended to represent established businessmen, while the Nkrumah faction represented what Richard Rathbone has called 'aspiring entrepreneurs' (Rathbone 1973).

In 1949 the UGCC split and Nkrumah's faction left to form the Convention People's Party (CPP) (ibid.). From this date we begin to see the emergence of a form of patronage politics that influences Ghana to this day. The CPP's business backers were local men of some standing who were able to mobilize a local following, and who expected to be rewarded once the CPP won power. The first opportunity came with the capture of municipal councils prior to the 1951 general election. At this juncture a slew of local government contracts was awarded to members of the CPP's political clientele: 'For the first time the usual names of brick-makers, carpenters, latrine builders, change in favor of new names, and many of these had strong links with the CPP' (ibid.: 397).

Nkrumah went on to form a national government, and then led the country to independence in 1957. A visionary socialist, he promised to 'make Ghana a paradise in ten years' (Killick 2010: 38). The plan was to use rents from cocoa, and income from forced savings, to finance a far-reaching economic transformation program, including the creation of heavily mechanized state farms and the growth of numerous new industries. These plans were in accord with the conventional development wisdom of the time, which envisaged, among other things, a 'big push' for development (ibid.: 59–60). The plans were also, unfortunately, hugely overambitious. The Ghanaian civil service, while relatively strong at independence, was not equipped to carry through the kind of far-reaching transformation desired by Nkrumah. The first seven-year plan (1962–69) was a technically flawed document based on insufficient data. There was a relative neglect of sector performance and programs, and there were no mechanisms to ensure coordination of the plan with annual and departmental budgets. The kinds of import controls the plan was premised on, for example, required a much more capable state than Ghana possessed (ibid.: 289–313, 359–97).

The plans, however, were not adopted for economic reasons alone: there was also a patronage dimension. When the CPP took power, it used the state to reward its supporters, greatly expanding the number of jobs in the civil service and public enterprise. Economic policies, such as the decision to have a state farm in every parliamentary constituency, or to situate different components of a footwear industry in different corners of the country, were often made not on grounds of economic rationality, but for political reasons (ibid.: 249–56). Generally speaking, Nkrumah lacked both the means and the will to prevent his ministers from signing off on projects that had more of a political than an economic justification, and as a result the number of non-performing projects mushroomed (Berg 1971). Despite the massive levels of investment, economic performance was extremely disappointing, and after 1965 the economy entered a phase of profound imbalance (Killick 2010; Rimmer 1992).

Fearing dissent, Nkrumah had by this time taken steps to centralize political power. The trade union movement was neutralized, a Preventive Detention Act introduced, and in 1964 the country became a one-party state (Rathbone 1978). There was little time to test whether this centralized structure would permit a more judicious management of rents, however, since in 1966 Nkrumah was overthrown by a coup. The incoming National Liberation Council worked hard to restore some kind of economic rationality, overseeing some market liberalization and encouragement of foreign investment; but the economically unviable industries created by Nkrumah were never thoroughly overhauled. The economy was still fragile, then, when it was handed over to the avowedly liberal Progress Party (PP) government of Kofi Busia in 1969. Busia continued with liberalization, although haltingly, and raised the prices delivered to cocoa farmers, his main political constituency. There was a cocoa windfall, but because of insufficient political and economic control, this stimulated a surge in imports which led to a massive devaluation of Ghana's currency, in 1971 (Killick 2010).

In 1972, Busia was turned out of office by the Supreme Military Council of Colonel I. K. Acheampong. Acheampong pronounced Busia's liberal economics to be bankrupt, and initiated a return to far-reaching economic controls, including the nationalization of

Ghana's gold mines. However, rather than being used for long-term development, this system of rent centralization appears to have been almost invariably geared to short-term personal gain, and the regime came to be regarded as one of the continent's worst kleptocracies. At one point cocoa farmers were receiving only 10 percent of the world price, leading to declining crop purchases and widespread smuggling. As the economy plummeted, *Kalabule*, a term for black-marketeering, became the era's catchphrase (Austin 1996; Killick 2010).

In 1978 Acheampong was overthrown by Lieutenant General Fred Akuffo, and then Akuffo himself was overthrown by a junior officer, Flight Lieutenant Jerry John Rawlings, in 1979. Rawlings executed his two predecessors before restoring power to the civilian government of Hilla Limann later that year. Limann's government was unable to halt the economic slide, however, and Rawlings again took power in 1981. He was to rule Ghana for the next twenty-one years, first through the Provisional National Defence Council (PNDC), a military regime with popular organs throughout the country, and then through the National Democratic Congress (NDC), a political party that won democratic elections in 1992 (Jeffries 1996).

The first years of Rawlings's regime were ones of intense economic hardship for Ghanaians, but after 1983 the economy began to rebound. Rawlings had struck a deal with the IMF, and his finance minister, Kwesi Botchwey, was pursuing a series of liberal reforms. But despite a recovering economy, private investment remained depressed; most of the growth came from a resurgent public sector and cocoa economy, together with a rise in non-agricultural exports like timber and gold (Gibbon et al. 1993; Handley 2008; Rimmer 1992). This pattern continued until 1992, when macroeconomic management also began to deteriorate, making private investment more difficult still (Killick 2010).

Part of the reason was the persistence of the kinds of state–business relations present since the birth of two-party politics back in 1949. We have seen that Nkrumah used the power of the state to award contracts to his business supporters. In 1969, when the UGCC's conservative wing took power in the shape of Kofi Busia's Progress Party, privileges tended to be withdrawn from pro-CPP businessmen and steered to PP supporters instead. The pendulum swung back when Rawlings, whom many saw as the inheritor of the Nkrumahist mantle, assumed control in 1981. Old-regime businessmen were persecuted, and a new, pro-PNDC business class nurtured instead. Dozens of NDC stalwarts 'exploited the provision of loans, grants, lucrative contracts, implicit exemption from payment of taxes, acquisition of public enterprises, and other incentives to enter business' (Opoku 2010: 147). Examples include civil servants the Awhoi brothers, First Lady Nana Rawlings, presidential aide Tsatsu Tsikata, and politician Eddie Annan. 'In sharp contrast to the decline of opposition business,' Opoku says, 'NDC insiders flourished' (ibid.: 147).

With the return to multiparty politics in 1992, these trends were amplified. Opoku explains how local businessmen in Brong Ahafo, for example, were expected to contribute transport, money, food, drink, cold storage, and other resources to NDC election campaigns. Those that did so were sometimes rewarded with contracts, land, and a generally cooperative attitude from district authorities. Those that didn't, or those known or suspected of supporting John Kufuor's New Patriotic Party (NPP), were victimized in a variety of ways (ibid.: 161–87).[1]

In 2002, the NDC lost power to the NPP. Kufuor came to power promising a 'Golden Age for Business', and in the first few years of his regime the government managed the economy sensibly while making a number of regulatory changes to the benefit of private business. The economy responded strongly, but by 2008 macroeconomic management had once more gone off the rails (Killick 2010). Although the economy has continued to grow at a respectable rate, there remain question marks over how far the government is committed to the promotion of truly dynamic private business. Knowledgeable observers tend to agree that while Ghana is doing reasonably well, it could do much better.

Rents, industrial policy, and the investment climate

In this section we look in more detail at the climate for business in Ghana. Contrary to analyses that laud Ghana's economic success, we show that a pattern of decentralized, short-horizon rent management that has its roots in the country's political competitive clientelism creates major obstacles to productivity-enhancing investment.

Private sector development: 'best practice' or 'jobs for the boys'? One of the NPP's first acts on coming to power was to create a new Ministry for Private Sector Development. The ministry was tasked with developing and coordinating the implementation of a Medium Term Private Sector Development Strategy (PSDS) (2004–08), and in 2005 this gained significant donor support (Broemmelmeier et al. 2007). The Strategy was well aligned with conventional donor wisdom on strengthening the investment climate, and focused on enhancing Ghana's competitive position in global and regional markets, improving the efficiency and accessibility of national markets, increasing competence and efficiency at firm level, and strengthening public–private dialogue (Government of Ghana Private Sector Development Strategy 2010). It has been described as 'a show case for successfully managing business reforms' in Africa (Broemmelmeier et al. 2007: 7). Partly as a result, Ghana has made steady progress up the World Bank's Doing Business league table, from 81st out of 155 economies in 2005, to 67th out of 189 economies in 2011 (ibid.: 17; World Bank and International Finance Corporation 2010). In 2006 it was classed as a 'top ten reformer' in the areas of trading procedures, tax procedures, and land registry, and in 2007, it was a 'top ten reformer' in procedures related to starting a business, registering property, getting credit, reforming trading procedures, and enforcing contracts (Government of Ghana Private Sector Development Strategy 2010: 17). On almost all measures it outperforms other West African countries, and it was rated as the fourth-best place to do business in Africa in 2009 (Killick 2010: 459).

Yet problems remain. An evaluation of the PSDS remarked that the lack of demonstrable impact on 'bread and butter' issues made it difficult to attract and sustain political commitment, and some programs had been stymied by personnel changes, both of which contributed to patchy implementation of reforms.[2] Partly as a result, Ghanaian firms remain smaller and less competitive than their African rivals, and the country stands at 114 in the World Competitiveness Index, behind comparator nations like Tanzania, Kenya, and Uganda (Government of Ghana Private Sector Development Strategy 2010: 5).

At the time of writing, arrangements were in place for a PSDS2. This was divided into two components: Component 1, which focused on the Business Environment, and appeared to be close to conventional investment climate wisdom, and a more heterodox Component 2, which focused on Enterprise Growth and Job Creation, and included programs in skills development, rural finance, and an agricultural value chain facility (Danish Ministry of Foreign Affairs/

Danida 2009). However, in April 2011, when the fieldwork for this chapter was conducted, progress was at something of an impasse. Some of our informants questioned how high private sector development ranked among the government's priorities, while others attributed the delays to management problems in the Ministry of Trade and Industry (MoTI).[3]

To understand this we need to step back a little and review the broader landscape of Ghanaian politics. Ghana today has a highly competitive two-party system. In 2000, the NPP seized power from the NDC, presidential candidate John Kufuor winning the run-off with a fairly slim 56.6 percent of the vote (Nugent 2001). Then in 2008 the NDC won power back, this time with a margin of less than 1 percent! Competition for votes is obviously intense, and this puts local-level activists, known in Ghana as 'footsoldiers', in a strong position vis-à-vis national party leaders (Whitfield 2011b: 33–6). Another point we need to grasp is that most Ghanaian voters expect their representatives to deliver private or club goods, such as money, jobs, or roads, rather than public goods like legislative scrutiny, macroeconomic stability, or a friendly environment for business (Lindberg 2009). When combined these two phenomena have a detrimental impact on government–civil service and government–business relations.

To take the civil service first, some commentators have argued that bureaucracy in Ghana functions less as an instrument for achieving social or economic goals, and more as a patronage resource for the government of the day (Killick 2005). Like other African states, Ghana has had a number of donor-driven programs to strengthen the public sector and public finances over the past twenty years, but none of these has gained much traction. According to Opoku, for many years the public service has been handicapped by 'the persistence of a bureaucratic ethos of deliberate delays, an aversion to transparency, and tendency to privatize office for personal gain. Public officers in Ghana often treat their workplace like their personal domain and make their own "rules" which supplant laid down procedures and rules' (Opoku 2010: 197).

In interviews in Ghana in 2011, we heard complaints that although the regulatory arms of the state had improved, customs, tax inspection, land administration, and other services still left much to be desired. In addition, some of the special agencies created to help Ghanaian exporters, such as the Ghana Export Promotion Council and the Free Zones Board, were under-resourced and lacking capacity. The Free Zones Board, for example, was tasked with setting up industrial parks in four regions of the country, but because of resource shortages and difficulties acquiring land, only one of these, at Tema, was fully operational. In addition, business costs in the zones tended to be high, partly because infrastructure services were supplied by a private contractor.[4] The Ghana Export Promotion Council, in spite of some success in boosting non-traditional exports, had had its budget cut, and external funding had dried up.[5] We are not suggesting here that these special agencies were rendered ineffective by direct competitive clientelist pressures. Rather, we are suggesting that a regime focused on winning elections by dispensing private and club goods is unlikely to devote sufficient supervision and resources to state agencies that are likely to deliver benefits only in the long run.

Another reason that 'best practice' business reforms receive only vacillating political support is that the underlying logic of Ghanaian politics inclines leaders toward cronyistic relations with businessmen, and businessmen to short-term, politically opportunistic investments. This is a problem that pre-dates political liberalization, but the close-run nature of recent electoral contests seems to have intensified it. As Buur and Whitfield explain,

> Increasing vulnerability of ruling coalitions to losing power at the next election resulted in two tendencies. First, the ruling elite focused on extracting as many rents through political office as possible. Sometimes this involved creating their own businesses to take advantage of opportunities created by state regulation or intervention, but often in areas that were not directly productive. Second, businesses attached to the ruling coalition have short time horizons, with entrepreneurs focused on sectors with quick, certain returns to investment (again, often not in production). (Buur and Whitfield 2011: 24)[6]

Our interviews confirmed this analysis. Informants characterized business–politics relations in terms such as the following: 'the domestic private sector wants easy concessions from government. Pro-regime businesses get favors, others are systematically left out';[7] 'An unfortunate impression has been created that you need to court government for your business to prosper';[8] 'The parties are like private companies, competing for power and then paying themselves back. We have to learn not to award contracts to our cronies who are inefficient and become moneybags.'[9]

Despite the NPP's proclamation of a 'Golden Age of Business', much in the pattern of business–politics relations remained the same. Pro-NDC stalwarts like Eddie Annan found themselves out of favor, while old supporters of the liberal tradition were back in the fold (Opoku 2010: 221). Among the measures government introduced to help business was a Ghana Investment Fund, but there are allegations that this was distributed along cronyist lines (ibid.: 223). Certainly, questions have been asked about several of the biggest business deals of the NPP era, awarded under such favorable terms that it is hard not to suspect foul play. One is the concession granted to Kosmos Energy to exploit Ghana's most promising oilfield, at a royalty rate substantially below that levied on other Ghanaian fields (Arnold and Wallis 2010). Another is the deal in which Vodafone acquired Ghana Telecom, apparently in the absence of a level playing field and for a knock-down price. Ghana Airways' best routes were sold to GIA, an obscure group of investors who came only fourth in the official assessment of bids. Zakhem International Ltd is alleged to have received $150 million of taxpayers' money for the Kpone Power Project, but has made little progress to date (Murray 2010). A deal under which Balkan Energy refurbished the Osagyefo barge and leased it back to the government at a huge mark-up has also come under scrutiny. Balkan's owner, Gene E. Phillips, has previously stood trial for racketeering in the USA (ibid.).

After the NDC returned to power in 2008, it began to query some of these dubious deals. It quickly suspended and opened for investigation several of the NPP's pre-election contracts.[10] In the words of one informant, 'The minister is signing contracts only for the next minister to throw them away.'[11] In addition, it worked in other ways to punish pro-NPP business, such as Databank Services Ltd, about which it issued a damaging report.[12] That this was a manifestation of competitive clientelism, rather than a genuine concern for issues of probity, is suggested by the hullaballoo surrounding some of the contracts the NDC itself has awarded: for example, a $10 billion loan from Korea to build public housing using a Korean company (Otchere-Darko 2011), and $15 billion worth of contracts with China for infrastructure and oil and gas development.[13] Meanwhile old NPP stalwarts like Eddie Annan are now back in business after being sidelined for eight years.[14]

A further effect of election-induced competitive clientelism is to upset macroeconomic stability. Ghanaian governments ran large budget deficits in 1992, 1996, 2000, and 2008 (Killick 2010). The result has been rising inflation and interest rates, and an unstable exchange rate. In 2010, for example, interest rates were in the region of 30–40 percent, and all the businessmen we spoke to in 2011 bemoaned the high cost of credit, regarding it as a major blot on the business landscape: 'The government tells us the private sector is the engine of development, but it is an engine without oil!' quipped one.[15]

The potential for an intensification of Ghana's patronage politics was magnified in 2007, with the confirmation of lucrative hydrocarbon reserves off Ghana's coastline, a discovery that generated a quasi-religious response among politicians and public alike (McCaskie 2008). Oil began pumping in December 2010, and it stands to make a significant contribution to Ghana's public finances, conceivably providing the basis for a much more ambitious industrial policy than hitherto. However, given the current dynamics of Ghana's competitive clientelist politics, there are well-founded concerns that these revenues will be mismanaged, only exacerbating Ghana's current macroeconomic instability. A potential portent came in March 2011, when legislators passed the Petroleum Management Bill. The original draft of the bill contained a provision which prevented the Ghana government from using oil as collateral for loans. After heated parliamentary debate the provision was replaced with one that permitted the exact opposite (Anonymous 2011).

In the next section we home in on some of Ghana's more and less successful economic sectors, with a view to understanding more about the government's commitment to transformative growth.

Sector evidence

Patronage politics impacts on Ghana's sectoral economic performance in different ways. In some sectors, political rationality and economic rationality dovetail; in others, the pickings are too slim to be of much interest to politicians; and in others, political considerations tend to overwhelm economic rationality. In the subsequent paragraphs we will illustrate these points with studies of the cocoa, horticulture, and industrial sectors respectively.

Cocoa Since the onset of economic liberalization in the 1980s, Ghana's most successful economic sector has been agriculture. It has grown at over 5 percent a year for the past twenty-five years, making it the world's fourth-best performer, ahead even of countries such as Brazil, China, and Vietnam (Wiggins and Leturque 2011: 3). At the center of this story is the revival in fortunes of the Ghanaian cocoa sector. Ghana entered independence as the world's leading cocoa producer, but direct and indirect taxation, used to siphon rents from cocoa into government and industry, led to declining production and sales. In 1975 farmers were receiving only 10 percent of the world price for cocoa, and many responded by diversifying into other activities, or smuggling the crop across borders.

Economic reform in the 1980s saw the beginnings of a reversal in that trend. The most important element was a sustained devaluation of the cedi, which reduced the implicit taxation of cocoa farmers, and raised the real price they received (ibid.: 13). When combined with tough measures to tackle inflation, this meant that farmers' incomes grew.

Another factor raising real prices was reform of the marketing system. By the early 1980s, the state marketing agency, COCOBOD, was a bloated and inefficient organization employing 130,000 people. Over the next decade staff numbers were reduced to just over 10,000, and then to 5,100 in 2003 (ibid.: 14). At the same time, COCOBOD's monopsony on cocoa buying and input distribution was lifted and the industry opened to private competition. Farmers' share of the cocoa export price increased from 21 percent in 1983, to 40 percent in 1995, and 50 percent in 2001. The real price received by farmers consequently tripled (ibid.: 14). COCOBOD meanwhile focused its energies on plant-breeding and disease control (ibid.: 14–15).

Why have Ghanaian politicians supported the cocoa industry? Buur and Whitfield explain its success by reference to its economic and political importance. As a major source of foreign exchange, state revenue, and rural incomes, the crop is crucial to political survival. Early Ghanaian regimes were slow to learn this lesson, but since the 1980s cocoa has received sustained political support (Buur and Whitfield 2011). Wiggins and Leturque emphasize the strong, authoritarian leadership of Jerry Rawlings, who, freed in the 1980s from the threat of impending elections, was able to take tough decisions in the long-term interests of the sector (Wiggins and Leturque 2011: 12). For Buur and Whitfield, this also involved standing up to the IMF and World Bank over the details of cocoa sector reforms, insisting on a staged and *partial* liberalization, and allowing the cocoa board, which is staffed by competent and experienced officials, to retain quality-control functions. Thanks to these controls, Ghanaian cocoa earns a premium on the international market, and the board is supported by international buyers (Buur and Whitfield 2011). Wiggins and Leturque note that by the time Rawlings faced the voters in 1992, enough had been achieved to secure him significant rural support (Wiggins and Leturque 2011).

Horticulture Horticulture has also been something of a success for Ghana, but in contrast to its involvement in cocoa, government has been largely indifferent to its fate. This can be illustrated by the shifting fortunes of its pineapple sector, analyzed in an important paper by Lindsay Whitfield. Pineapple exports increased from around 650 tons in 1984 to over 70,000 tons in 2004 (Whitfield 2010: 7), before stagnating. By the late 1980s, Ghana had captured 60 percent of the market in air-freighted pineapples to Europe, based on its production of the 'smooth cayenne' varietal (ibid.: 17). Exports of smooth cayenne had been pioneered in the early 1980s by a small group of public servants, professionals, and businessmen who were looking for something to export so as to acquire foreign exchange. At that time pineapple exports from Africa to Europe were dominated by Côte d'Ivoire, which had a strong state-supported pineapple sector. However, the pioneers realized that Ghana had a comparative advantage over Côte d'Ivoire in one respect: access to cheap air freight. By air-freighting pineapples directly to Europe, Ghanaian producers were able to earn a premium. Once the pioneers had demonstrated that it was possible to earn profits this way, new producers began to enter the market and production began to take off (ibid.: 16–17).

The sector was assisted at this juncture by some well-timed government support. The Ministry of Trade and Industry, at the minister's personal initiative, financed and organized access to planting material from Côte d'Ivoire, and a concessionary credit facility for the eight largest producers financed pack-houses, irrigation facilities, farm equipment, and agrochemicals. This one-off rent was provided at a time when the industry was beginning to stagnate because of unproductive competition, helping pineapple growers overcome a crucial coordination and collective action problem. The industry also received some small support from the Ghana Export Promotion Council, which linked producers with buyers and arranged study tours of exporting and importing countries. But government support began to wane after 1989, when the minister left the government. Unlike cocoa production, pineapple production lacked the backing of the top political leadership (ibid.: 18).

Over the 1990s Ghana's comparative advantage in air-freighting began to erode. In time, a group of some fifty exporters was able to arrange for refrigerated sea freight, but the industry could not maintain its rapid growth. Part of the problem is that issues of quality are magnified over the course of a long sea journey, and post-harvest quality control in Ghana was weak, mainly because of inadequately trained staff and the lack of packing sheds and cold stores at the port. Côte d'Ivoire and Central American producers had an advantage here, and continued to outperform Ghana (ibid.: 18–23). Part of the reason Ghanaian producers failed to upgrade was a lack of access to working capital, and part of the reason was that producers had become complacent. At the same time nobody in government was pushing the industry to remain competitive. The 2000s were characterized by 'a motley assortment of uncoordinated and incoherent donor-funded (and -driven) projects and programs implemented by different Government and private agencies' (ibid.: 27).

This was the period in which Ghanaian producers faced their stiffest challenge. Across the Atlantic in Costa Rica, Del Monte had developed a new breed of pineapple, MD2, which was cheaper, sweeter, more pest resistant, with a longer shelf life and a more attractive appearance than smooth cayenne. Thanks to an aggressive marketing campaign supported by the Costa Rican government, MD2 had soon displaced smooth cayenne from most European supermarket shelves. The Ghanaian pineapple industry was badly affected (ibid.: 29–30). Belatedly, Ghanaian producers began to make the shift to MD2, but the new breed requires more precise agronomic practices than smooth cayenne did, and most struggled. They were not helped by a comparative absence of government support, and a general business environment that furnished high-cost credit, poor infrastructure, problems with land acquisition and land security, and a lack of skilled horticultural labor.

Since 2009, pineapple production has begun to rebound, but it is now dominated by a smaller number of firms with a higher degree of foreign ownership (ibid.: 30–4). Smooth cayenne has enjoyed a modest revival, it now being recognized that it has some advantages over MD2. According to Whitfield, increased government support for smooth cayenne at an earlier date might have saved the industry from recession. But 'since the early 1990s, the Government has done almost nothing outside of donor-negotiated projects to support the pineapple export industry, or horticulture more broadly' (ibid.: 36). As a result, industry actors have been unable to surmount the collective action problems inhibiting enhanced technological capability development (ibid.: 38–41).

The President's Special Initiative Encouraging and assisting producers to upgrade their technological capabilities requires, as we have seen, an industrial policy. Although the government has lacked such a policy in the horticulture sector, it has been more active in other areas. In 2001 John Kufuor launched the President's Special Initiative (PSI), an industrial policy designed to 'spearhead the expansion and deepening of the economy, create jobs, and reduce poverty (especially in the rural sector) through agribusiness and export in Ghana'. It included projects in garments and textiles, salt mining, cotton production, oil palm production, cassava starch production, and distance learning, aiming to create 'a critical mass of growth oriented internationally competitive firms'. 'Moderate' projections indicated that upon maturity, the various schemes would contribute an additional $6–10 billion a year in exports (Ghana Investment Promotion Centre n.d.). However, performance has fallen well short of expectations.

The Garments and Textiles initiative, for example, aimed to take advantage of the USA's African Growth and Opportunity Act by accelerating the development of the garment industry, making it a lead exporter. It aimed to attract and assist ten large-scale foreign investors to relocate in Ghana, to assist and build the capacity of 100 medium-sized companies by the end of 2004, and to create a pool of garment subcontractors. The initiative was supposed to directly create 70,000 jobs and generate 3–5 billion cedis in forex earnings over four years.[16] As part of this plan, the government created a 'multi-functional Garment Village and Export Processing Zones'. The Village, with 110 factory units, was completed in 2007, three and a half years behind schedule. As of 2009, there were five factories operating in it, and another fifteen or so operating in other zones with the assistance of the PSI. Most were employing between 200 and 500 workers (Tettehfio 2009). It is not clear whether the number of garment manufacturers has increased or declined since that date, but our interviews suggested that there were only five or six garment factories functioning in the zones.[17] We have not been able to find figures for garment and textile exports, but tellingly in 2010 they did not rank among Ghana's top-ten non-traditional exports (Bank of Ghana 2011a).

Industrial starch production, using cassava as a raw material, provided another initiative. In 2002, the Ayensu starch factory began production with an investment of $7 million. However, by 2006 it had stopped operations because of technical difficulties – caused primarily by frequent power outages that damaged its machines – and an inability to procure sufficient cassava to supply the factory. Apparently farmers were not motivated to sell cassava to the factory at prevailing prices. In 2008 the factory was rehabilitated with the assistance of the Export Development Investment Fund and the Swiss food giant Nestlé. The management had also acquired 2,000 acres of land to grow the requisite cassava (Adadevoh 2008).

Why have the PSIs underperformed? Inadequate funding, inadequate capacity in MoTI, and unrealistic projections and project planning – an old problem in Ghana – are all reasons. But another important reason is patronage politics. Informants told us the PSIs' problems were partly caused by the fact that they were the pet projects of Allan Kyeremanteng, the then minister for trade and industry who was vying to be the NPP's next presidential candidate. They thus tended to be overwhelmed by short-term political considerations instead of economic rationality.[18] This point is supported by Buur and Whitfield, who detail the ways in which the president's oil palm initiative became embroiled in a tug of war between the minister and other factions of the NPP (Buur and Whitfield 2011: 27–31). There may also have been purely selfish motives at work. According to one source, 'PSI went wrong because [Kyeremanteng] played politics with it and went against his own principles which was to let the private sector [do it]. You're not going to pick winners by picking your cousin, your girlfriend, etc.'[19]

In spite of these problems, the Ghanaian government's appetite for industrial policy remains undeterred. In July 2011 the NDC government announced a $346 million Industrial Policy and Industrial Sector

Support Programme, including a $296 million Industrial Development Fund, to be accessed mainly by the private sector (Republic of Ghana 2011). The policy was designed to ensure that the country did not squander its recently acquired oil and gas reserves (MacDougall 2011), using them instead to transform Ghana into 'an industry-driven economy that delivers high levels of productivity as well as decent jobs, on a scale significant and widespread enough to achieve equitable social and economic development' (Republic of Ghana 2011: 8). The policy aimed to create a modern productive economy, expand productive employment and technological capacity in manufacturing, transform agriculture through agro-industries, provide consumers with competitive, quality products, and to promote the spatial distribution of industrial development (ibid.: 8).

The strategy involved eighteen different projects under the broad thematic areas of 'production and distribution', 'technology and innovation', 'incentives and regulations', and 'cross-cutting issues'. It envisaged the state collaborating with the private sector in activities such as expanding the production of agricultural and non-agricultural raw materials, improving entrepreneurial and management skills, providing venture capital, supporting strategic industries, and acquiring land for industrial development. It was to be implemented by the Ministry of Trade and Industry, in collaboration with other key ministries and agencies, and with involvement of the private sector in a biannual review process (ibid.). The policy appears impressive on paper. Nevertheless, doubts must remain about the government's current capacity to implement it, given the previously identified problems of macroeconomic imbalance, a focus on short-run political pay-offs, weak civil service capacity and commitment, and the tendency for private business to seek easy concessions, all of which are conditioned by the dynamics of Ghana's patronage politics.

Economic performance

The economic performance of Ghana over the past two decades has been mixed, and appraisals of it are not uniform. On the positive side of the balance sheet, Ghana has been growing at an average rate of over 5 percent a year for the past sixteen years, a feat unprecedented in the country's history. This translates into per capita income growth of 2.8 percent per annum (Republic of Ghana 2010: 4). Because this growth was reasonably inclusive, it has had a significant impact on poverty. The poverty headcount index fell from 52 percent in 1991/92 to 29.5 percent in 2005/06 (ibid.: 8), meaning that Ghana is well on track to meet the Millennium Development Goal of halving poverty by 2020. Export-oriented farmers experienced the biggest poverty reduction over the period, followed by public sector workers (ibid.: 10). Urban poverty stands at just 10 percent, while rural poverty as a whole remains at 39.2 percent, and is concentrated in non-export crop regions, especially in the country's north (Wiggins and Leturque 2011: 7–9). Unemployment also appears to be falling, although a large informal sector means that much underemployment persists (Government of Ghana Private Sector Development Strategy 2010: 4).

Less encouragingly, there has been little sign of structural transformation (Republic of Ghana 2010: 4). The main change has been an increase in the share of services in the economy; indeed, services are now the biggest sector of the economy, larger in 2010 than agriculture and industry combined (Bank of Ghana 2011b). Growth sub-sectors include tourism, telecommunications, and financial services. The share of industry meanwhile has remained more or less constant, increasing to 27.7 percent of GDP in 2008, up from 26.7 percent in 1995 (Republic of Ghana 2010: 6). Within industry, the share of mining and construction has increased, while the share of manufacturing has declined (Bank of Ghana 2011b). In 2009 it represented about 9 percent of GDP, and was growing at only 5 percent a year (Ghana National Commission for UNESCO n.d.).

Perhaps the most worrying aspect of Ghana's current pattern of growth is its failure to diversify its export base in significant ways. The country's exports remain dominated by primary commodities. Cocoa, timber, gold, and other minerals account for 48 percent of GDP and 90 percent of export earnings (Government of Ghana Private Sector Development Strategy 2010: 4). In December 2010 the country began pumping oil, which was expected to contribute another 6 percent to the government's budget in 2011 (Economist Intelligence Unit 2011b). It would also intensify the country's reliance on primary exports, at least in the short term.

As we have seen, Ghana's governments have struggled to maintain fiscal balance and to manage debt. The fiscal deficit rose from 4 percent of GDP to 8.6 percent in 2000; it declined to 2 percent of GDP in 2005 before spiking to 11.3 percent of GDP in 2008. Inflation reached 18 percent that year, before falling to 10.9 percent in 2010. Government debt stands at around 50 percent of GDP (Various Authors 2011c). Large fiscal and balance of payments deficits also put downward pressure on the cedi. The combined effects on inflation, credit availability, and exchange rates all militate against the creation of an investment climate appropriate to long-term investment in higher-value manufacturing.

Conclusions

In recent years Ghana has been performing reasonably well, economically, posting fairly high rates of economic growth and making significant inroads into poverty. However, these gains are mainly attributable to better management of the cocoa industry, and increases in the price of Ghana's main mineral export, gold. Services have also been growing apace, but as of yet there is little sign of a breakthrough into high-value-added manufacturing, or higher-value-added exports in general. Indeed, we have seen one case, pineapples, where a promising experiment stagnated because of government neglect. It seems, then, that despite Ghana's best efforts to implement conventional investment climate policies, which have seen it shoot up the league table for Doing Business, investors remain conservative.

A large part of the problem is that the Ghanaian polity currently provides the wrong incentives. The system of competitive two-party clientelism generates huge demands for election funding, which leads on the one hand to an expansion of the government budget and large fiscal deficits in election years and, more insidiously, exacerbates a business culture in which entrepreneurs look to get quick returns from government contracting. In cases where the government has attempted to undertake more ambitious industrial policies, for example in textiles or starch production, they have fallen victim to these kinds of political pressures.

Ghana has now begun pumping oil, and the government has announced a suitably ambitious industrial policy to prevent the squander of oil resources in the manner of some neighboring countries, for example Nigeria. However, it remains to be seen whether Ghanaian politicians will have the self-discipline, and whether the Ghanaian civil service has the capacity, to allow industrial policy to be conducted along sensibly technocratic lines. All the signs are that it too will get swallowed up in the struggle for electoral patronage.

In many respects Ghana represents an ideal investment destination

– coastal, peaceful, close to Europe, reasonably resource rich, and with a comparatively well-educated population. It should arguably be receiving more productive investment than it does. It is Ghana's system of competitive clientelism, its decentralized, short-term rent management, which appears to be the main factor holding it back. What, then, is the solution?

The kinds of rent centralization under a dominant party that we will encounter in due course in Ethiopia and Rwanda, and which may yet be possible in a country like Tanzania, are not feasible in contemporary Ghana: its two-party system is too well entrenched. Consequently, the country must seek the functional equivalent of these arrangements. One way of doing this would be to search for institutions that will mitigate short-term political pressures without extinguishing democracy. An idea which has been mooted in-country is increased government funding for political parties, although this comes with its own problems (Gyimah-Boadi 2009). Another would be legislative or constitutional lock-in measures that restrict government's discretionary spending opportunities, of the kind that were recently defeated in the petroleum bill. Another might be an agreement that the managers of industrial policy organs be appointed either by cross-party or politically neutral bodies, and that the latter be subjected to forms of political scrutiny that are not of a partisan kind. Another might be an electoral system that attenuates the clientelistic nature of the ties between an MP and his constituents. Another, given Ghana's recurrent inflation problem, would be increased measures to strengthen the independence of the Central Bank.

Whatever functional equivalents are chosen, it seems clear that the measures will not work without the painstaking creation of a cross-party consensus on the need to combat competitive clientelism and the short-horizon rent management it drives.[20]

4 | ETHIOPIA: RENT-SEEKERS AND PRODUCTIVE CAPITALISTS

Our third case study, Ethiopia, lies in the Horn of Africa and is Africa's second-largest country, with a population of over eighty million people. It is one of Africa's poorest states, and GDP per capita stood at just $358 in 2010.[1] The country has more than sixty ethnic groups, from which the large Oromo, Amhara, Tigray, Afar and Somali groups have historically made an explosive mix. Economically, it is largely agricultural with a poorly integrated non-agricultural periphery. Highland areas are very fertile in years with good rainfall, though vulnerable to famine in years of drought. There is a 'perpetual cycle of drought and plenty' and serious problems of soil degradation (Economist Intelligence Unit 2008a: 32). Much of the rest of the country is unsuitable for arable farming, and here pastoralists predominate. Oil exploration is under way and the country has some mineral resources: gold, coal, potash, and natural gas, but these are only beginning to be developed. Ethiopia is landlocked, and, since the breakdown of relations with Eritrea, the only viable route to the sea has been through neighboring Djibouti. This raises the cost and difficulty of doing business.

In spite of these comparative disadvantages Ethiopia has been growing extremely rapidly over the past decade. Interestingly, it has done this by ignoring a great deal of conventional donor advice, claiming to be following an Asian development model instead. In this chapter we examine the political and economic antecedents of the country's incipient economic turnaround, and provide evidence to show that it has put in place a structure for centralizing rent management and gearing it to the long term. This has helped it to operationalize an ambitious industrial and development policy, something we illustrate with examples from agri-business, and from what in Ethiopia are called 'endowment companies'.

Historical context

The current Ethiopian state can trace its roots back almost two thousand years to the kingdom of Axum. It was not until the late nineteenth century, however, that it acquired something close to its present form, when Emperor Menelik of Shoa reunited and expanded its fragmented possessions (although Eritrea was lost to Italian colonial rule). Menelik began to modernize Ethiopia, a process continued by his successor, Emperor Haile Selassie. Through administrative and educational reforms, Selassie succeeded in creating a centralized autocracy that curbed the power of the regional aristocracy, restored Ethiopian independence in the wake of Mussolini's five-year occupation, and reincorporated Eritrea, while all the while maintaining the constitutional premise of a divine right of rule (Bahru Zewde 1991; Donham and James 1986; Paul and Clapham 1967; Tekeste Nagash 1997; Various Authors 2007).

Centralization of political power was accompanied by economic development. In 1954/55 the emperor established a National Economic Council designed to boost agro-industrial productivity and living standards, and three five-year development plans focused on boosting the development of the private sector (Mulatu Wubneh 1991). There were investments in commercial agriculture, construction, and a small manufacturing sector. Large foreign investors, including the Dutch sugar giant HVA, and the British automotive firm Mitchell Cotts, were lured in with tax incentives, import-export privileges and finance. Mixed-origin communities (particularly Ethio-Italian, Ethio-Greek, and Ethio-Armenian) also played important economic roles. In 1963 a Government Investment Committee was established as an independent decision-making body, and legislation extended concessions to domestic investors, who were emerging from the regional aristocracies. Although there was little attempt to centralize rents or tie them to the learning or development costs associated with domestic market or sector expansion, growth was respectable, averaging 4 percent per annum between 1960 and 1974 (Alemayehu Geda 2005: 6).[2] Many influential Ethiopian private entrepreneurs, whose personal or family businesses were established during this time, still consider the period a 'golden age'.

In the early 1970s, serious cracks began to appear in this economic and political edifice, driven by a number of factors, including Eritrean nationalist opposition, iniquitous landholding and surplus accumulation by traditional and foreign elites, the neglect of rural famine in the north, and the domination of state positions by Amharic-speaking Christian highlanders (Bahru Zewde 1991; Iyob 1995; Markakis 1974).

In 1974 the emperor was overthrown by a military committee known as the 'Dergue',[3] backed by radical students and much of the urban population. It quickly nationalized land, a step that was initially very popular (Clapham 1988). However, it rejected a series of leftist groups emerging from the influential student movement, and the resulting periods of 'White' and 'Red Terror' saw the deaths of over a hundred thousand intellectuals (Zewde 2009).

In 1977, military support provided by the USSR against an opportunist invasion from neighboring Somalia saw the Dergue ideologues adopt a Marxist approach to 'safeguard the revolution'. The government embarked on a disastrous development strategy designed around a command economy. This involved the wholesale nationalization of industries and property; the collectivization of production; and the state control of marketing (Eshetu Chole 1994; Mulatu Wubneh 1991). Peasant farmers were organized into cooperatives under a highly centralized system of local government (Clapham 1988), often involving compulsory villagization or resettlement (Clay and Holcomb 1986; Gebre Yntiso 2009; Wolde-Selassie Abbute 2009). As in socialist Tanzania, policy mistakes easily outweighed the potential benefits of rent centralization here. The government was soon embroiled in an armed struggle with ethno-nationalist rebel groups around the country (Gebru Tareke 2009), and the local structures of the state became increasingly militarized and repressive in a system of mass conscription and 'garrison socialism' (Markakis 1987). As the cost of these multiple civil wars escalated during the 1980s, famine loomed larger than ever, and the economy ground to a halt. Growth slowed to an average of 2.3 percent between 1974 and 1991 – expansion more than swallowed up by the growing population (Alemayehu Geda 2005: 7).

In the late 1980s the withdrawal of Soviet economic and military support spelled the end for the Dergue, and in May 1991 it was finally defeated by the combined onslaught of its various ethno-nationalist opponents. Of these, the Tigrayan-led coalition, the Ethiopian Peoples' Revolutionary Democratic Front (EPRDF), emerged the strongest of a disparate collection of ethnic organizations with which it joined in a Transitional Government (TGE).[4] The latter set its face against the centralizing logic of a century of pan-Ethiopianism, granting independence to Eritrea, and introducing a radical form of multi-national federalism based on the country's major language or ethnic groups (Aaron Tesfaye 2002; Vaughan 2011). This was one of three sets of fundamental reforms to which the new government declared itself committed: the others were liberalization of the economy and democratization of politics. Socio-economic advancement, decentralization, and democratization were all seen as mechanisms for the resolution of conflict and removal of its deeply rooted causes; all have encountered fundamental challenges and some shortcomings over the last two decades.

The introduction of federalism was also key to the building of a ruling coalition, apparently offering seats at the table to a range of armed movements (including Oromos, Somalis, Sidamas, Afars, etc.) and to the representatives of other ethnic groups which had not fought the Dergue. But when the EPRDF attempted to win seats in elections in areas where it had not previously been active, a number of groups left the government. EPRDF meanwhile consolidated its position among supporters from across the country who won unprecedented access to rents in the form of governmental positions and resources, as the infrastructure of the state was decentralized, and nine federated units established (Vaughan 2006).

The first federal government came to power in 1995, establishing a constellation which has remained effectively unchanged ever since: EPRDF administering the central highland regions, and affiliated groups loyal to it ruling the peripheries. Economic policies designed to move the highly centralized and state-dominated Ethiopian economy in a more plural direction were far reaching (World Bank 2009b). Reforms included: the removal of price controls and liberalization of commodity distribution, particularly agricultural produce; the gradual devaluation of the Ethiopian birr and introduction of a regular foreign exchange auction; the reduction of tariffs on imported goods; the reform of tax policy, and labor and employment law; the sale of public enterprises under a program of privatization which is still ongoing; the introduction of legislation allowing the establishment of privately owned banks and insurance companies; and, crucially, the introduction of a land-lease system, designed to be more 'market oriented' and to foster commercial investment, while retaining land in public ownership (Mulatu Wubneh 1991).

Nevertheless, doubts persisted about the commitment of EPRDF to an economic transition (World Bank 2009b). The privatization program in particular was criticized as slow and lackluster, and excluded important sectors (notably banks, telecoms, power and water distribution, and air transport) either from foreign or from private investment. In addition, quantitative restrictions have remained on certain imported goods – for example, cement (Access Capital 2010b: 5). In retrospect, the EPRDF seems to have paid rather careful attention to some of the ways in which its predecessors lost control of rent centralization, and attempted to learn from and counter these experiences. Thus since 1991, the Ethiopian government has been slow or unwilling to divest in strategic sectors, and cautious about rents accruing internationally, particularly from finance and infrastructure (Vaughan and Gebremichael 2011).

In 1998 Ethiopia embarked on a war with Eritrea that was to have major economic ramifications. The international, human, and economic implications were severe, with hundreds of thousands mobilized or displaced, and capital budgets for local investment across Ethiopia cut at a stroke. Perhaps of most lasting import was the serious factional conflict which erupted within the EPRDF, for which the war was something of a catalyst. This was ended when Prime Minister Meles Zenawi's faction outmaneuvered its opponents and many of them were detained for several years on flimsy corruption charges. Party power structures which had been implicated in the dissidence were emasculated, replaced by a bureaucratized capacity-building structure under the state (Vaughan and Tronvoll 2003).

The period of party 'renewal' after the split in 2000 marked the beginning of a period of strong economic growth, and increased spending. Feeling increasingly secure, the EPRDF took steps to liberalize the political field in the run-up to a third round of federal elections in May 2005. It was surprised by the strength of opposition support that emerged from the poll – especially support for pan-Ethiopianist parties opposed to the system of ethnic federalism itself, and enjoying the support of the middle class and private sector (Vaughan 2011). Facing electoral defeat in Addis Ababa, a recalcitrant opposition determined to seize a disputed national poll victory, and urban agitation for a transfer of power, the government responded with a severe crackdown (Aalen and Tronvoll 2009; Abbink 2006a).

A series of opposition politicians were tried on charges of crimes against the constitution and treason, with most of them pardoned and released only a year later. In the meantime, the ruling party took a range of steps to rebuild the infrastructure of its political and party institutions, distinct from those of the state. Veteran politicians were reassigned to oversee the energetic process of party reconstruction, and by 2008 the organization was reporting the successful recruitment of more than 4.5 million members (Aalen and Tronvoll 2009). At the time of writing, EPRDF membership is understood to be in the region of six million, more and more of whom are new graduates of the country's expanding public university system. With the scope of the political choices open to them now clear, electorates overwhelmingly returned ruling-party representatives in local and regional elections in 2008, and in federal elections in 2010, which returned only a single opposition candidate (Lefort 2010).

If the first decade of EPRDF rule had been marked by the establishment of ethnically based federated states, the second has focused on the capacitation and expansion of demographically defined local districts or '*weredas*', the third tier of government. Local civil servant numbers grew from around 150,000 in 2004/05 to over 350,000 in 2009/10, and a system of 'block grants' channeled directly to this level sought a dramatic increase in the presence of the local state. Decentralized service delivery expanded exponentially, and strong progress was made toward some of the MDGs. More problematically, levels of development-induced displacement and disruption have been increasing, particularly in parts of the periphery (Pankhurst and Piguet 2009).

Today, the social base of the elite includes the many peasant farmers, youth cooperative members, school and university students and graduates who have been recruited into the party. Party cadres form an important core of the federal and regional civil service, with an increasing number of political appointments at every level of government. Despite several programs of military recruitment which have diversified the profile of the armed forces over the last two decades, its leadership continues to involve a significant number of those who fought for the EPRDF against the Dergue. In the last few years, EPRDF has also won a degree of support in the commercial sector (albeit still a minority), with significant private donations to the party a feature of the 2010 campaign. Among a growing number of others, the large MIDROC bloc, owned by Saudi-Ethiopian investor Sheikh Mohammed Al Amoudi, has long been consistently and generously supportive. As we will discuss in more detail later, the party also has close links to the series of regional 'endowment funds' which own large commercial companies in strategic development sectors (Vaughan and Gebremichael 2011).

Opposition to the ruling party, meanwhile, is concentrated among educated urbanites, and a range of private business people and professionals employed in non-governmental sectors (Vaughan 2011). A recently formed front, Medrek, represents a range of opposition groupings whose leaders include academics, professional people, and a number of the excluded EPRDF faction leaders. While these groups have continued to pursue their interests through legal electoral means, a radical opposition fringe, enjoying strong diaspora support, has also attempted a more direct approach. These armed groups share Eritrean backing and regional logistics support with a number of ethno-regional groups, of which the two most important are the Oromo Liberation Front, and the Ogaden National Liberation Front (ONLF). The ONLF hit the headlines in 2007 with an audacious attack on an oil exploration camp, killing Chinese as well as Ethiopian nationals, and eliciting a heavy-handed counter-insurgency campaign in the central areas of the Somali Regional State. These conflicts wreck lives and livelihoods but do little to threaten the regime.

Together these groups present a potentially serious internal challenge to the regime, but what they lack is organizational power or cohesion. So long as the government maintains its current dominance over the political economy, and provided that political economy continues to furnish the regime with resources, its longevity seems ensured. This is particularly the case since Western powers regard Ethiopia as a key regional ally in the war against terrorism, despite its dismal human rights record (Economist Intelligence Unit 2011a).

Rents, industrial policy, and investment

Since coming to power in 1991, and especially after the post-2001 party renewal, the Ethiopian regime has dedicated itself to an ambitious program of economic transformation. Although receiving large amounts of aid from the West, it has eschewed a Washington-based development program, preferring to look east for inspiration. Japanese and Korean advisors have assisted with development policy (Altenburg 2010: 16), and more recently the prime minister has lauded the achievements of China, claiming that 'the process of reform and development in China has provided an alternative paradigm for Africa's development' (Schaefer 2011: 17). The Ethiopian take on this is known as Agricultural Development Led Industrialization, laid out in the Industrial Development Strategy (2002) and the Plan for

Accelerated and Sustained Development to End Poverty (2006–10), now superseded by the Growth and Transformation Plan (2011–15) (Berhanu Abegaz 2011).[5] It focuses resources on rural areas, aiming to improve agriculture, rural infrastructure, and agro-based industries.

As well as the Asian example, the policy is inspired by the Tigrayan People's Liberation Front's (TPLF's) own experience of organizing the war against the Dergue in the 1980s. There, the TPLF gained 'a clear understanding of the value and potential of coincidence of interest between peasant populations benefiting from socio-economic development, and the party consolidating its support base as a result of being seen to provide the means of such development' (Vaughan and Tronvoll 2003: 119). Reflecting this, the government currently devotes around 64 percent of its budget to pro-poor sectors such as education, health, agriculture, water, and roads (Altenburg 2010: 7).[6] More recently, however, a focus on the peasant sector has been supplemented by the provision of incentives for large-scale commercial farming (Access Capital 2010b).

Successful rent centralization Development policy has been facilitated by a formidable concentration of political and economic power. Following the internal party strife in 2001, technocratic ministers were replaced by political appointments, and a series of new 'superministries' created at federal level for Capacity Building, Infrastructure Development, Rural Development, and Federal Affairs (Vaughan and Tronvoll 2003: 89). The ministers of these four ministries, together with the prime minister, constituted the core leadership of the government's development and state capacity-building program through the first half of the decade (ibid.: 89). Although the scope of the 'superministries' was scaled back in 2005/06, and the Ministry for Capacity Building was replaced with a more technically oriented Ministry of Civil Service in 2010, the political impetus behind public sector reform and the expansion of service delivery has remained high – and centralized. The power of the federal executive is deconcentrated through bureaus and departments replicated at regional and district level, with the district becoming an increasingly important and capable third level of government. A series of EPRDF and governmental 'advisors' has been attached to the executives of each of the four peripheral areas (ibid.: 107, 134), where there is little room for alternative political viewpoints, and state-building initiatives increasingly extend the strategies of the highlands.[7] The legislature, meanwhile, has to date played only a limited role in policy-making or policy scrutiny (ibid.: 97), despite a dramatic expansion of local legislative membership at district level in 2008.

The regime receives little in the way of challenge from other political parties or civil society. As we saw in the previous section, the former were subjected to severe reprisals following the disputed election of 2005, and these have continued. In 2009, at least thirty-three government opponents were sentenced to long jail sentences and five were sentenced to death; more arrests came in June 2011 (Various Authors 2011e). NGOs and civil society organizations, meanwhile, have been brought firmly into line with government policy through the 2009 Charities and Societies Proclamation, which curtails the scope of their activities if they receive more than 10 percent of their operating budget from foreign sources (Schaefer 2011: 15). Freedom of expression and assembly are further constrained by the Mass Media and Freedom of Information Proclamation of 2008, and the Anti-Terrorist Proclamation of 2009 (ibid.: 15). The country has one of the worst records of press freedom on the continent, and journalists and editors are frequently harassed or subject to arrest (Economist Intelligence Unit 2008a).

The civil service has also been overhauled. In the early 1990s it was common to hear EPRDF officials commenting that the civil service was 'the next enemy we have to fight now that we have overcome the Dergue' (Vaughan and Tronvoll 2003: 94). A Task Force for Civil Service Reform was established in 1994 and a home-grown Civil Service Reform Programme implemented from 1996, and given new impetus from 2003 under the ambitious Public Sector Capacity Building Programme (PSCAP). According to Altenburg:

> The reforms tackled the major issues required to design appropri-ate industrial policies, to improve implementation, and – very important – to create safeguards against political capture. Among other measures, a program for results-based monitoring and evalu-ation was initiated; an employee appraisal system was introduced; tools to benchmark public sector performance were established; and instruments to increase transparency and accountability were introduced at the federal, regional, and local levels. (Altenburg 2010: 12)

In addition, a Civil Service College was created, offering degrees in Law, Business and Economics, Technology, and later in Public Administration and Management. In its early years it recruited heavily among former EPRDF fighter students, and utilized 'the EPRDF-favored technique of collective evaluation by "criticism and self-criticism" (*gem-gema*)' (Vaughan and Tronvoll 2003: 95). More recently it has earned an impressive reputation in the professional training of civil servants identified by the state governments.

Complementing the civil service reform, and an important component of PSCAP, has been financial sector reform. The government has devised a public financial reform program to build on what already existed, marshaling foreign technical assistance only as and when needed. Today Ethiopia apparently has the third-best financial management system in Africa (Peterson 2011), something which has allowed for the decentralized allocation and management of the rapidly growing government block grants for service delivery to district level. Concerns remain over competence and turnover at local levels, but progress in building local capacity for public financial management has been dramatic.

Economically, the government has retained a great deal of control over the principal levers and strategic sectors of the economy, rather in the manner of an East Asian developmental state. For example, the state-owned enterprise (SOE) sector remains comparatively large, comprising around 130 companies. Key fields such as telecoms, utilities, civil aviation, and financial services remain solely or largely in the public sector (Berhanu Abegaz 2011: 32); in 2006 SOEs accounted for some 72 percent of total manufacturing value-added (Altenburg 2010: 9). The government recently passed a new competition law, but this maintains the privilege of SOEs by shielding products and enterprises that are regarded as 'having a significant impact on development' from competition (ibid.: 8).

The government also influences the strategic direction of economic development through party-linked holding companies, or 'endowment companies', as they are known in Ethiopia. These are private businesses started by members of the ruling party during the transition from the Dergue, building on resources captured during the war. In 1995 they were transformed into charitable trusts, but they continue to play an important strategic role in the government's overall policy. As we shall see in the next section, they have invested in areas where the private sector has been reluctant, and some of them seem to demonstrate high standards of business probity and payment of taxes. The best-known endowment company is the Endowment Fund for the Rehabilitation of Tigray (EFFORT), which has investments in a wide range of sectors, including cement, pharmaceuticals, and textile production, engineering and construction, and crop marketing and transport. Although the company is formally delinked from the TPLF, coordination of aims and activities is secured through overlapping membership of both organizations (Berhanu Abegaz 2011: 41), which makes politically unsanctioned commercial activity unlikely (Vaughan and Gebremichael 2011: 33). The government also enjoys close relations with Ethiopia's largest private investor, Mohammed Al Amoudi, head of the MIDROC business empire. In 1997 MIDROC was awarded a $175 million license to exploit the country's largest gold mine at Lega Dembi, and has a range of other investments in real estate, cement, and manufacturing (Economist Intelligence Unit 2008a).

The financial sector is also tightly controlled. The three largest banks are state owned (although some have had foreign, private managers), and, while private concerns now account for 40–45 percent of the market, some of the larger ones, such as Wegangen Bank, are linked to the ruling party (Altenburg 2010: 16; Berhanu Abegaz 2011: 33; Economist Intelligence Unit 2008a). The board of directors of the Commercial Bank is appointed by the government, and its lending policy is based on strategic economic criteria. In the early 2000s the bank faced financial meltdown on account of its high percentage of non-performing loans to state companies, but it was subsequently restructured and management handed to the Royal Bank of Scotland (Economist Intelligence Unit 2008a). In 2011 the government attempted to shore up its finances by ordering commercial banks to buy bonds worth 27 percent of their loans from government at an – effectively negative – 3 percent interest rate (Groum Abate 2011). Then in September it raised the minimum capital requirement for commercial banks by a massive 566 percent, citing 'overcrowding' in a sector that has recently grown extremely rapidly as the reason (Economist Intelligence Unit 2011a). The party is also deeply involved in micro-finance, with nearly 90 percent of the gross loan portfolio accounted for by the five biggest micro-finance institutions, all of which are institutions with close connections to the ruling coalition (Berhanu Abegaz 2011: 42).

SOEs and endowment companies have been active in recent years in a massive program of infrastructural expansion, much of which has been financed and in some cases implemented by the Chinese. There are ambitious programs for the development of transport networks, and hydropower generation in the escarpments, taking advantage of Ethiopia's position as the 'watertower of Africa' (Schaefer 2011: 17; Vaughan and Gebremichael 2011). As of 2008 the Ethiopia Electric Power Corporation and its chosen contractors were building four major dams, with a combined cost of around $1.5 billion, in addition to the massive Gilgel Gibe III station, scheduled to cost up to $2 billion (Economist Intelligence Unit 2008a). The current flagship dam project is the giant Millennium Dam on the Nile, projected to produce 5,250 megawatts in 2017.[8] In education, the country has ploughed large resources into both vocational and higher education sectors: there are said to be over 800,000 students in the former and the construction of twenty new universities has facilitated a massive expansion in the latter (Altenburg 2010: 17). Investments such as these constitute the foundations of an ambitious industrial policy, some examples of which we will consider in the next section.

Naturally, this magnitude of government control and intervention creates significant opportunities for rent-seeking and corruption. The latter is controlled with the help of the Federal Ethics and Anti-Corruption Commission, established in 2001. This institution played a pivotal role in the political purge that followed the TPLF internal dissensus, arraigning on corruption charges Central Committee members, private businessmen, and senior civil servants (including managers of the Commercial Bank of Ethiopia and the Privatization Agency) (Vaughan and Tronvoll 2003: 101). Although these prosecutions were widely perceived as being politically motivated, Ethiopia does seem to do better on corruption than most of its regional competitors. The Corruption Perception Index ranks Ethiopia at 126 out of 180 countries, while the World Bank's Enterprise survey found that only 12 percent of firms state that public officials expect them to make informal payments in order to get things done, compared to an average of 41 percent for sub-Saharan Africa as a whole (Altenburg 2010: 13). According to Altenburg, 'Ethiopia is anything but a predatory state whose Government pillages the economy. There is no hard evidence of systematic abuses of political regulation and support programs for illicit personal enrichment of political elites' (ibid.: 2).

In light of this array of developmental attributes, some might question whether the Ethiopian developmental experience is 'patrimonial' at all. In fact, Ethiopia arguably retains some significant neo-patrimonial dimensions. These center on the concentration of power around the person of the prime minister, long-standing traditions of hierarchy and secrecy, a large state apparatus in which patronage is used as a resource for securing political support, and a blurring of the lines between the public and the private spheres. Long-term observers of the Tigrayan political scene, for example, have noted 'the prevalence of deeply personalized politics based on close-knit patronage systems around a small group of key individuals and families' (Vaughan and Tronvoll 2003: 125), while Jan Abbink has identified the resurrection of an old tradition of authoritarian neo-patrimonialism, driven by economic scarcity, the fusion of political and economic power, and the zero-sum nature of political competition: 'the country and its politics are treated as the privileged domain of power holders who operate in an informal and often non-transparent manner, and over which the formal institutions do not have a decisive say' (Abbink 2006a: 196).[9] One concrete example is the massive expansion of posts in party and local government following the 2005 election debacle. Today, some 30 percent of the rural population hold posts that may entitle them to a share of the rents from this highly managed political economy (Tronvoll 2008).

Weaknesses of the Ethiopian model The Ethiopian model is not without weaknesses. Civil service reforms have not met their highest ambitions, for example, and doubts remain about the extent to which the ruling party really desires a competent civil service. Altenburg reports that: 'It seems that the Government, while fully aware of the need to enhance the efficiency of its civil service, still values political loyalty higher than merit. There is a general perception that party affiliation and loyalty have become even more important since the 2005 events' (Altenburg 2010: 13). Vaughan and Gebremichael, meanwhile, state that the combination of professional competence and independence characteristic of developmental bureaucracies is often in question in Ethiopia:

Civil service morale and willingness to 'speak truth unto power' were both dented in the wake of post-election controversy in 2005.

The broad scope and regular recycling of political appointments across all levels of government service, combined with long-standing hierarchical patterns of Abyssinian socio-political culture that do not encourage dissent, challenge the strength of Ethiopian technocratic integrity. (Vaughan and Gebremichael 2011: 16)

Corruption is also a concern. As we saw above, it is probably lower than in neighboring countries, but it does exist. *The Economist*, commenting on the country's 2007 Transparency International score of 2.8 out of 10, has gone so far as to describe it as 'rampant' (Economist Intelligence Unit 2008a: 30). New areas of economic opportunity, such as telecommunications and pharmaceuticals, appear to be particularly vulnerable, while land management, tax, procurement, and customs are other problem areas. While there is anecdotal evidence that egregious offenders are quietly disciplined, a certain level of 'enrichment' is widely regarded as acceptable (Vaughan and Gebremichael 2011: 29–30).

One of the distinctive features of the Ethiopian brand of developmental patrimonialism, and arguably one of its weaknesses, is its generally antagonistic relations with private business. In the government's view, businesses can be divided into 'rent-seekers' and 'productive capitalists', and it aims to withdraw opportunities from the former while promoting the latter (ibid.: 15). As such, it commonly denounces practices such as hoarding and price gouging, together with the general reluctance of the private sector to enter into risky areas. On occasions it has taken quite draconian measures against these practices, most recently when it imposed prices on a basket of basic foodstuffs in 2011. On the private sector's side, there is much criticism of government. *The Economist* reported in 2008, for example, that 'the predominance of party-owned companies in key sectors is bitterly resented by independent private entrepreneurs' (Economist Intelligence Unit 2008a: 37).

Partly in consequence, businessmen flocked to the political opposition in 2005. The government later retaliated for this act, refusing to extend the license for the Ethiopian Manufacturing Industries Association, and installing a new leadership at the National Chamber of Commerce. Since that time business associations and chambers have continued to function and to enjoy audiences with ministers and even the prime minister, and a public–private partnership (PPP) forum was established in 2010 (Altenburg 2010; Various Authors 2011e). But whether these will serve as a forum for the kinds of 'embedded autonomy' characteristic of other developmental states is open to doubt. According to some of Altenburg's informants, 'they serve as communication channels through which Government officials propagate their decisions rather than as a platform to exchange views, solve immediate problems and jointly develop long-term strategies for industrial development' (Altenburg 2010: 14).

These shortcomings are reflected, perhaps, in the government's recent regulatory performance. While policy has been relatively stable, its enforcement and implementation are occasionally erratic, especially in the case of land administration, and price controls. Added to this has been a recent devaluation of the birr, restrictions in bank credit, changes to windfall taxes, and retroactive application of new legislation, alongside changes to urban land leasing legislation in late 2011 (Vaughan and Gebremichael 2011: 12, 25). More generally, Ethiopia performs relatively poorly on conventional 'Doing Business' indicators, ranking 104th out of 198 countries, considerably below Ghana and Rwanda, although more than twenty places ahead of Tanzania (ibid.: 24).

Government's relations with foreign private investors appear to be more cooperative. Ethiopia has received billions of dollars in investment from Saudi Arabian, Indian, and Chinese investors among others in recent years. There have been investments in electronics and textiles, and the government is trying to diversify foreign investment into agro-processing, energy, infrastructure, tourism, and mining (Schaefer 2011: 17–18). Major investments in commercial agriculture are also planned, and these are proving controversial, with a reported total of 3.5 million hectares of land placed in a 'land bank' under federal government control (other concessions below the threshold of 5,000 hectares are available from regional state governments), and a further comparable area projected for additional leasing over the coming three years (Desalegn Rahmato 2011: 11). A series of international companies, including Indian, Saudi, Malaysian, Italian and other investors, have taken long-term concessions on up to several hundred thousand hectares, alongside smaller-scale but more numerous domestic investors. Much of the land in question is located in the lowland periphery, and critics have expressed concern about the potentially negative impact on indigenous communities, which – albeit sparsely distributed – occupy very particular ecological niches. Government policy seems to be driven by the desire to introduce new mechanized technology and jobs to remote areas, boost agricultural production, improve energy security from biofuels, and generate hard currency from exports. Critics, meanwhile, have focused on the local social impact of what they consider to be unethical foreign 'land grabbing' (Oakland Institute 2011). What is beyond doubt is the profound impact of the policy in terms of state reshaping of the agrarian structure of the country, and associated land rights (Desalegn Rahmato 2011).

Sectoral examples

As we have seen, the current Ethiopian regime envisages itself as an East Asian-style developmental state, and it plays a correspondingly active role in industrial policy. Not only is it providing large-scale infrastructural and educational investments with a view to boosting the overall investment climate, it is also actively undertaking a number of interventions to encourage private investment in sectors regarded as having special developmental significance, or growth potential.

Floriculture Over the past decade the exported flower industry in Ethiopia has begun to take off. Currently about eighty-five companies are operating (Altenburg 2010: 24),[10] of which around three-quarters are foreign (ibid.: 25). Between 400 and 1,200 hectares acres of flowers are under cultivation, with a few large companies having over one hundred hectares, and many smaller ones cultivating around ten hectares each. As of 2008 the industry was employing between 30,000 and 60,000 people, mostly women (ibid.; Gebreeyesus and Lizuka 2010; Getu 2010). Exports have expanded from less than $2 million in 2003 to $170 million in 2009/10, despite a slowing world market. This is equivalent to about 1.2 billion stems a year, or thirty-seven freight planes a week (Access Capital 2010a). The figures show that Ethiopia is now the second-largest exporter of cut roses in Africa, and the sixth-largest in the world, having overtaken more established producers such as Uganda, Zambia, Tanzania, and South Africa (Altenburg 2010; Gebreeyesus and Lizuka 2010; Getu 2010).

Rapid growth has been driven by a combination of ecological factors and government policy (Getu 2010: 241). Experiments in flower production were first conducted by the Dergue regime and later by two domestic entrepreneurs, but were unsuccessful. It was not until Golden Rose – an Indian investor contracting specialists from Israel – entered the market that the industry's commercial viability was proved. Later, Dutch producers entered, including Sher-Ethiopia, which has become the country's largest developer of greenhouse production (Altenburg 2010: 25).

At this stage government support (aside from the usual tax breaks offered to exporters) appears not to have been particularly instrumental. But once the government became apprised of floriculture's export potential, significant incentives were provided (ibid.: 26). In what Altenburg refers to as a good example of neo-patrimonialism in industrial policy-making, the prime minister took a personal interest. He met regularly with growers to discuss their problems, and granted the Ethiopian Horticulture Producers Export Association (EHPEA) a direct line to him (Altenburg 2010, 2011). Subsequently, the government set a target of achieving 1,000 hectares under flowers after five years, and committed itself to removing all intervening obstacles (Gebreeyesus and Lizuka 2010: 2). A key constraint at that time was access to land close to Addis Ababa airport, with investors having to lease small plots from individual farmers. After becoming aware of this problem, the government assisted investors to find appropriate land at a lease price of only $18 per hectare. A second bottleneck was uncompetitive air-freight rates. The government assisted here by securing an arrangement with Ethiopian Airlines to subsidize air freight. With the removal of these two bottlenecks, the industry began to change gear (ibid.: 4). When horticulture producers began to experience congestion at Bole airport, a new $35 million cargo terminal was opened (Economist Intelligence Unit 2008a). Concessional credit was also made available, although this has now ended (Altenburg 2010: 26).

In 2008, the government created a new Ethiopian Horticulture Development Agency. This is a semi-autonomous agency designed to operate as a one-stop shop for investors, and to have the independence to act with alacrity in response to investor concerns. It reports directly to the Export Committee headed by the prime minister (ibid.: 26). Other assistance has come in the form of dedicated research and agricultural extension services. Although these have yet to pay dividends, and Ethiopian producers still lag behind foreign investors in technological know-how, a new capacity-building program at Jimma University, undertaken with assistance from EHPEA, Wageningen

University, and the Horticulture Development Agency, is a step in the right direction. The government has also assisted EHPEA in agreeing and enforcing a code of conduct among its members, which helps protect the image of Ethiopian flower production abroad (ibid.; Gebreeyesus and Lizuka 2010; Getu 2010). Government has also assisted with market search, and the Ethiopian industry has now diversified its export destinations beyond the EU to Japan, the Middle East, and Russia (Gebreeyesus and Lizuka 2010: 5).

Industrial policy in floriculture appears to have generated some positive externalities. These have come in the form of propagation of planting materials, packaging factories, fertilizer and chemical suppliers. Foreign airlines have now also entered the market. Knowledge gained in rose production has begun to be used in summer-flower production, and there is hope that it will spill over into increased horticultural production generally (Altenburg 2010; Gebreeyesus and Lizuka 2010). There are some concerns, however, that industrial policy in floriculture has outlived its usefulness. Now that the pioneering work has been done, the positive externalities from knowledge spillovers would appear to be limited, in which case the Ethiopian government's generous grants of land and subsidized air freight might be regarded as a wasteful use of rents. The issue is difficult to judge, however, since contextual technological innovation and adaptation are not yet exhausted, meaning that a rationale for providing special incentives to new investors can still be found (Altenburg 2010: 27).

Leather products The government has been even more active in the leather and leather products industry, partly because the problems of the sub-sector demand a more encompassing approach. Ethiopia is well placed to develop this sector, having the largest cattle population on the continent, and numerous local tanneries and leather goods factories. However, the industry suffers from a number of disadvantages when it comes to breaking into international markets. To begin with, hides are generally small, and of poor quality, partly because most Ethiopian cattle suffer from ecto-parasites and other hide-degrading diseases. Secondly, local practices of branding and backyard slaughtering, together with inappropriate storage and transport of hides, reduce quality still further. Local tanneries suffer from diseconomies of scale, fail to meet international environmental standards, and lack knowledge of fashion trends in international markets (ibid.: 23).

The government has introduced a comprehensive upgrading program, with support from GTZ, UNIDO, the Italian government, and other international agencies. One major initiative centers on the Ethiopian Leather and Leather Products Technology Institute, which provides consultancy and training to tanneries in areas that include factory management, effluent disposal, and marketing. It also works on productivity enhancement through a benchmarking program. Another is the Engineering Capacity Building Programme, which operates a leather value-chain upgrading program, consisting of ten working packages that cover areas such as ecto-parasitic control, international exposure for Ethiopian firms, and firm-level support for productivity improvement (ibid.: 24).

In footwear, there already appears to have been something of a breakthrough. In the 1990s, Ethiopian producers lost most of the domestic market to Chinese imports, but by the early 2000s they had won most of it back. They began exporting on a regular basis in 2004/05, with exports reaching $10 million by value three years later (ibid.: 22). Today several firms are exporting in bulk to Italy as well as to other European and non-European markets, and exports look set to grow. In 2011 the government announced that it was banning the export of semi-processed 'crusted' leather, another example of the EPRDF using state power to encourage a move into sectors with higher job and value-creation potential (Economist Intelligence Unit 2011a).

Endowment companies We turn now to the endowment-owned companies, and especially EFFORT, the Endowment Fund for the Rehabilitation of Tigray. As we touched upon in the previous section, EFFORT has its origins in a variety of private companies established by prominent TPLF members between 1991 and 1994, using resources amassed during the war against the Dergue. Soon afterwards, questions began to be asked about these companies' legal profile and political affiliation, and in 1994 the government responded by passing legislation that prohibited political organizations from running businesses. Shareholders of the TPLF-linked companies subsequently 'donated' their shares to EFFORT, in a move widely seen as respecting the letter rather than the spirit of the law (Vaughan and Gebremichael 2011: 35–6).

EFFORT is formally governed by a council of fifty-five to seventy-five members, made up of representatives of the regional government,

local governments, and other associations. Overall strategic management, however, is controlled by a board of between nine and twelve
members, all senior TPLF members and leaders. When the fieldwork
for this chapter was being conducted, the board chairman was head
of the political office of the TPLF in Tigray and EFFORT's CEO was
a former regional vice-president; both were long-standing members of
the TPLF socio-economic committee and TPLF politburo members.
When it comes to EFFORT's individual companies, however, many
are managed by professionals with significant private sector experience
and good business training (ibid.).

EFFORT's stated objectives encompass a variety of economic and
social goals that include: using the resources of the people of Tigray
for the economic, social, and cultural development of the region;
generating income for the families of the martyrs and other war
victims, as well as other vulnerable citizens; acting as an instrument
to promote the industrialization of Tigray, given that most investors
prefer the service sector; opening up new sectors into which private
sector businesses could follow, once infrastructure and a precedent
have been established; and contributing to the development of human
resources in Tigray, especially to the establishment of research and
training institutions (ibid.: 37). In some ways, then, EFFORT sees
itself as the kind of 'first mover' that heterodox industrial theorists
are so keen to support.

Currently EFFORT owns sixteen companies that report some $360
million in assets and $160 million in working capital (ibid.: 37). They
are organized into five clusters or 'commercial business units', namely
Engineering and Construction, Manufacturing, Services, Agroprocess-
ing, and Mining. From our point of view, the most interesting are
Guna Trading, TransEthiopia, Mesebo Cement, Mesfin Industrial
Engineering, Almeda Textiles and Garments, Hiwet Mechanised Agriculture, and Sur Construction.

The first thing to note about these companies is that some operate in highly profitable, not terribly risky areas. For example, Guna
Trading imports and exports seeds, pulses, coffee, fertilizer, and other
key commodities, while TransEthiopia operates a large truck fleet.
EFFORT is able to use the profits generated in these reliable money-
spinners to subsidize some of the riskier investments, which are also
assisted through subcontracting.

The second thing to note is that party linked companies (whatever their protestations to the contrary) are widely seen as enjoying a range of advantages over normal private businesses. According to Berhanu Abegaz these may include a soft-budget constraint, the preferential allocation of public tenders and contracts, the steering toward them of aid organization and other business, preferential access to government credit facilities, preferential treatment in obtaining licenses and customs clearance, and the crowding out of private competition in high-profit, easy-entry areas (Berhanu Abegaz 2011: 42). EFFORT managers are quick to point out that they now face competition in most areas, that they are successful with only a percentage of their tenders, and that, like other private companies, they also sometimes experience difficulty obtaining credit (Vaughan and Gebremichael 2011). A plausible conclusion is that the playing field, while not always level, is not as steeply pitched as most observers assume.

The third and perhaps most important point to note from our perspective is that EFFORT companies are part of a deliberate industrial policy of structural transformation and upgrading, and that as such there is a high degree of integration and complementarity among them. Take Mesebo Cement Factory. This was started in 1997, the aim being to reduce the regional price of cement and to create spin-off industries. As part of this endeavor, it switched in 2009/10 from imported furnace oil to locally produced coal and petcoke, reducing costs in the process. Mesebo struggled initially, but with rising cement prices it has now entered a period of strong profitability, and has about a 30 percent share of the local market. A $180 million expansion is planned, and the company hopes one day to export to the region. The company has also generated retail opportunities for youth cooperatives and mass associations (ibid.).

Mesebo's coal-firing plant was built by another EFFORT company, Mesfin Industrial Engineering. Mesfin's main activities have been the construction of cargo bodies and trailers, where it dominates the local market. However, it has also been involved in more ambitious projects such as the aforementioned Mesebo contract, manufacture of sluice gates for hydropower projects, design and erection of Ethiopia's eight new sugar factories, design and erection of an EFFORT-owned tannery, and work on Addis Ababa airport, among others. It has grown from a small undertaking of thirty employees to one with 650 permanent employees and 350 casual or contract workers, and with assets of almost $50 million (ibid.).

One of EFFORT's most ambitious projects, meanwhile, is Almeda Textile and Garmenting, the country's only integrated textile and garmenting factory, which cost almost $100 million to commission. Like Mesebo, it initially struggled, experimenting with both Chinese and Pakistani management teams, and has yet to enter profitability. Nevertheless, there are signs that it has turned a corner, and an expansion to create 4,000 extra jobs is planned. The plant is designed to take advantage of local supplies of high-quality cotton, a sector in which EFFORT is also involved. The main company concerned is Hiwet Mechanised Agriculture, a scheme to settle demobilized TPLF fighters in the West of Tigray. It employs 300 permanent workers and around ten thousand casual laborers, growing cotton, operating a ginning factory which processes about two thousand tonnes of cotton per annum, and experimenting with irrigated agriculture.

EFFORT has also created companies to drive and take advantage of Ethiopia's huge infrastructure investments, namely Sur Construction. Sur employs 1,500 permanent staff and 6,000 daily laborers, and has been involved in the construction of hydropower plants, airports, universities, garmenting factories, and roads, often in partnership with Chinese contractors (ibid.).

Given the breadth of its commercial activity, it comes as no surprise that EFFORT is the biggest employer and taxpayer in Tigray. Only a rigorous social cost–benefit accounting could determine whether the creation of domestic capacity in new areas with potential high value-added, plus the realization of other social goals, justifies the implicit subsidies, or rents, the company receives. However, it is relevant to note that we found no credible evidence that rents are being squandered in corrupt ways, or that individual party members have been enriched by way of the rents accruing to EFFORT.[11] In this respect, Ethiopia seems to refute the conventional wisdom that African states cannot be trusted with interventionist industrial policy because of unproductive rent-seeking and corruption. Rather, the allocation and use of profits, dividends, benefits and rents seems to be conceived and managed strategically to resource the wider socio-economic and political objectives of shaping and enhancing 'developmental state' outcomes (ibid.: 36).[12] In this sense, a centralized structure of rent management has at least created the enabling conditions for a productive use of economic rents.

By 2010 EFFORT was reporting that during the five-year period following its 2005 return to profitability, it had expanded by reinvesting 3 billion birr (about $178 million).[13] Mesebo was expected to begin full production of 36,000 quintals of cement per day in September 2010 (EFFORT 2010). In January 2011 it was announced that the Development Bank of Ethiopia would loan Mesebo another 316 million birr during the coming financial year for its further expansion program to develop a second factory (Addis Fortune Newspaper 2011). We have already reported on expansion at Almeda Textiles. In addition, Sheba Leather upgraded its facilities to produce finished leather and leather products, and Abergelle Livestock expanded its slaughterhouse capacity to 240 cattle and 960 goats a day with an investment of 150 million birr. Sur Construction and Addis Pharmaceutical also reportedly received additional investment worth tens of millions of birr (EFFORT 2010).

EFFORT has ambitious plans for its future. Its expansion strategy envisages it becoming competitive in the world market, helping to lift Ethiopia to middle-income status, and turning an annual profit of more than 3 billion birr within fifteen to twenty years, by increasing its production and investment capacities, creating partnerships with other businesses, and focusing on human resource development (ibid.). EFFORT's leadership, all still senior members of the leadership of the Ethiopian ruling party, continue to see themselves as playing a key role in contributing to Ethiopia's economic transition, not least in helping to boost, inspire, rein in, discipline, and control an entrepreneurial sector regarded as weak, conservative, mercurial and politically unreliable. As such EFFORT and the companies it owns are increasingly integrated into the wider fabric of economic, political, social and developmental actors involved in promoting the economic agenda of 'revolutionary democracy'. This is an idea and a strategy with long-horizon resilience.

Economic performance

For several years now, Ethiopia has been one of the world's fastest-growing economies. Between 2004 and 2008, GDP growth was in double digits. It dipped somewhat to 9.9 percent in 2009, and to 8.8 percent in 2010, but this was still better than that of almost any economy in the region (Various Authors 2011d). Growth has been broad based, with agriculture, industry, and services all recording double-digit expansion for much of the past decade (agricultural growth has slowed recently, partly because of severe drought). FDI has been comparable to that of Tanzania and Uganda, and better than that of Kenya (Economist Intelligence Unit 2008a). Unlike in Tanzania, however, the government's record in reducing poverty has been strong. In 1995 some 61 percent of the population were estimated to be below a $1.25 (PPP) a day poverty line, but by 2010 that had fallen to 29 percent (Altenburg 2011: 15). Thanks to both growth and effective social spending, government is on track to reach Millennium Development Goals 1, 2, 4, and 6, and likely to be on track for goals 3, 5, and 7 (Various Authors 2011e).

The impact of growth on structural transformation, however, has been less impressive. Although industry has grown, and there has been an increase in the share of larger firms relative to smaller firms, its share in the economy as a whole has remained broadly constant, at around 13 percent. As in other African economies, the major growth area has been services, which now account for more than half of GDP, with retail trade and financial intermediation growing particularly strongly (Access Capital 2010b). In industry, manufacturing, especially agro-processing, was the fastest-growing sub-sector for much of the last decade, but it still contributes only 4.9 percent of GDP.

Nevertheless, there are some signs that the government's industrial policy is bearing fruit, particularly when we look at the level and composition of exports. In 2004/05 exports stood at only $800 million, but after strong year-on-year growth (2008/09 excepted) they reached $2 billion in 2009/10. More encouragingly still, Ethiopia has begun to diversify its export base. While coffee is still in top spot, it now produces five other commodities (oilseeds, gold, khat, flowers, and pulses) that bring in more than $100 million each. Another fifteen products realize sales of more than $10 million each, including textiles and garments with $22 million, and leather and leather products, with $15 million (Access Capital 2010a).[14] The upsurge in production of flowers, garments, and leather products demonstrates an ability to move into higher-value-added sectors, and suggests an impact for industrial policy on technological upgrading. China is making a serious move into manufacturing, and there are plans to open a special economic zone south of Addis Ababa which, if successful, will create 20,000 new jobs (Various Authors 2011e).

Export growth and FDI have been assisted by generally sound macroeconomic management. For much of the last decade there was an emphasis on exchange rate stability and low inflation. However, in the last few years problems have begun to emerge, some but not all of which are of the government's own making. The fiscal deficit has been widening, for example, on account of the government's ambitious development program (ibid.). Inflation has also been a problem, and reached a very high 40.6 percent in 2011 (Economist Intelligence Unit 2011a). This is driven largely by food prices, which have been at record levels, mainly owing to drought. The government has used a variety of monetary instruments, including a cap on private sector credit, to tackle the issue, but it remains a problem (ibid.; Various Authors 2011e).

Ethiopia's external balance has also been deteroriating. In 2010 the current account balance deficit stood at over 8 percent of GDP, and foreign exchange reserves were equivalent to only two months' imports (Economist Intelligence Unit 2011a; Various Authors 2011e). The government's five-year plan targets agriculture to grow at over 8 percent a year and industry at 20 percent a year for the next five years, which should lead to export growth of 36.6 percent in 2010/11 and 28.4 percent annually in the remaining plan period (Various Authors 2011e). Even accounting for exchange rate devaluation and the government's huge infrastructural investments, it is clear that these are extremely ambitious targets. Nevertheless, the World Bank has pledged to support the plan, calling its ambitions 'appropriate' (Economist Intelligence Unit 2011a).

More positively, Ethiopia's external debt ratio fell from 7.3 percent in 2002/03 to 1.2 percent in 2007/08 on account of debt relief. However, it has subsequently begun to grow again, with much of the new debt coming from non-traditional partners such as China (Various Authors 2011e).

In sum, Ethiopia is performing well in terms of growth and poverty reduction, although less impressively when it comes to structural transformation. There are signs, however, that that may be about to change, with at least some progress registered in the sectors that have been targeted by government industrial policy. The most immediate threat to that progress is macroeconomic imbalance, which has taken a worrying turn in recent months, although most commentators remain optimistic that this can be rectified (see, for example, Economist Intelligence Unit 2011a).

Conclusions

This chapter has shown that Ethiopia's EPRDF regime has succeeded in centralizing economic rent management to a considerable degree. Power within government is concentrated in key ministers who are all personally and politically close to Prime Minister Meles Zenawi, and subsequently deconcentrated throughout the regions. Economically, the government retains control over a large number of state industries, including in key strategic industries such as power and banking. There are also close links between the ruling party and other major economic players, such as the endowment companies. This degree of centralization has permitted some ambitious experiments in industrial policy which appear genuinely focused on the long term, and appear not to have fallen victim to the usual struggle for short-term rents that characterizes many other African economies. Ethiopian development policy appears to have a drive, momentum, and coherence that are lacking in some of our other case studies, notably Ghana and Tanzania. We therefore surmise that these industries have a reasonable chance of success, and that they will in time make a significant contribution to structural transformation, which is currently lagging behind growth and poverty reduction.

Rent centralization is driven by a regime that is controversial to large sections of the population, but which has chosen to pursue legitimacy primarily through broad-based development. Unfortunately the country's ethnic geography does not make that an easy task, and while the EPRDF has tried to balance broad-based development strategy with constitutional concessions to Ethiopia's powerful ethno-national traditions, these measures are neither universally popular nor entirely successful in resolving particularly chronic and intractable conflicts. In some ways, a low-growth strategy that focused on providing narrow patronage pay-offs to ethnic groups would be much easier, but for reasons that are probably both social and ideological, the regime has tried to steer clear of that.

Its preferred strategy, in the meantime, faces some definite challenges. One is the political subservience of the civil service, which may prevent it from offering sound technical advice to the leadership. With such a strong government presence in the economy, it is obviously important that the government makes good technical choices, and there is some concern about this. Another is the government's relations with the private sector. Although a disdainful attitude to private business is a not uncommon feature of developmental states – see, for example, some of the literature on Japan and Taiwan (Johnson 1982; Wade 1990) – recent research suggests that the technocracy should be reasonably well embedded with the private sector if it is to maximize the potential for constructive industrial policy (Sen and te Velde 2011; Whitfield and Therkilsden 2011). In other words, politicians are much more likely to pick winners in consultation with business, than on their own. A final problem is the question of political succession. The prime minister has now been in power for twenty years, and after recent reshuffles, is one of the last surviving leaders of the TPLF old guard. It is not clear whether recent changes are part of a far-sighted policy to secure a smooth intergenerational transition, or whether the prime minister is surrounding himself with less capable but more loyal juniors. One cause for concern is the signal regarding the potential personalization of power sent by the recent replacement of the chief executive of EFFORT by the wife of the prime minister, also a senior member of the ruling party. Such concerns highlight the possibility that centralized rent management, while a powerful developmental tool in the right hands, can quickly go off the rails and into ruin.

A further concern is with human rights. Although the regime is making strong progress on addressing the social and economic dimensions of development, it performs consistently poorly in the field of civil liberties. Ethiopian politics, unlike Ghanaian politics, has no strong liberal tradition, and it is unclear whether a more liberal regime could even survive, let alone preside over the levels of social and economic progress which Ethiopia is apparently witnessing. At the same time, it is far from clear that the levels of repression Ethiopia currently experiences are absolutely necessary to its developmental strengths. At some stage the regime will need to open up, and it is true that in recent years the EPRDF has tried to broaden its social base by recruiting millions of new members; but a likely effect of this is to increase the pressure for unproductive rent distribution, providing another source of strain that could pull developmental patrimonialism off track.

5 | RWANDA: THE PARTY LEADS, THE MARKET FOLLOWS

In our final case study we turn our attention to Rwanda. An East African country of 10.5 million people, Rwanda suffers from a number of quite severe disadvantages. Landlocked, under-endowed with natural resources other than land and climate, and with an exceptionally unfavorable person–land ratio, it continues to be extremely poor in per capita income and human-development terms.[1] With an extremely small formal sector and a limited urban informal sector, the economy has an overwhelmingly pre-capitalist character. Its domestic market for goods and services other than food is tiny. At the end of the war and genocide in 1994, decades of previous advance were wiped out.

In spite of this it has seen excellent economic growth figures and improving social indicators over the past ten years. Rwanda has made considerable efforts to reform the regulatory environment to conform with orthodox investment climate views – in 2011 the World Bank ranked it as the fourth-best country in Africa in which to do business, following only Mauritius, South Africa, and Botswana (World Bank and International Finance Corporation 2010). And yet there remain aspects of its business–politics relations that are very unconventional, not least the heavy involvement in business of the ruling party itself, through its holding company, originally called Tri-Star Investments.

In the following pages we discuss the political-economic background to Rwanda's growth experience, before explaining the place of the party companies in the wider picture of investment, and investment-promotion efforts, in Rwanda. We show how the ruling party uses its private sector operations to effect a centralized management of economic rents, and then take a closer look at how the more orthodox and more interventionist approaches seem likely to be applied in the mining and horticulture sectors.

Historical context

The contemporary Rwandan state has its origins in a centralized kingdom dating back to at least the early nineteenth century. In 1890 it became a German colony, before being transferred to the Belgians after World War 1.

Although Rwandan history is a hotly contested topic, current scholarly evidence suggests that from around 1860 there were two main ethno-political groups in Rwanda: Tutsi, who dominated the political leadership and were mainly cattle keepers, and Hutu, most of whom were politically subservient agriculturalists. Under the influence of colonial rule these distinctions were ossified, entrenching a system of Tutsi privilege (Pottier 2002: 12–15).

In the run-up to full independence (1962), the Belgians transferred their support to Hutu elites, and in 1959 the Tutsi king was over-thrown. Large-scale killings of Tutsi by Hutu took place at intervals between 1959 and 1966, sometimes in response to armed actions by Tutsi groups. The Hutu-led regimes which controlled the country up to the 1994 genocide had different regional power bases. President Grégoire Kayibanda (1961–73) drew support from the south and his successor Juvenal Habyarimana (1973–94) hailed from the northwest. However, both regimes placed restrictions on Tutsis in the name of Hutu emancipation, and there were additional episodes of ethnic killing, notably in 1973 following the large-scale massacres of Hutu in neighboring Burundi the previous year (Kamukama 1997; Prunier 1999).

The pre-1994 regimes quickly adopted single-party rule and in other respects too followed, by and large, the orthodoxies of the period. Habyarimana was influenced by Nyerere's version of African socialism, built up the parastatal sector, promoted compulsory community labor (*umuganda*), and was something of a donor darling until the economic recession of the late 1980s (Uvin 1998).

The introduction of multipartyism came only at the end of the 1973–94 Habyarimana regime, helping to destabilize it. Before that, single-party rule did not prevent the prevailing clientelistic rent-seeking from being competitive and disorganized. Businesses needed 'godfathers' within the administration or the military, and through this mechanism the small business sector financed politics.[2] The *Akazu*, the notorious clique which formed the apex of the clientelist system, was close to but not controlled by the president (Golooba-Mutebi 2008; Prunier 1999; Uvin 1998).

Facing discrimination at home, many Tutsi had fled to neighboring countries and farther afield. In Uganda, some were early recruits to Museveni's National Resistance Army, where they hoped to gain military experience that would serve them in an eventual return to Rwanda. Several individuals, including future president Paul Kagame, rose fast in the military hierarchy and became influential figures in Uganda after Museveni's victory in 1986. Eventually, the prominence of the Rwandans became a political liability for Museveni, and they were encouraged to expedite their return to Rwanda.

In 1990 a force calling itself the Rwandan Patriotic Army (RPA) invaded northern Rwanda, displacing many thousands of people before a ceasefire was brokered by the international community. There followed an internationally sponsored attempt to bring about a democratic transition, scuppered when the plane carrying Habyarimana and the president of Burundi was shot down on April 6, 1994. Almost immediately, a planned genocide against Tutsi and a spate of other mass killings were unleashed. As many as 800,000 people including politically moderate Hutu were murdered. By July, the invading RPA had succeeded in capturing large parts of the country, a large-scale French intervention (Operation Turquoise) had cordoned off other parts, and hundreds of thousands of Hutu refugees, some of whom had participated in the genocide, had fled to neighboring countries.

Between 1994 and 2000 a 'Government of National Unity' led by the Rwandan Patriotic Front (RPF) consolidated its domestic power while pursuing its enemies abroad. On the domestic front, it incorporated the few remaining moderate Hutu politicians, and a Hutu RPF member, Pasteur Bizimungu, became president. It sought new foreign sponsors, distancing itself from France, which had strongly backed the previous regime, and drawing increased support from the UK and the USA. It cooperated, fitfully, with the International Criminal Tribunal for Rwanda, which was established to try the leading figures of the genocide, while launching its own national trials, eventually accompanied by a grassroots restorative justice program called *gacaca* (Clark and Kaufman 2008). As well as garnering substantial amounts of aid from foreign donors, it engaged the support of the pre-1994 Rwandan diaspora to kick-start economic recovery and development, as we shall see in more detail later.

On the external front, it joined with Uganda in a successful struggle, fronted by Laurent Kabila, to overthrow Zairean dictator Mobutu Sese Seko. When it later fell out of Kabila's favor, it launched an attempt to overthrow him. Rwanda's role in the conflict in eastern Congo remains a source of bitter controversy (Prunier 2009; Reyntjens 2009). There has also been an economic dimension, in that the Rwandan army stands accused of profiting massively from trading in Congolese minerals during the years in which its forces and surrogates occupied the east of the country (UN Panel 2002).

Around 2000 the politico-military leadership of the RPF, headed by Paul Kagame, fell out with several of its former collaborators, including Pasteur Bizimungu and other leading public figures. Departures from the ruling coalition included both RPF members and members of smaller allied parties. People of both Hutu and Tutsi background were among those forced out. New adherents to the regime also came from several quarters, including some political and military leaders from the Habyarimana era who were wooed back by the RPF. Kagame assumed the presidency of a government which remained a coalition but whose political complexion was significantly transformed.

Under Kagame's leadership, the RPF-led regime has been distinguished by a ruthless determination which has won admiration and disapproval in more or less equal measure. Its power rests ultimately on control of the army and security services, the leadership of which are carefully vetted for their loyalty to Kagame (Economist Intelligence Unit 2011c). Party politics is tightly controlled: parties that fail to comply with strict, and some would say partial, rules on non-ethnic campaigning are banned or not allowed to register, with the effect that most parties permitted to contest are regarded as RPF allies. At the same time, the government has shown drive and determination in the implementation of economic and social policies, resulting in visible improvements in public service delivery, especially in the health and education fields.

In this context, Paul Kagame won presidential elections easily in both 2003 and 2010. Naturally these successes have appeared tainted, although most observers concede that Kagame's overwhelming endorsements reflect, more than anything else, an appreciation of the peace, security, and broad social and economic progress that have accompanied his rule (in his day, Habyarimana also commanded overwhelming support from the rural masses).

The regime is generally considered to exercise a strong grip on civil society and on press freedom. Especially in pre-election periods, journalists and opponents of the regime have been vulnerable to arrest on charges of fomenting 'genocide ideology', which tends to be broadly interpreted. Several once highly placed Tutsi, including senior military commanders, have fled the country, preferring exile to what they assume will be rough justice in Kigali.[3] An intense and highly polarized debate continues to take place in the international media and on the Internet around human rights issues, including responsibility for murders at home or abroad of individuals who have fallen out with the regime.[4]

Another distinguishing feature of RPF rule is what happens after elections. Under the 2003 Constitution, ministerial posts, which cannot be held by MPs on a separation-of-powers principle, are shared among the legal parties in proportion to their seats in the Chamber of Deputies, with the majority party (the RPF) holding no more than 50 percent of the portfolios (Rwanda 2003: Art. 116). By convention, the prime minister, the speaker of Parliament, the president of the Senate, and the president of the Supreme Court are also expected to be of a different party or tendency from that of the president.[5] The effect is that all governments are coalitions. The RPF is dominant but perhaps no more than in the national unity governments established after the war. The winner-takes-all approach, which was a feature of both the Kayibanda and Habyarimana regimes in Rwanda, as well as of most post-election scenarios in sub-Saharan Africa, is avoided. This has the effect of softening the sense of exclusion among losing parties, and of enabling cabinets and parliaments to work cooperatively with a view to shared long-term interests.

The progress achieved in Rwanda since 2000, as measured by overall economic growth and improvements in social indicators, has been substantial. The regime appears genuine in its efforts to build a society based on a common Rwandese national identity. While Tutsis from the former Ugandan exile group dominate the higher ranks of the army, there have been genuine attempts to break down ethnic differences. The aim, as we shall see, is to transform Rwanda both economically and socially in order to at least reduce the sharpness and political salience of the old distinctions. The Rwandan government is pursuing this vision in a single-minded fashion, which makes it popular with several official donors, who find in Rwanda an exceptionally serious and effective partner.

Debate about Rwanda tends to be polarized, therefore, between two views. One says that the government is a dictatorship in which there is little political space and therefore little chance of genuine reconciliation. The other accepts at least in part the government view that Rwanda cannot afford adversarial politics accompanied by unrestricted campaigning, and that the model being followed will in due course justify its results, including a new dispensation in which the old ethnic politics is generally rejected. Thus, for example, the submission by Human Rights Watch to the International Development Committee of the UK Parliament in May 2011 (Human Rights Watch 2011) reproached DfID for conceding too much to the second viewpoint while itself firmly espousing the first.

The sharpness of the international debate around Rwanda can give the impression of a highly fluid, if not unstable, situation. However, that would probably be misleading. The leadership of the regime has a virtual monopoly of organizational as well as military power. As long as it does not permit greater political opening, or suffer more serious internal splits than have occurred so far, it can be confident of remaining in power for a long time. This makes a difference to its ability to take the long view that we argue is crucial to successful promotion of economic and social transformation, the topic to which we now turn.

Rents, industrial policy, and investment

In the introduction to this chapter we touched on some of the development challenges facing Rwanda: landlocked, land poor, and with a history of social and economic devastation. Against this backdrop, the RPF-led regime is making strenuous efforts to develop agriculture, industry, and services along lines mapped out in ambitious Vision 2020 and growth strategy documents (Government of Rwanda 2000, 2007). Discussion continues on whether the balance of the vision is right. It contains bold ideas about technological leapfrogging and the 'Singapore' model, which, at the very least, remain to be tested (Asche and Fleischer 2011). As elsewhere in the region, it is doubtful whether sufficient public resources are yet being directed at the key task of transforming the productivity of smallholder agriculture (Booth and Golooba-Mutebi 2012b). However, the feature of the policy vision which distinguishes it most clearly is not the content but the seriousness with which implementation is addressed month on month and year on year.

The formal structure of government in Rwanda is conventional. It has the division of labor now usual in the region, with an executive president and a prime minister convening a cabinet of ministers. The cabinet is small by regional standards, and there is a strict separation of government, parliamentary, and party posts. Ministries, with a powerful Ministry of Economy and Finance (MINECOFIN) at the apex, are supported by a range of public agencies with specific executive responsibilities, for example, the Rwanda Development Board (RDB) discussed below. The way this structure functions, however, involves some unusual elements: active management of the cabinet by the president, heavy use of government retreats to update and review progress in policy implementation, and a very public display of accountability for performance at sessions of the annual National Dialogue.[6]

As in other countries, the division of labor between line ministries, public agencies, and local authorities is quite complex. According to the conventional theory, ministries set policies and monitor, and executive agencies implement at the national level, while district and lower tiers of local government provide many of the front-line services. However, the substance of these relationships is different from what is observed in other countries in the region.

One difference is that, from ministers downwards, the civil service and public agencies are regulated by an actually functioning system of performance contracts and targets. *Imihigo* contracts – modern performance agreements supported by a significant component of moral pressure and a neo-traditional[7] gloss – propel a public administration that is remarkably effective in the delivery of the public goods and services it has chosen to prioritize.[8]

At the front line of public service provision and regulation, local authorities have limited autonomy; they are not free to set their own priorities even in theory. Rather, they are subject to a fairly high degree of control and direction by the center. Mayors and councilors are elected on an individual merit, not party, basis, and both mayors and local civil servants are involved in *imihigo*. In these ways, the center gets local governments to do what it considers most important in terms of implementing priority programs and activities. These formal features are consistent with and help to support the most significant feature of the political economy of contemporary Rwanda – the way economic rents are deployed and managed.

Two approaches to investment promotion The Rwandan government's approach to investment promotion is currently a rather unusual hybrid of two elements. Policies and institutional arrangements promoted as best practice by the World Bank's Doing Business surveys have been adopted with vigor, with the effects on the country's rating by the Bank noted at the beginning. It takes only three days to start a business in Rwanda, for example, the eighth-shortest time in the world (World Bank and International Finance Corporation 2011). This coexists with a more activist strand of policy thinking manifested in the use made of the RPF holding company, Tri-Star Investments, but also reflected in the government's evolving approach to privatization and joint ventures.

Conventional, arm's-length investment facilitation in Rwanda has been, since 2008, the responsibility of the Rwanda Development Board (RDB), a composite of several pre-existing state agencies. The RDB and its predecessors did impressive work simplifying and modernizing the regulatory regime for private enterprise, which was once as gargantuan and as prone to corruption as anywhere in Africa. There remain gaps and weak points in this effort, but together with the country's low crime and corruption levels, it makes Rwanda in conventional terms a star investment destination. The extreme weakness of indigenous formal private enterprise – one of the several factors making it difficult to capitalize on this stardom – is being addressed by a government initiative to kick-start interest representation and capacity development among small and medium firms, the Private Sector Federation.

As a whole, the set-up just described is consistent with the international conventional wisdom of the last quarter-century in which the role of government is limited to policy-making, regulation, and the provision of a limited set of core public goods (public order, courts, roads, schooling, etc.). In contrast, Tri-Star grew in part out of the RPF leadership's response to a succession of critical market failures going well beyond those conventionally recognized.

The holding company Tri-Star Investments/CVL is fully owned by the RPF.[9] Its initial funding came from political contributions from supporters, especially in the diaspora. Within a few years of the RPF's accession to power, companies owned wholly or mainly by Tri-Star were in metals trading, road construction, housing estates, manufacture of building materials, fruit processing, mobile telephony, and printing, as well as furniture imports and security services.

At the beginning, in 1994/95, Tri-Star companies were created to respond to the acute material shortages which characterized the immediate post-war situation, using the reserves of the RPF's pre-war and wartime production department to import supplies and even pay civil servants' salaries. Soon, they moved into addressing politically crucial needs, including providing housing for returnees and offering private security services. Investments in basic import substitution followed (e.g. bottled water and basic dairy products).

During the Congo wars, a Tri-Star subsidiary, Rwanda Metals, ran a profitable operation buying minerals from Congo-based traders and selling them on international markets. It was in this period that the dominant role of Tri-Star moved from shoring up the government with the help of surplus funds from the RPF's war chest to doing business on behalf of the party. In its more interesting later phases, Tri-Star-financed companies combined the meeting of urgent socio-political needs with specific economic objectives, including demonstration effects aimed at other private operators. In due course, the activities of several of these firms stimulated other investment by private or public bodies in new or defunct sectors of the economy.[10]

In all cases, the Tri-Star subsidiary was at first a pioneer in activities in which there was little interest from the domestic private sector. No doubt these firms profited from some unhindered access to government and other large contracts – as well as preferred-client treatment within the group (concerns often expressed by critics of the model). In some respects, however, these were advantages that would have been enjoyed by any first-comer. Being first on the scene also meant taking risks and assuming learning costs. Correspondingly, there was the possibility of earnings over and above those that would have been attainable under competitive conditions – in other words, rents.

It would seem, in fact, that most of the firms were not highly or even moderately profitable. Although they operated like private companies, they were run by party cadres with little or no business experience, and were probably not very efficient. The introduction of the accounting and reporting systems that would allow us to judge the matter only came later. What is clear is that the operations were to a greater or lesser extent risky and involved heavy initial learning costs. The major contribution of Tri-Star and its biggest advantage over would-be competitors was its financial power (a combination of its own resources and its credibility as a borrower from national banks) and its willingness to use this to fund investments with high expected social benefits or economic externalities and significant initial learning costs.[11]

These generalizations apply quite clearly to the most important early Tri-Star investment, the one which brought the South African cell phone network MTN to Rwanda. Tri-Star largely funded the initial establishment of the MTN network in Rwanda at a time when neither MTN nor any of the other global operators found the size of the country's subscriber base potentially interesting.

The results of this venture were spectacularly successful, leading the MTN parent company to expand its equity share. Not long after setting up in Rwanda (July 1998), it went on (October 1998) to establish a network in Uganda, with Tri-Star as one of the shareholders. Initially, Tri-Star held approximately 65 percent of the equity in the Rwandan operation and MTN South Africa 26 percent, with the government of Rwanda through the then parastatal Rwandatel contributing the balance. In the following years, Tri-Star progressively transferred holdings to the parent company, reducing its share to 50 percent and 40 percent by 2007. That year, anticipating the entry into the market of two new providers – Tigo and the now privatized Rwandatel – MTN International assumed majority control (55 percent) when Tri-Star sold it a 15 percent stake. Tri-Star got back five to ten times its original investments from these sales.[12] In October 2011, the remaining 10 percent government stake and a further 15 percent Tri-Star (now CVL) holding in MTN Rwanda was sold to the South African parent company, leaving CVL with a 20 percent stake.[13]

In other words, Tri-Star contributed to a demonstration effect and learning experience in which one of the beneficiaries was an international firm. It thereby ensured not only that Rwanda entered the world of mobile telephony earlier than it would otherwise have done, but also that the network that was established was at least partly owned by domestic capital. There have been spillover benefits for the wider information and communications technology field, with new IT firms being established by Rwandese entrepreneurs who cut their teeth negotiating with MTN on behalf of the government.[14]

In other sectors, too, the emphasis has been more on using financial clout to enable local players to undertake the risks and learning associated with getting established in competition with international suppliers. This is particularly applicable to building and road construction, where some international firms, including Chinese companies, have not only experience but a financial capacity which allows them to be free of risk-averse Africa-based banks. As experience in Uganda confirms, operational competitiveness with international and particularly Chinese firms in these sectors is close to impossible to achieve for local firms in the subregion in the absence of a mechanism for financing start-up costs and learning-by-doing (Booth and Golooba-Mutebi 2009).

In all of these operations, there is awareness that competitiveness depends not only on having a supportive and patient financial backer. Tri-Star firms have had extremely open recruitment policies for managers, engineers, and other technical specialists. In a number of cases, diaspora professionals have been headhunted, but increasingly the firms recruit by means of open advertising within the East African region and beyond. They can and do hire globally to meet needs in some technical areas. A willingness to hire internationally for the sake of creating competitive national firms has been noted as a distinguishing feature of regimes that we have elsewhere characterized as 'developmental patrimonialisms' (Cammack and Kelsall 2011). It would appear to be one of the features that distinguish the policies of such regimes from those of the African modal pattern, in which 'jobs for the boys' and jobs for locals take precedence over firm efficiency and competitiveness.

In this respect and others, the operational management of Tri-Star/CVL has gone through at least three fairly distinct phases. In the earliest phases management styles within the group resembled those of the parastatal sector, but progressively the companies have come to be managed according to the norms of the private sector. Increasingly, the model is that of 'early-stage venture capitalism'. The orientation is toward creating firms that are attractive partners for international direct investors, not just large players in domestic terms. The pressure is on to raise efficiency and management reporting to the necessary standards.[15]

Today, CVL has a 50 percent stake or more in eleven companies operating in Rwanda.[16] These are mostly in the position of being the leading national company, their competition coming primarily from either regional (usually Kenyan) or international (including notably Chinese) firms. In 2009, group turnover, referring to majority shareholdings only, was about $35 million. Group profits in this restricted sense were around $7 million after payment of $0.8 million in taxes. With the contributions from minority shareholdings, including in the Rwanda branch of the cellphone company MTN, turnover was $167 million, post-tax profits $47 million and taxes paid $24 million. While the majority-owned CVL firms represented well under 1 percent of Rwanda's $5.3 billion GDP, the whole group represented over 3 percent, a significant proportion given the limited size of the formal sector as a whole.[17] The taxes paid by the larger group were equivalent to around 9 percent of all direct taxes paid in fiscal year 2009/10.[18] In addition, CVL has two investments in the USA and owns an air charter company in South Africa.

Leading from the front The recognition that the private sector needs to be driven forward and not just facilitated with the provision of a business-friendly environment is entrenched in several parts of the Rwandan system, not just the Tri-Star/CVL set-up. Under Kagame, the government of Rwanda has been quite strongly committed to the private sector as the engine of development. Nearly all of the parastatals inherited from the Habyarimana era were privatized between the late 1990s and mid-2000s. However, the privatizations were actively supervised. A number of privatized firms, including Rwandatel, were intervened in and then reprivatized when the first buyers proved incapable of providing the promised injections of capital and know-how. More recently, Rwandatel went into receivership after Libya's Lap-Green failed to meet some of the conditions of its purchase, and is to be sold for a third time. Policy today is more tough minded about the likely benefits of privatization, and there is stronger interest in the option of bringing private sector disciplines into the remaining, and some newly created, state-owned companies.

The regime has also adopted a relatively activist stance in at least two other areas. First, it encouraged the army to create an investment arm with which to undertake socio-economic projects and create productive enterprises. The result was another holding company run on private corporate lines, Horizon Group. Secondly, it brokered the creation of a large private investment consortium bringing together a group of the richest domestic and diaspora entrepreneurs. The consortium is known as the Rwanda Investment Group (RIG).

Horizon Group's first venture was a construction company established with an initial gift of equipment from the government and a team of military engineers seconded from the army. It undertook a series of projects for the government, including building irrigation dykes and constructing coffee-washing stations, 'to avoid the Chinese doing everything'.[19] At an early stage, it established a cassava-growing operation and a dairy (Laiterie Nyabisindu). Subsequently, it moved into comprehensive urban site development, first on land bought from the Housing Bank in Kigali and later in collaboration with CSS-Zigama, the military's micro-finance initiative. Horizon is now also in pyrethrum processing, as the owner of the Sopyrwa plant in Musanze, the former Ruhengeri Province, which is linked to twenty-four large producer cooperatives in the area.

Horizon Group is run as a private firm. Even its board does not include serving military officers, although its CEO was seconded from the army following a previous posting with the military bank. However, as with Tri-Star, its social and political purposes are important, and profitability is no more than a co-equal objective. The interest in rural construction arose from the perceived imperative to restore export agriculture to something approaching its previous condition. Urban housing was signaled as a vital matter when competition between returnees and displaced people for access to the limited housing stock became acute in the later 1990s. The intervention in pyrethrum was necessary to avert the collapse of a privatized parastatal which would have had harmful employment and smallholder income effects in the still politically fragile mountain region of the northwest. Like Tri-Star, Horizon has a robustly internationalist approach to filling skill gaps in its firms, with business efficiency and the meeting of strategic social objectives taking precedence over commitments to local hiring and capacity development.

RIG is again a holding company but of a different character. It was created in May 2006, at the instigation of President Kagame and in response to the difficulty of raising funds for large projects in the absence of a local capital market. Currently, it has forty-one shareholders, including thirty-one individuals, four medium-sized companies and six institutional investors, including the Rwanda Development Bank, major insurers and Crystal Ventures Ltd. The initial start-up capital totaled $25 million.[20] In effect, it brings together 'nearly all' of the richest and best-known individual business people of Rwanda and the diaspora along with the major public financial institutions.[21] At present it operates with a fairly restrictive minimum subscription ($3.6 million) but the intention is to seek international partners and in due course float shares publicly.

RIG's mandate is to raise capital for investments of particular national interest without relying on international capital markets or the local branches of foreign banks. Social objectives are less prominent than in the cases of CVL and Horizon, but 'economic patriotism' is part of the group mission. Such an approach appeared necessary at the time when the country's largest cement factory, CIMERWA, a Chinese–Rwanda government joint venture under the Habyarimana regime, was being privatized and needed a substantial capital injection. RIG has a 90 percent stake in CIMERWA, with the government of Rwanda holding the balance.

RIG subsequently invested heavily in peat mining and methane gas extraction from Lake Kivu (both potential solutions to Rwanda's acute electric power shortage). It is in a public–private partnership with the government for the establishment of the Kigali Industrial Park and several other schemes.[22] These are all initiatives which funding sources with no 'patriotic mandate', or willingness to underwrite risks, might well have considered unsuitable.[23]

As RIG illustrates, the allocation of privileged or protected economic opportunities to large private businesses which are not fully owned by Tri-Star/CVL is a feature of the Rwandan political-economic model. However, these are risky, first-comer investments, not an easy ride, and the private partners are under political as well as economic pressure to perform.

Unlike the conventional, arm's-length approach, the interventionist style associated with Tri-Star/CVL, Horizon and RIG tends to worry donors. The default viewpoint among donors stresses the importance of a 'level playing field' for private firms and would prefer a limited regulatory role for state and quasi-state agencies. Tri-Star, in particular, has attracted a good deal of hostile commentary over the years, not only because of the Congo connection, but also because in some particular instances its behavior has been judged to have been anti-competitive. There is a pervasive view that, somehow, the involvement of a ruling political party in private sector business operations is particularly to be feared and deplored.

The donor default position is, however, grounded in now increasingly questioned elements of the so-called Washington Consensus. It is out of line with the views of a large and growing group of economists influenced by Asian experience and 'new structuralist' theory, who, as we saw in our opening chapter, maintain that an active and forward-looking public policy is a precondition for achieving the agricultural transformation and industrial upgrading (as distinct from mere economic growth) that poor economies need (Amoako 2011; Chang 2002; Khan 2007; Lin 2011b; United Nations Economic Commission for Africa 2011; Van Donge et al. 2012).

As we saw in Chapter 1, the most persuasive standard objection to the new economic thinking has been that African politicians cannot be trusted with state interventionism. Until the reforms of the 1980s and 1990s, state failure in the form of widespread administrative inefficiency and corruption was a more prevalent and immediate problem in Africa than market failure. What confidence can we have that this problem has gone away? The view that underpins this book is that it is unwise to give a blanket answer to this question; it depends what kind of regime is being considered. In the Rwandan case, most observers accept that there is relatively little unproductive 'rent-seeking' for short-term personal or political gain.

Moreover, the way the ruling RPF does gain directly from its ownership of Tri-Star/CVL seems to be part of the secret of the regime's success in maintaining a tight grip on administrative and political corruption. Most observers agree that corruption in Rwanda is much lower than in most countries of sub-Saharan Africa, and this is confirmed by the standard perception data used by Transparency International. How has this been achieved? Elsewhere in the region, electoral competition has become increasingly expensive, creating large needs for party funding that can be met only by large-scale scams and other theft of public resources, which in turn set the standard that applies in public life at every level. Although Rwanda's limited political competition undoubtedly reduces the extent to which the regime must engage in corruption to win elections, we think the relationship between Tri-Star/CVL and the ruling party is an important part of the story too.

In Rwanda, elections are still relatively cheap. However, they are not cost free. In that context, it matters that the RPF, by far the largest legal party, has a reliable source of income. As mentioned earlier, the notion that the holding company has been consistently and massively profitable is largely a myth. Nonetheless, the part of its usually modest profits that is not reinvested is remitted annually to the RPF, as the only shareholder. This provides the party with a source of funds for its running costs and election campaigns. The

RPF's financial solvency obviates the need for party officials to engage in election-related corruption, which in turn allows the party to take a very tough line on corruption among its leading supporters and in the bureaucracy. As one example of this, government spending on key areas of its Economic Development and Poverty Reduction Strategy is in line with its budgetary commitments: 'perhaps a unique record of achievement in the region' (Various Authors 2011a: 8). There has been a concomitant fall in the expenditure share of wages and salaries, and a rise in the share of public investment (ibid.).

In summary, the involvement of the ruling party in the private business sector has benefits going beyond the particular way it has helped to kick-start private investment proper in telecommunications and other sectors. It has helped to enable the regime to manage the public investment portfolio, including Horizon and joint ventures with RIG, in ways that contribute to the diversification of the economy while maintaining high standards of public probity and discipline.

As in Ethiopia, the leadership has strong reasons for wanting to implement ambitious development plans, reasons which have their roots in bloody historical experiences of recent memory. However, achieving what we have called centralized, long-horizon rent management calls for more than just political will. It calls for institutional arrangements which enable the necessary disciplines to be established and maintained within the ruling elite. Even more clearly than in Ethiopia, the arrangements we have been describing seem to provide that.

Sectoral examples

We have seen that Rwanda seems to have acquired institutional arrangements that make an active 'industrial policy' both economically and politically sustainable. At the same time, it has come to be viewed as a star performer in terms of orthodox, arm's-length investment facilitation. The organizations that have been vehicles of this transformation, such as the Rwanda Development Board (RDB) and Private Sector Federation (PSF), will naturally want to capitalize upon it. Moreover, having been firmly led from the front for years, the small and medium-sized firms which are represented in the PSF are showing signs of acquiring an independent voice and influence within government. As a result, there may in the future be more of a domestic constituency for 'level playing field' arguments and more resistance to further expansion of state and party enterprises (Gökgür 2011; Private Sector Federation 2011).

This raises the question of Rwanda's likely future direction of travel. Will CVL, Horizon, and RIG turn out in the end to have been a post-conflict flash in the pan? Or will they be a permanent feature of the country's development model for some time yet? There seem to be strong reasons for accepting the second, but different sectors of the economy have different needs and possibilities, so the direction of travel will not be uniform. We illustrate this with a discussion and interpretation of what has been happening in two dynamic economic sectors, mining and horticulture. In both sectors, government policies and practices in recent years have been highly supportive of private initiative, in sharp contrast to the conditions in the countries discussed earlier in this book. However, the form of support has been different between the two sectors and seems set to become more so.

Mining and quarrying constituted a mere 1 percent of GDP in 2010, but were the second-largest export earner by value after tourism ($68 million as against $201 million), exceeding both coffee and tea ($56 million each) despite the continuing effects on mineral demand of the world downturn of 2009 (MINECOFIN 2011; NISR 2011). Sector employment is estimated at 35,000 (Hesselbein 2011; MINIRENA 2008).

In contrast, there has been little previous development of commercial horticulture in Rwanda, even though a large variety of fruits and vegetables have always been available in local markets (G&N Consultants 2008). In developing commercial horticulture, Rwanda is starting from a very low base, compared with its neighbors Kenya, Tanzania, Uganda, and Ethiopia. However, horticulture is now one of the fastest-growing export sectors. The government hopes that current exports of around $3 million per annum will rise to $9 million by 2015 (MINICOM 2011).

Mining: getting the right framework Mining has been a significant activity in Rwanda since the 1930s, when a number of Belgian firms were awarded production concessions, especially for wolfram (tungsten) and casiterite (tin). In the 1960s, mining accounted for between 25 and 47 percent of export earnings, second only to coffee, declining in relation to tea thereafter. Privatization of state-owned concessions became a government priority in the early 2000s, but made difficult headway because information on the production potential was frequently lacking. Overcoming this obstacle was the main objective of a new mining law passed in 2009, which retains the distinction between research and production concessions but improves the incentive to engage in prospecting. Other aspects of the investment promotion regime are heavily focused on information supply, regulation, and certification (MINIRENA 2009).[24]

Mining has become, probably indefinitely and for good reasons, a redoubt of arm's-length facilitation. There may well be good technical reasons for this, given the technology- and knowledge-intensity of the business. In any event, with the controversy around trading in Congo minerals in the background, this is probably the field in which the government of Rwanda will be most unwilling for some time ahead to permit itself a more interventionist role. Arguably, also, this is a field in which backward and forward linkages are typically handled on a within-firm basis, making externalities less of a concern than they are in other sectors, especially agriculture in general and export horticulture in particular. The results of the approach being taken have yet to be seen. However, the outlook is at least promising, with several large international prospectors now at work, with interest in gold and coltan (tantalite) as well as wolfram and casiterite. Avenues for value addition are also being pursued.

As in other countries, the mining sector of Rwanda is highly stratified. There are no large operations on the scale of, for example, big gold in Tanzania, but several medium-scale exploitations, surrounded by a mass of artisanal producers. The larger firms include some joint ventures between foreign capital and returnee Rwandans. They are organized in their own association, with small producers separately represented by mining cooperatives. The medium-scale operators seem to consider themselves well supported by the government; when they encounter snags, they pick up the telephone and arrange a meeting with the minister.[25]

Horticulture: the challenge of market coordination In the case of horticulture, too, the policy approach until now has been mostly of the 'hands-off' type. However, the limitations of such an approach have become increasingly apparent.

A specialized agency under the Ministry of Agriculture, the Rwanda Horticulture Development Authority (RHODA), works alongside the general agency for agriculture (RADA). Through RHODA and the RDB, the government is making a strong play to make Rwanda the place where international and regional investors will go after exhausting the horticultural potential of Kenya and Uganda. This is a reasonable ambition, given that for a number of horticultural crops Rwanda is already competitive in terms of yields without yet having made large investments (RDB/RHODA 2010). One of the Crystal Ventures companies, Inyange Industries, has moved from processing of water, milk, and imported fruit concentrate into processing of locally procured fresh fruit and promoting contract farming. However, the aim and the need is for investment on a broad front, with domestic private operators like the celebrated Gérard Sina and regional firms like East African Growers taking increasing shares of the regional and, to a limited extent, the global markets for horticultural crops and processed products.

A number of steps have been taken to set a suitable legal and regulatory framework. RHODA is proactive in promoting the opportunities that Rwanda offers and in brokering partnerships at various points in the value chain. There are good links with related aspects of policy for agriculture, including the development of an appropriate model of rural cooperation and a vision for cooperative-based contract farming. Some investors have been allocated land.

The government has supplied some of the infrastructural conditions for Rwanda to become a global player, and has generally played an active facilitating role. For example, it has constructed a cold storage facility at Kigali airport and a flower park is under construction.[26] RHODA and RDB with the support of a Belgian Technical Assistance project have enabled Rwandan horticulture investors to attend agricultural trade fairs in Germany. A Rwanda Horticulture Inter-professionals Organization (RHIO) was formed with official support in 2009, and has sixty business and technical professionals as members. RHODA has contracted a Kenyan firm to advise on quality control in contract farming and it subsidizes use of the certification services of Global Gap, which are essential to realizing the best international prices.[27] Subsidized fertilizer is being delivered to areas judged particularly suited to specific crops, along with awareness campaigns about necessary volume and quality standards.[28] There is an active and much-needed program of research led by the Institut des Sciences Agronomiques du Rwanda (ISAR) on planting materials and disease control.[29] Finally, agreements in principle have been reached with several air freight companies, and the national carrier Rwandair has been encouraged to invest in two new wide-bodied planes to serve routes to Dubai and Kinshasa, both target destinations for Rwandan horticulture.[30] But in spite of these positive measures the uptake of opportunities is beginning to be viewed as disappointing. Limitations of the current approach are being recognized. There are increasing references to unresolved 'chicken-and-egg problems'; that is to say problems of market coordination.

The most important bottleneck of this kind seems to be the volume and continuity of production that are necessary to sustain any processing operation using modern technology and aiming to be competitive in a regional or international market. Land availability in Rwanda is not considered sufficient for the establishment of centrally managed plantations. The model being promoted is therefore contract farming by smallholders organized in member-controlled cooperatives around a centrally managed home enterprise. But the organization of contract farmers on a sufficient scale and at sufficient production standards is challenging even for firms that are well embedded in the local environment, such as Sina's Urwibutso enterprise and Inyange. Those firms are themselves in the learning phase and having to cover their learning costs.

Another much-cited cluster of chicken-and-egg problems concerns post-harvest aggregation, storage, and marketing for the domestic market, and cold storage and international air freight for international destinations. We have seen that the government has taken steps to address these, but at present the government cold storage facility at the national airport is underutilized and freight rates are high on account of low volumes. A modern market facility to serve the national market is under construction, but there are some doubts about the ability of even this infrastructure to be able to attract a sufficient volume of produce out of the informal local and cross-border channels through which most of it flows at the moment. In several respects, these are the challenges also affecting the government's wider project of transforming smallholder agriculture by encouraging it to become more commercial.

Against this background, there are signs that the government will adopt the technical advice being offered from various quarters that it is time for it to undertake joint ventures with a few international investors in which the authorities will underwrite and if necessary subsidize the learning costs and risk-taking. With a larger share of the national budget now being allocated to agricultural support, it is to be hoped that this will be accompanied by a sharp increase in the capacity of the public extension system to engage with smallholders and smallholder organizations, a critical ingredient in all previous 'green revolutions'.

The viability of the proposed approach relies on the possibility that some relatively large regional investors will be attracted and that, bringing relevant know-how with them, they will be prepared to bear the initial investments, including in respect of negotiating agreements with and providing ongoing technical extension services to groups of producers. This is in fact the model that has been followed by the existing processors, Urwibutso Enterprises, Inyange Industries and Shakina Enterprises, each of which has agreements with producer groups. The Kenyan supermarket Nakumatt, which is now established in Kigali, has some local producer agreements, although much of its sourcing is still regional.[31] In the case of Urwibutso, the agreements include the provision of free or subsidized social services and a significant research and demonstration undertaking on the home farm. One well-known regional investor, East African Growers of Kenya, has established a contract-farming operation – experimenting with irrigated French bean production, their stock-in-trade.[32] However, it appears that others are watching and waiting.

If and when a breakthrough occurs on volume and quality of fruit and vegetable growing, bottlenecks will quickly appear on the processing side. Inyange Industries, the largest processor and an affiliate of Tri-Star Investments/Crystal Ventures Ltd, the holding company owned by the ruling RPF, has recently invested in a $30 million state-of-the art pineapple and passion-fruit juicing plant. This has enabled the firm to establish agreements which are more remunerative for the producer groups and more easily supervised for quality. It is predicted that this will force the previous market leader in fresh juice, Urwibutso Enterprises, to upgrade its technology.[33] However, it will remain the case that Rwanda has no plant for concentrating surplus passion fruit juice, and only one tomato processor.[34]

This is an incomplete story. At this point, it is not clear that the idea will pass the various levels of scrutiny that it is likely to attract. The modalities of the investment and the institutional form of the government's involvement (or that of CVL or perhaps RIG) will need to be defined. The necessary massive scaling up of extension services is particularly challenging. But until these challenges are met, storage and transport facilities will be underutilized, resulting in unit costs which cannot beat the competition from Uganda and elsewhere.[35] While the government and supporting donors have gone some way toward bearing those costs centrally, it is not clear that this will be sufficient to give Rwandan producers the competitive advantage they need.[36] Unlike most others in the region, however, the RPF regime may prove to have both the determination and the working models with which to pull it off.

Economic performance

To what extent are these developments reflected in official statistics of economic performance? The overall picture is one of sound macroeconomic management and strong growth, albeit with some concerns about external dependence, external balance, and structural transformation. GDP growth averaged 6.8 percent per year between 2002 and 2010, for example, and is forecast to continue at around 7 percent for the next few years (Various Authors 2011a). Sectorally, the biggest gains, as in much of the rest of Africa, have been in services, with the financial sector, transport, and communications featuring particularly strongly. Construction has been another lead sector, driven in part by large infrastructural investments. Manufacturing also performed strongly in 2010, growing by 10.9 percent, although its total share of the economy fell slightly between 2005 and 2010, from 7.5 percent to 6.7 percent.

Externally, exports grew at the impressive rate of 26.1 percent per year between 2005 and 2009. The Economist Intelligence Unit records Rwanda's principal exports in 2010 as coffee ($56.1 million), tea ($55.7 million), tin ore ($42.2 million), and coltan ($18.5 million). Seventy-five percent of Rwanda's exports are accounted for by five products, all of them primary commodities; as of yet there is little evidence of a move into higher-value exports. Moreover, export growth has not been sufficient to keep pace with increases in imports, about two-thirds of which are capital or intermediate goods. The current account deficit was 8.4 cent of GDP in 2009, with a trade deficit of 15.8 percent (ibid.). More positively, the balance of payments is being helped by rapid increases of FDI to over $100 million a year, the country has foreign reserves to cover more than six months' imports, and its external debt, at under 5 percent of GDP, is one of the lowest in the region (ibid.).

External assistance is integral to Rwanda's development strategy. In 2009/10 parliament approved a budget of 35 billion Rwandan francs (about $630 million) – slightly more than half of which was provided from external sources. In the same year, Rwanda received $934 million in ODA, almost double what it received in 2004. Tax revenue, meanwhile, was equivalent to about 12.3 percent of GDP in 2009. There was a fiscal deficit equivalent to 2.2 percent of GDP, forecast to fall to 1.6 percent of GDP in 2012/13 (Economist Intelligence Unit 2011c). Total debt as a percentage of GDP was 14.2 percent, with debt service equivalent to 1.8 percent of exports.

Thanks in part to this external assistance, together with strong financial control, macroeconomic management in Rwanda has been better than in most of the rest of the region, especially its East African neighbors, all of which have experienced double-digit inflation and plummeting currencies (ibid.). Inflation stood at 10.3 per cent in 2009, but was predicted to fall to 2.3 percent and 5.2 percent in the subsequent two years (Various Authors 2011d).

Perhaps the most impressive aspect of Rwanda's economic performance, or of the government's overall political economic strategy, to be more precise, is its impact on poverty. The country is said to be on track to halve the amount of people living on under a dollar a day by 2015, and is also on track to meet five of the other seven MDGs (United Nations 2011), a pattern confirmed by the most recent Household Living Conditions Survey. The same survey also shows inequality coming down. Progress has been attributed to improved agricultural production, increased agro-business activity, increased farm wage employment, increases in the preponderance of non-farm wages, increases in income transfers, slowing population growth, and improvements in physical infrastructure (Murangwa 2012).

Conclusions

This chapter has shown that the RPF regime in Rwanda has achieved a remarkable degree of rent centralization, thanks mainly to its tight grip over the polity, and its domination of the private sector, in which the innovative use of its party holding company, Tri-Star/ CVL, is particularly notable. This unparalleled control also provides the space for the regime to orient rent management to the long term.

The exceptional seriousness with which the leadership approaches this task can be explained by the unusual severity of the threats it faces. Confronting a genocidal political opposition abroad, and a potentially hostile ethnic majority at home, its position is comparable to if not even more vulnerable than that of certain Northeast Asian developmental states, in particular Taiwan. In this context, a strategy designed to mitigate the severity of ethnic distinctions by means of long-term broad-based development seems a rational response.

This policy has come bundled with a highly regulated political system which prompts sharp criticism from democracy and human rights monitors. Restrictions on political participation seem to go farther than required for the success of the regime's development strategy; at the same time it seems probable that a regime that lifted all restrictions on political campaigning would soon be swept away by another wave of ethnic violence. In any case, the government has made significant strides in enhancing social rights, for example by reducing rates of maternal mortality in rural areas.

Economically, also, its strategies show some promise. The use of Tri-Star and Horizon appears to have been crucial in restoring growth in the post-conflict period. To some extent these companies are also leading the way in new sectors with considerable growth potential, such as horticulture, and it is probable that they would provide a suitable vehicle for more ambitious industrial policies in other sectors too. There is little evidence that they have crowded out competitors, been instruments of embezzlement, or been characterized by a high degree of waste. At the same time, another interesting feature of the regime is that its exceptionally strong grip on the polity has permitted it to pursue conventional investment climate reforms in a more serious way than any of the other countries in our study. We have argued that by itself this strategy is unlikely to realize the kinds of transformation that Rwanda desires, but for sectors like mining it is probably the most sensible approach, and should help the country steer clear of the kinds of uncertainty generated by an uneven implementation of best-practice policy, as seen, for example, in Tanzania.

For the past ten years the economy has been managed extremely prudently. It is growing at a solid rate. This growth is being translated into reductions in poverty, although not as fast as would be the case with heavier investments in smallholder agriculture. There is as yet not much evidence of productivity-induced structural change, and the country remains heavily dependent on aid. It is too soon, therefore, to talk about Rwanda in terms of economic miracles. Nevertheless, on the basis of the evidence we have collected, we believe that Rwanda is much closer to realizing its economic potential than Ghana and Tanzania, and while Ethiopia's development plans are in many ways more ambitious, they also come with a greater degree of risk attached.

There are two main threats to Rwandan development prospects, as we see it. One is the question of donor support. If donors cut back on aid, influenced perhaps by Rwanda's limits on personal freedoms, the government would find it much more difficult to balance its budget, and progress, especially in the social sectors, would slow. The other main threat is the question of political succession. Rwanda is not a classic neo-patrimonial state insofar as the government does tend to follow formal rules and procedures. Nevertheless, the Rwandan experiment is still extremely closely identified with the person of President Kagame. Some of the recent defections from the military are seen by some as challenges to his position, and it is not clear that the RPF will have the cohesiveness to steer a steady course once Kagame steps down as president. For the Rwandan success story to be sustainable, therefore, an increased institutionalization of power is probably required.

6 | CONCLUSION: CHALLENGING THE ORTHODOXIES ON BUSINESS AND POLITICS IN AFRICA

We began this book by examining the debate about economic performance in Africa. Although the past decade has seen a welcome upturn in growth, there are well-founded concerns that this will be unsustainable. Particularly worrying is the failure of African economies to increase productivity in agriculture, structurally transform their economies, and move into more sophisticated, higher-value areas of manufacturing and services. The standard policy advice to African governments is to redress this failure by continuing to make the environment for business friendlier, reducing costs, risks, and barriers to entry, and reducing opportunities for rent-seeking and government failure, in line with the goals of 'best practice' and 'good governance' (World Bank 2004). Heterodox advice, by contrast, is to develop enhanced capabilities for smart industrial policies that will correct market failures and stimulate technological learning and productivity growth, implying an increased role for the state in development (Noman et al. 2011). Successful developed states including France, the USA, Japan, and South Korea all took this path, whatever neoliberal ideology would have us believe (Chang 2010).

Opponents of industrial policy in Africa reject this. They argue that even if it is true that market failure presents a constraint to development, and even if it is true that the successful developers mentioned above pursued industrial policies, there is a big difference between those states and African states. Whereas the former were well-governed countries with competent bureaucracies, the latter suffer from a syndrome of 'neo-patrimonial' governance, characterized by personal rule, clientelism, and corruption. Under such arrangements industrial policies inevitably fall prey to unproductive rent-seeking, and are consequently best avoided, at least until greater progress has been made on conventional 'good governance' reforms. Heterodox thinkers, meanwhile, tend to downplay the significance of neo-patrimonialism, viewing it as purely a structural and transitional phenomenon, or even implying that it doesn't exist at all (Khan 2011b; Olukoshi 2002).

Revisiting our argument

This book was conceived as an intervention in that debate, an attempt to explore the conditions under which neo-patrimonialism – which we think succeeds in capturing an important aspect of reality in most African countries – might be compatible with strong economic performance. Our inspiration came mainly from East Asia, where several states have developed extremely rapidly in spite of having governance arrangements similar to those of African states, and partly from a re-evaluation of the African record itself, which shows that since independence some African states have performed strongly for significant periods.

In Chapter 1, therefore, we conducted a review of clientelism, rent-seeking, and economic performance in a dozen Asian and African countries. We found that almost all the successful developers had managed to centralize the management of economic rents and orient that rent management to the long term, even though they remained neo-patrimonial in significant respects.

These findings allowed us to construct a model of rent management, which generated four different regime types according to the degree of rent centralization and the horizon to which rent management was steered. Decentralized, short-horizon rent management regimes were associated with a type of competitive clientelism in which no one took the long view: investors could expect numerous, uncoordinated, parasitic demands, and the climate for investment was also liable to be undermined by macroeconomic and political instability. Decentralized, long-horizon regimes, by contrast, were ones in which the leadership had a serious long-term vision for development, but in which it had been unable effectively to control the creation and distribution of economic rents. The result was likely to be an ineffective developmental state, fighting a losing battle against corruption, and unable to coordinate economic rents in judicious ways. Centralized, short-horizon regimes were different again. Here, the leadership had succeeded in gaining control over the main rent sources, but for one reason or another, perhaps acute political insecurity, behaved as a kleptocracy, squandering these on short-term goals. Finally, we discussed centralized long-horizon rent management, an economically successful type of regime we glossed as 'developmental patrimonialism'.

It is worth reconsidering at this juncture just why centralized long-horizon rent management is an asset to development. There are at least three reasons. First, an effective centralized structure provides the leadership with an instrument for disciplining rent-seeking, ensuring that it doesn't run out of control, leading on the one hand to instability in the macroeconomic environment, and on the other to unpredictability in investors' relations with state and non-state actors. This was present in Suharto's Indonesia, for example, but not in Sukarno's Indonesia or the First Republic in Nigeria. Secondly, an effective centralized structure provides the leadership with an instrument for allocating and reallocating rents to sectors that are likely to enhance development, as we see, for example, in the successful industrial policies of a state like South Korea. Thirdly, an effective centralized structure provides the leadership with an efficient instrument for channeling payments or other forms of compensation to political groups with the ability to disrupt the development process. An example is UMNO's redistributive policies toward indigenous Malays in Malaysia.[1] Obversely, a long-horizon orientation ensures that leaders use rent centralization in the service of long-term development goals, and have a vision or plan that shapes how they do so.[2]

The enabling conditions for long-horizon rent centralization were the presence of a strong, visionary leader; a constrained yet inclusive political system; top-down patron–client networks; and a competent, vertically disciplined economic technocracy. A country needs a strong, visionary leader (or leadership group) in order to grasp the nature of the development challenges it faces, and to fashion the right kind of polity, patron–client network, and bureaucracy to overcome these. A constrained polity is important because it helps limit the demands from powerful groups for unproductive rents, and permits development policy to be steered to the long term; at the same time the polity should be inclusive enough that none of the most powerful groups feel so excluded that they undermine it, for example through political violence. Top-down patron–client networks are important because they control the scramble for spoils and permit some discipline to be imposed on rent-seeking, and also because they can be an efficient way of steering compensatory rents to development's potential losers. Finally, a competent, vertically disciplined, self-confident economic technocracy is important in order to respond to the political leadership's developmental vision, to craft and implement sound economic and industrial policies, and to warn the leadership when its ideas are unsound.

We proceeded to flesh out these insights by providing narrative examples from Côte d'Ivoire, Malawi, and Kenya, which charted the ways in which visionary post-independence leaders reined in their political systems, building top-down patron–client networks and competent bureaucracies that allowed them to keep a lid on rent-seeking, spread the benefits of development around, and run reasonably effective industrial policies. All three countries saw significant expansion in their agricultural sectors, together with the beginnings of structural transformation as industry, supported by a range of state agencies, gained an increased presence in national accounts. Economies grew and in Kenya and Côte d'Ivoire, at least, poverty decreased. Unfortunately these gains were not sustained, since each of these classic developmental patrimonial states sooner or later degenerated into other types of rent management regime, with deleterious consequences for economic performance. Policy mistakes and succession crises lay at the heart of this process.

Reflections on our cases and our model

In Chapters 3–6 we used our model to illuminate political and economic developments in Tanzania, Ghana, Ethiopia, and Rwanda. On the face of things, there is not a huge amount to choose between these states in terms of economic performance: all have performed reasonably well, or better. Ethiopia has had the fastest growth, followed by Tanzania and, only slightly behind, Rwanda. Macroeconomic management, in terms of fiscal balance and inflation, appears to have been strongest in Rwanda, followed by Tanzania; Ghana has quite serious problems of macroeconomic imbalance and Ethiopia, otherwise sound, a serious inflation problem. When it comes to external balance, the countries are quite evenly matched, with Ghana's predicament perhaps giving the most cause for concern. Tanzania has a more diversified export base than the three other countries, but the rate of export growth is highest in Rwanda and Ethiopia. When it comes to poverty reduction, Ghana has the lowest percentage of its citizens falling below a $1.25-a-day poverty line, with Ethiopia not too far behind. Rwanda and Tanzania are doing considerably worse,

TABLE 6.1 Selected economic indicators: Tanzania, Ghana, Ethiopia, Rwanda

	Annual real GDP growth (2002–10)	Budget balance (2007–09)	Inflation (2009) (%)	Current account deficit as % of GDP (2007–09)	Number of products accounting for more than 75% of exports (2009)	Annual export growth (2005–09) (%)	% of population living on less than $1.25 (PPP) per day (2011)
Tanzania	7.0	−2.9	12.1	−9.63	31	6.0	67.9
Ghana	5.9	−10.1	19.3	−14.9	7	10.9	30.0
Ethiopia	8.6	−2.47	36.0	−5.03	7	15.3	39.0
Rwanda	6.8	−1.73	10.3	−5.53	5	26.1	76.8

Sources: UNDP (2012); Various Authors (2011d)[3]

although recent data presented in Chapter 5 suggests that Rwanda is successfully remedying this state of affairs.[4]

It is important, however, not to take these statistics at face value. To begin with, we must recognize that Tanzania and Ghana are countries that are politically stable, comparably rich in natural resources, and with long coastlines. It is fair to say that they have considerably more economic potential than Ethiopia and Rwanda, which have more troubled political histories, are landlocked, and not as well endowed with natural resources. In addition, Tanzania and Ghana have been reforming their economies since the mid-1980s, whereas in Rwanda and Ethiopia, that process is more or less a decade behind. When viewed in this light, it is perhaps remarkable that Ethiopia and Rwanda are close to matching Ghana and Tanzania on some economic indicators, and are outperforming them on others.

Moreover, statistics do not tell the whole story. For what our case studies have shown is that Ethiopia and Rwanda have been able to operationalize some relatively ambitious industrial policies. We see the beginnings of this in the horticulture sector in Rwanda, and clearly in the floriculture and leather goods industries in Ethiopia. We also see it in the range of investments undertaken by ruling-party-linked holding or endowment companies, in sectors as diverse as fruit processing, cement manufacture, and textiles. It is too soon to say whether or not these policies are going to be sufficient to lead Ethiopia and Rwanda to an East Asian-style economic take-off. Much depends on the success of local industrialists in learning how to use new technologies, the amount of crowding out of other types of private investment, and the strength of the state in withdrawing rents from favored sectors at appropriate times. There are also uncertainties in the wider policy and political environment that could yet derail the initiatives. But what we can say with some confidence is that these endeavors attempt to capitalize on latent comparative advantage, to maximize knowledge spillovers and learning effects, and to coordinate complementary investments, just as modern advocates of industrial policy recommend. By contrast, in Tanzania and Ghana more ambitious attempts to develop new sectors and transform productivity appear to be failing. Mining, horticulture, and irrigated rice production in Tanzania, horticulture and the various President's Special Initiatives in Ghana, have all disappointed.

Underlying these differences in the type and success of industrial policy, we think, are differences in the structure of rent management. Ethiopia and Rwanda have established centralized rent management structures that not only allow them to put some limits on corruption, petty and grand (and very strict limits in the case of Rwanda), they also have institutions at hand, not least the party-linked companies, that can act as vehicles for strategic industrial goals. Arguably, these structures depend on these states' respective regimes ignoring a great deal of conventional donor advice on issues such as good governance and best-practice investment climate reforms. Tanzania and Ghana, by contrast, have gone farther in liberalizing their political systems than Rwanda and Ethiopia, and as a result economic management tends to fall victim to short-term electoral goals. This tends to lead to a permissive attitude to corruption, and an emphasis on political rather than economic considerations in industrial policies and relations with private business generally. If Tanzania and Ghana had institutions like the party-linked holding companies in Ethiopia and Rwanda, they would almost certainly be used for short-term parasitic ends.[5] In Ethiopia and Rwanda, however, *there is little evidence to date to suggest that industrial policy initiatives have fallen prey to the kinds of unproductive rent-seeking the conventional wisdom associates with neo-patrimonial states*, and that is one of this study's most significant findings.[6]

Development management is not perfect in any of these countries. In Rwanda, there are a few problems. One, arguably, is an oversensitivity to donor-promoted 'best-practice' investment climate models. We have seen how Rwanda has done extremely well on conventional Doing Business indicators. However, we have also seen that a more heterodox approach may be needed to overcome market failures and realize latent comparative advantages in sectors like horticulture. There are signs that this is beginning to happen, but more perhaps could be done. There are also concerns that the regime places insufficient weight on agricultural development in its long-term vision, although this too may be beginning to change (Booth and Golooba-Mutebi 2012b). Perhaps the most potentially damaging problem is the over-association of Rwanda's current development model with current president Paul Kagame. The country is already at something of an advantage when it comes to development management since the presidential term limit is two installments of seven years. There is speculation that Kagame may try to extend his tenure beyond the current two-term period (Duval Smith 2011), but only time will tell whether this will be possible, and if it is not, whether his successor will approach questions of development with the same seriousness and vigor.

It is worth mentioning at this point that Rwanda is not a classic neo-patrimonial state in the mold of Houphouët's Côte d'Ivoire or Kenyatta's Kenya. While it may be true that the president is extremely dominant, that he depends partly for his security on the personal loyalty of the military, that there was *in the past* a blurring of relations between public and private through institutions like Tristar, and that certain aspects of Rwandan governance, such as the *imihigo* performance contracts, have a neo-traditional or neo-patrimonial veneer, in other ways the regime is quite different. Most importantly, the desire to transcend patron–client politics and win legitimacy through programmatic delivery of public goods, the near-zero tolerance for corruption, and the seriousness with which rules and procedures are followed, including by the president, distinguish the RPF regime. Consequently, developmental patrimonialism may be best understood as a cluster of subtypes in which the personalistic dimension of rent management is a variable (Booth and Golooba-Mutebi 2012a: 5).[7]

Problems in Ethiopia are both similar and different. Prime Minister Meles Zenawi is also very closely associated with Ethiopia's current development trajectory. Unlike Kagame he does not face constitutional term constraints. Nevertheless, he has been in power now for more than twenty years, and as time wears on questions about succession will inevitably grow louder. As a post-liberation movement, the EPRDF is arguably better institutionalized than some of the more personalized party structures that emerged from independence handovers in classic neo-patrimonial states such as Kenya, Côte d'Ivoire, and Malawi. It is not obvious, however, that it has the wherewithal to manage a smooth succession.

Succession issues, however, are not the most pressing of Ethiopia's development problems. The regime has gone a long way toward centralizing rents, and it is clear that its vision is focused on the long term. Many of its policies to date have appeared sensible and in accord with modern industrial policy advice. However, if policy becomes overambitious, or takes a turn for the worse in other ways, the concentration of economic power in the hands of the leadership could easily turn from being an asset to a liability. Recently there has been a spate of measures signaling that this is a real possibility:

increasing budget deficits, external imbalance, and inflation, coupled with measures that surprise and dismay the private sector, such as price controls and orders to buy government bonds. Underlying these developments may be the generally supine nature of the civil service, which imperils the quality of technical advice.

Let us turn now to Tanzania. Like Rwanda and Ethiopia, Tanzania has a dominant ruling party that has been in power for a long time. Also as in Rwanda and Ethiopia, there has been significant success in centralizing rents at a macro-level, in Tanzania's case through the expedient of cash budgets. In addition, rent-seeking is loosely centralized within the CCM, insofar as it is difficult to get access to major rents if you are not associated with the party, plus there are some lines in the sand concerning how much it is permissible to steal (or, more accurately perhaps, to be seen to steal). However, unlike Rwanda and Ethiopia, Tanzania has undergone a relatively genuine form of political liberalization over the past two decades. The political playing field is far from level, yet the presence of the opposition still strengthens the position of lower-level factions within the ruling party. This increases the amount of resources needed to win both internal party and multiparty elections, and provides an incentive to the leadership to turn a blind eye to many different acts of unproductive rent-seeking and corruption. Tanzania, then, appears to be a mixed type when it comes to our rent management model, having some of the characteristics of centralized long-horizon rent management, and some of the characteristics of decentralized short-horizon rent management.

Is this fatal to our model? We think not. If we follow Max Weber's lead and think of the model as a constellation of ideal types, the aim of which is not to 'capture reality', but to provide 'a logical construct that documents patterned action, establishes clear points of reference and orientational guidelines against which a given piece of reality can be compared and measured' (Kalberg 1994: 87), then the fact that Tanzania diverges significantly from any of its pure types is not a problem. Weber also recognized that divergence between the real world and logically consistent ideal types sometimes necessitates the creation of 'mixed' or 'compound' types (ibid.: 88). In previous work we struggled to describe Tanzania as an instance of decentralized short-horizon rent management (Kelsall et al. 2010; Kelsall 2011), when really a mixed type would have fitted better. Indeed, when we described a new 'modal type' of African rent management we were already dimly aware that this combination of reasonably strong control in the Ministry of Finance with a more relaxed attitude to rent-seeking outside of it is prevalent in an increasing number of African states (Kelsall et al. 2010: 9; Kelsall 2011). A modified version of this modal type, which we call 'mixed rent management', on account of its dual personality, is represented in Figure 6.1.

We saw in Chapter 2 that not only has the Tanzanian economy been growing strongly, but the beginnings of structural transformation are also discernible. Best-practice investment climate and industrial policies can take some of the credit for this, especially the creation of export processing zones. With this foundation, it is not impossible that Tanzania will continue to grow and even 'take off', especially if it can address production bottlenecks in agriculture, and magnify the knowledge spillovers from foreign investment. However, as we hope to have shown, weaknesses in the prevailing system of rent management make this unlikely. Tanzania needs to tighten up its rent management structure, probably through reforms within the ruling party, before these obstacles can be overcome.

Ghana is another type of case. Its competitive clientelist politics places it closer to the short-horizon decentralized ideal type of rent management than Tanzania. Although there are few signs of structural transformation in the country, in certain other respects, such as poverty reduction, it is performing well. This is something of a surprise for our model. The anomaly is partly solved when we realize that poverty reduction is largely a product of successful management of the cocoa industry.[8] But this raises an interesting question. For if Ghana can get its cocoa industry right, couldn't it get other industries right, and couldn't it develop on the basis of islands of effectiveness amid a wider pattern of decentralized rent management?

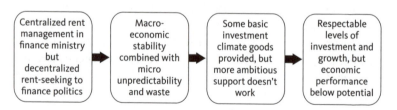

6.1 Mixed rent management – the new African modal type

Our earlier literature review of Southeast Asia provides some clues. In Chapter 1 we touched on the fact that despite making huge strides in recent years, Vietnam appears not to have a strongly centralized system for managing rents, while there is also evidence that Thailand developed very rapidly without such a system. However, there are significant differences between Ghana and these two countries. To begin with, both have experienced a large part of their economic growth under authoritarian rule. Secondly, these countries' ruling classes arguably had a cultural unity and spirit of nationalism stronger than in Ghana. Taken together, these two factors encouraged leaders to take a long time horizon, even if rent management was partly decentralized.[9] Another interesting difference concerns the character of local entrepreneurs in these three countries. In Thailand and Vietnam local business classes are larger and more capable than in Ghana, and, as in the rest of Southeast Asia, they are able to draw on transnational networks of Chinese capital. This has helped them to enter and succeed in areas of light manufacture without a great deal of government support.[10] Arguably the Ghanaian business class would need better and more coordinated government assistance if it is to compete internationally, and it is hard to see this happening without some mitigation of the competitive clientelist tendencies of the sort we identified in Chapter 3. Here, it is worth reminding ourselves that key reforms in the cocoa sector were initiated under Jerry Rawlings's authoritarian rule, when the regime was rather closer to the bottom right quadrant of our model.

If this is right, then building pockets of efficiency will not be a viable approach in all states, including, probably, in states like Ghana. Where rent management is highly short-termist and decentralized, it is hard to see how such pockets can survive. There must be some threshold of centralization and long-termism that a regime must cross before such an approach becomes feasible. It is possible, of course, that this threshold *has already been crossed* in a large number of states that are better centralized than Ghana, contemporary Africa's 'modal' states, for example – but that question requires more empirical research.

Beyond the model

If our rent management model has provided some insight into the kinds of relationships that are needed to stimulate transformative development in Africa, and if it has identified some of the institutions and processes needed to support these, the model doesn't tell us very much about which kinds of regime take the pains to create centralized, long-horizon rent management in the first place. That question was not the primary aim of our research project, so we will limit ourselves here to making a few remarks on the work of others who have addressed the question in more depth.

Mushtaq Khan has developed a model that explains why certain political settlements are more growth-promoting than others, which we echo in our interpretation of Thai and Vietnamese success above. The crucial variables are the relative 'holding power' of groups and organizations contesting the distribution of resources in society, including patron–client organizations and the structure of the ruling coalition, and patron–client networks and the political power of (emerging) capitalists. The configuration of these networks will affect where a state stands on its 'growth-stability trade-off curve', and thus the possibilities for growth-enhancing governance (Khan 2010). Whitfield and Therkilsden develop this model further to show why ruling elites try to develop some productive sectors and not others, and why those efforts are more and less successful. They argue that sectors get government support when they are regarded as being crucial to the ruling coalition's political survival. The success of that support, meanwhile, depends on a number of other factors, including organizational and electoral exigencies, whether elites share a common interest with productive entrepreneurs, and whether they are able to create pockets of efficiency in the bureaucracy (Whitfield and Therkilsden 2011). A not dissimilar approach comes from Williams et al., who identify a number of factors likely to push developing-country governments into nurturing growth rather than engaging in predation or distributive rent-seeking and patronage, including the availability (or non-availability) of receipts from minerals, oil, or foreign aid, whether the system is autocratic or democratic, the structure of organized interest groups outside the state, and whether the regime is vulnerable to political violence (Williams et al. 2009). Other variables such as public expectations of government, political attitudes toward business, and the nature of the bureaucracy may also play a role (ibid.: 23).

In our view all of these approaches are highly promising, and can be squared, for the most part, with our own insights about the structure of rent management. The ruling-party leaderships in Ethiopia and Rwanda, for example, have amassed great organizational power, and this permits them to pursue long-term growth over short-term stability. In addition, being relatively resource poor, it is perhaps natural that they regard industry as crucial to their future survival. In addition, in both these countries the local private sector is weak, providing the government with considerable leeway in economic policy. By contrast, in Ghana the main party leaderships are organizationally weak vis-à-vis their own foot soldiers, and this inclines them to a short-termist view of economic management. One of the few areas where a strong bureaucratic capacity *has* been developed is in cocoa, and this, as we saw earlier, is because it is crucial to ruling-coalition survival. Tanzania provides another variation. Here, historically high receipts from foreign aid have been more crucial to regime survival, and this helps explain why comparatively little attention is given to strengthening productive sectors.

While the approaches sketched above do not explain everything, they do provide an excellent starting point for understanding why some countries choose development over predation, and how far the factors behind that choice are mutable. This understanding can be combined with the insights provided by our own model to suggest paths of political and institutional change that would put the more plastic countries on a path of sustainable development and poverty reduction.

A final issue that we have touched upon at various points throughout this book is the vexed question of human rights. This is not directly addressed by our model, but our analyses make clear that a constrained but inclusive form of politics has been a critical enabling factor for rent centralization. The reason, as should be clear by now, is that in current African conditions, highly competitive multiparty democracy tends to amplify clientelist demands, and make long-horizon rent centralization practically impossible. Does this mean that there is a trade-off between political and civil rights and social and economic rights? With the proviso that political constraint is a necessary *but not sufficient* condition for better economic development, we think the answer is probably 'Yes'. That does not mean, however, that any of our economically successful regimes has got the balance right. While it may be unrealistic to think that a vibrant multiparty democracy could even survive in the political contexts of Ethiopia or Rwanda, let alone oversee an equivalent level of development, it is less far fetched to think that those states could be governed with somewhat less repression than they currently employ, and yet still achieve most of their economic goals. The ambition should be progress on all types of rights, not necessarily equally or evenly, but without one taking precedence to the complete exclusion of the other.

NOTES

Introduction

1 Unless otherwise stated, 'Africa' in this book refers to sub-Saharan Africa.

2 In this book '$' denotes US dollars.

3 McKinsey records total GDP growth as 2.6 percent 1980–90, 2.6 percent 1990–2000, and 4.9 percent 2000–08 (McKinsey Global Institute 2010: 13).

4 Many African states have received an additional dividend in the form of increased aid flows and debt relief. Partly as a result, African governments managed to cut their foreign debt from 82 percent of GDP to 59 percent (ibid.: 12).

5 With the exception of tourism in a small number of countries.

6 Lin's appointment as chief economist at the World Bank in 2008 shows that heterodox views are finally gaining traction – but they have yet to displace the conventional wisdom at country level.

7 With the possible exception of Hong Kong. See Wade (1990).

8 Note that no Southeast Asian states, with the exception of Singapore, have made the transition to 'developed' status. We venture that this is because they have yet to develop the capabilities to move into the most sophisticated, highest-productivity areas, and that where high-tech production is carried out, it is under foreign ownership.

9 Although it does not follow that neoliberals proposed the correct solutions.

10 For a critique of the arm's-length approach to investment facilitation, see Moore and Schmitz (2008). For a comparison of neoliberal and heterodox approaches to export processing zones, see Stein (2011: 322–44).

11 North et al. have also argued that the political distribution of economic rents is a crucial solution to the problem of violence in all developing countries (2006, 2007).

12 www.freedomhouse.org/regions/sub-saharan-africa.

13 www.transparency.org/policy_research/surveys_indices/cpi.

1 Developmental patrimonialism?

1 The countries were Botswana, Burma-Myanmar, Cambodia, Congo-Zaire, Côte d'Ivoire, Indonesia, Kenya, Malaysia, Nigeria, South Korea, Tanzania, and Vietnam.

2 Burma-Myanmar is more complex. Devastated by World War II and civil war, its economy actually began to bounce back in the 1950s, growing at 4 percent a year. Nevertheless, land reform was marred by corruption and insurgency paralyzed development in outlying districts. By 1960 income had still not regained pre-war levels. This triggered a period of national autarchy and anti-capitalist ideology that, until the 1990s, spelled continued problems for the economy (Owen 1999: 139–200; Taylor 2009). However, since the early 1990s it has been growing strongly.

3 An exception appears to be Vietnam, where we are unable to say that rents are strongly centralized. Rather, there appears to be an ongoing but only partly successful attempt by

the center to keep rent-seeking under control (Gainsborough 2002: 353; Gainsborough 2003: 69–84; Painter 2005: 261–83). We will discuss some of the implications of this anomaly in a later chapter.

4 In power-sharing Cambodia there was not a coup as such. Rather, the political faction of co-Prime Minister Prince Norodom Rannaridh was militarily defeated by the army faction loyal to co-Prime Minister Hun Sen (Un 2005: 203–30).

5 Thailand appears to constitute one such exception (Khan 2000b: 101–4).

6 The management of some of these investments, such as the $5 billion steel plant at Krakatau, was notoriously poor (Crouch 1979: 571–87; 581). It did actually produce steel, however, unlike the even more expensive plant at Ajaokuta in Nigeria.

7 For more on the idea that informal, personalized relationships can act as a substitute for formal legal guarantees during early periods of economic growth, see Abdel-Latif and Schmitz (2009); Moore and Schmitz (2008).

8 There is some debate over just how long-term rent management must be. We hazard that it must be longer than a typical electoral cycle, i.e. five years or more.

9 In addition, centralized long-horizon rent management will not work for development if a regime has bad policies. In this respect we note the findings of the University of Leiden's Tracking Development program, which investigates development performance in twinned comparisons of Southeast Asian and African states. They find that three policy changes were crucial to launching Southeast Asian states on a trajectory of sustained growth: macro-economic stability, economic freedom for smallholders, and pro-rural spending, which typically took the form of massive

government programs to develop the countryside (Van Donge et al. 2012). We are persuaded by these findings for Asia, while noting that launching a process of sustained growth is not the same as maintaining it; in other words, sustained growth requires effective policies for industry, not just agriculture.

10 Strictly speaking it should be called 'developmental *neo*-patrimonial', but for ease of expression we prefer simply 'developmental patrimonial'.

11 Although Abdul Razak was only deputy prime minister prior to 1970, he also held the influential agricultural and defense portfolios.

12 Is political constraint a necessary condition for rapid, transformative growth? This is a question we will discuss in more detail later. At this point, all we will say is that even if it is a necessary condition, it is not a sufficient one. Nigeria, Sierra Leone, Burma, and Congo-Zaire were also dictatorships for long periods, but have economically underperformed.

13 The type of bureaucracy we refer to is captured well by Peter Evans's idea of 'embedded autonomy', although he perhaps underplays the extent to which most such bureaucracies are politically driven from above (Evans 1989: 561–87; Evans 1995). For a fuller discussion of the technocratic relationships required, see Cammack et al. (2010: 4–5).

14 For us, a resource-poor economy is one in which hydrocarbon or mineral exports account for less than 50 percent of export earnings.

15 Malawi does not feature in Schatzberg's study, but it clearly fits his model.

16 We tested the typology against a set of data drawn from seven African countries (Kenya, Tanzania, Ghana, Côte d'Ivoire, Rwanda, Malawi, Uganda), covering a time-span from independence to 2010. Our case selection was

motivated by the desire to find a set of countries that were roughly comparable, and that at the same time had enough institutional diversity to represent the different types in our model. We began our study with three dichotomous variables, eventually narrowing that down to the two main variables, and four subsidiary conditions discussed here. Once this conceptual refinement had been undertaken, the results were consistent overall with the findings presented for three countries here, although a greater number of 'fuzzy' cases make them slightly less clean. Kenya, Malawi, and Côte d'Ivoire come closest to illustrating the model in ideal-typical form. For early versions of our categorizations, some of which we have subsequently modified, see Kelsall et al. (2010: 76–87).

17 Our wider study, and in particular the case of Tanzania from 1967 to 1978, shows that centralized rent management is not *sufficient* for strong economic performance. We explain this anomaly in Chapter 2.

18 The PDCI, although drawing on the organizational power of the union, began life as the Ivorian branch of the West African Rassamblement Democratique Africaine (RDA).

19 To a large extent this had the characteristics of a Kikuyu civil war.

20 'During the years of the coffee boom, government officers had been able to overspend their budgets with the confidence that parliament would always vote a "Supplementary" to bail them out. Once the profligate habit of ignoring red ink had begun, it was difficult to reintroduce fiscal restraint' (Leonard 1991: 178).

21 'This African parable is only meaningful in the context of specific attributes of political power in Africa, in particular Côte d'Ivoire. Roasting peanuts assumes that, at some point in the process, the cook tastes them

for salt ... The Grand Master justified this patrimonial economy or the fast enrichment machinery by reference to the urgent need to constitute a class of substitute investors in an Ivorian economy hitherto dominated by foreign, in particular French, capital' (Akindes 2004: 11–12).

22 Médard opines that the exceptional stability of the political class, which in other countries appeared more like a game of musical chairs, allowed Houphouët's courtiers eventually to entrench themselves as barons, and 'to create autonomous economic bases while still preying on the national economy' (Médard 1991: 185–21; 204). In the former type of case the main problem is short-termism; in the latter it is decentralization. As we saw, Kenya under Daniel arap Moi provides an example of the former.

23 Interviews with senior politicians, Lilongwe and Blantyre, January 2010.

24 Interview with former senior civil servant, Blantyre, January 2010.

25 Interview with senior politician, Blantyre, January 2010.

26 Interviews with former civil servants, Lilongwe and Blantyre, January and July 2010.

27 For more on these terms, see Booth (2011b); Grindle (2004: 525–48).

2 Tanzania

1 Tanganyika became 'Tanzania' after the 1964 union with the islands of Zanzibar. The mainland's ruling party thus became the Tanzania African National Union, a name it retained until 1977, when it formally merged with Zanzibar's Afro-Shirazi Party to become Chama cha Mapinduzi (Party of the Revolution) (CCM).

2 The abolition of district councils in 1972, and of cooperative unions in 1976, was also consistent with this concern.

3 MKUKUTA has now been

supplemented by MKUKUTA 2 and MKUZA 2 (Various Authors 2011b).

4 Some authors query the recent fashion of placing inflation control at the center of economic policy. See Noman and Stiglitz (2011).

5 Steel manufacture has been growing in Tanzania recently. The Steel Manufacturers' Association currently has fourteen members, making products that include iron sheets, steel bars, and steel pipes. The industry has been stimulated by a heavy demand for construction materials, and by a 25 percent import duty on imported products. Together, these companies produced some 50,000 tonnes of steel products and paid 18 billion Tanzanian shillings in corporate tax. The industry sees significant opportunities for expansion, especially if coal and iron ore reserves in Mchuchuma and Linganga can be exploited. In May 2011 India's Kamal Group announced plans to open a $220 million steel mill in Tanzania that would employ 500 workers, the largest in East Africa. See Doya (2011).

6 A power system master plan sets out the strategic direction of the sector for the next twenty-five years, but warns of power shortages until 2012 (Economist Intelligence Unit 2008b). Given the acute shortages experienced in 2011, this seems optimistic.

7 Interview with senior TICTS employee, Dar es Salaam, March 2008.

8 These contests, though reasonably competitive, have not been entirely free and fair. Freedom House describes Tanzania as 'partly free', and *The Economist* describes it as a 'flawed democracy' (Economist Intelligence Unit 2008b; Freedom House 2012).

9 Therkilsden notes the growing influence of local-level CCM factions on initiatives like rice irrigation (2011: 12–13).

10 Interview with young Tanzanian executive, Dar es Salaam, April 4, 2009.

11 Sutton was later bought out by Barrick.

12 Interview with general manager of a large mining company, Dar es Salaam, October 2009.

13 The TRA is an executive agency, a supposed 'island of excellence' that was tasked with improving tax collection and thus the state of Tanzania's public finances. See Fjelstad (2003: 165–75).

14 Mineral Development Agreements are not recognized by TRA because they are not the subject of parliamentary scrutiny, unlike tax rates.

15 Meeting of British Business Group, British High Commissioner's residence, October 2008.

16 Interview with general manager of a large mining company, Dar es Salaam, October 2009.

17 'Trouble brewing in mining review team?', *Thisday*, Dar es Salaam, May 21; interview with Tanzanian accountant, Dar es Salaam, December 10, 2009. In all, the tax expert provided twenty-six critical comments on the Committee's report.

18 See Deo Mwanyika, 'Successes, challenges and prospects: Tanzanian mining sector', Tanzania Chamber of Minerals and Energy, Powerpoint presentation, Dar es Salaam, October 2008. In March 2010 Barrick listed a new company, African Barrick Gold (ABG), on the London Stock Exchange. ABG's assets are Barrick's Tanzanian mines. Some observers saw the move as a way of separating the underperforming Tanzanian assets from the parent company.

19 UN Comtrade, comtrade.un.org/db/, accessed June 1, 2010. Different sources give very different figures, suggesting a definitional problem. In Tanzania Horticulture Association (2009), Arusha reports total horticulture exports of $67 million in 2004 and $140 million in 2007. UN Comtrade Data

(2010) gives $45 million and $89 million for the same years.

20 Interview with expatriate farm owner, Arusha, December 2009.

21 Occasionally, no amount of local lobbying will succeed, as demonstrated by the case of Stewart Middleton and Sarah Hermitage, a pair of British investors who fled Tanzania in 2006, following a long campaign by their farm's former owner, a well-connected individual, to run them off their land. See Cooksey and Kelsall (2011); Cooksey (2011a).

22 A disputed claim requires the claimant to deposit one third of the amount disputed, with no interest or guarantee of getting the money back promptly.

23 Interview with expatriate farm manager, Arusha, June 2010.

24 Ibid.

25 Interview with TAHA staff member, Arusha, June 2010.

26 An expatriate farm manager cited the risk of relying on KLM, currently the only international airline landing at Kilimanjaro International Airport, to upload a consignment of flowers. Interview, Arusha, June 2010.

27 Interview with TAHA staff member, Arusha, June 2010.

28 The Arusha–Namanga road repair contract was terminated by TANROADS, leaving large stretches unsurfaced. At the time of writing, another contractor is finishing the job. The Arusha–Dar road is in good condition, but there seem to be substantial delays at the Chalinze weighbridge.

29 This is partly the result of a stimulus package to counteract the effects of the global economic crisis (Various Authors 2011b).

3 Ghana

1 For further analyses of state–business relations, especially in the Rawlings era, see Handley (2008); Hart and Gyimah-Boadi (2000); Sandbrook and Oelbaum (1999).

2 Note that the PSDS had not been helped by the fact that donors had failed to deliver some of the monies they had committed, while they retained much larger funds for bilateral programs (Government of Ghana Private Sector Development Strategy 2010).

3 Interview with private sector development consultant, Accra, April 2011; interview with European development partner, Accra, April 2011.

4 Interview at private sector advocacy organization, Accra, April 2011; interview with private hotelier, Accra, April 2011; interview with official at Free Zones Board, Accra, April 2011.

5 Interview at Ghana Export Promotion Council, Accra, April 2011.

6 See also Whitfield (2011b, 2011c).

7 Interview with leading Ghanaian political scientist, Accra, April 2011.

8 Interview with European development partner, Accra, April 2011.

9 Interview at economic think tank, Accra, April 2011.

10 Interview with leading Ghanaian political scientist, Accra, April 2011.

11 Focus group interview with Ghanaian financial journalists, Accra, April 2011.

12 Interview with leading Ghanaian political scientist, Accra, April 2011.

13 See Center for Chinese Studies, Weekly China Briefing, October 1, 2010, www.ccs.org.za/wp-content/uploads/2010/10/Weekly-China-Briefing-1-October-2010.pdf.

14 Interview with leading Ghanaian political scientist, Accra, April 2011.

15 Interview at private sector advocacy organization, Accra, April 2011. Ghana has an Export Development Investment Fund, created by the government to provide concessionary finance to exporters, but the fund is

administered by commercial banks, which bear the risk and are reluctant to lend. Interview at Ghana Export Promotion Council, Accra, April 2011.

16 At the time of writing there were 1.74 Ghanaian cedis to the US dollar.

17 Interview at Ministry of Trade and Industry, Accra, April 2011. See also Abdallah (2010).

18 Interview at Ministry of Trade and Industry, Accra, April 2011; focus group interview with financial journalists, Accra, April 2011.

19 Interview with NPP party member, Accra, April 2011. Note that this was not an unbiased source, and we have been unable to corroborate the allegation. Something similar is hinted at, however, by Murray, when he says, 'I would like to know how industrial development funds were given to a network of companies the ultimate ownership of which traced back to the Minister of Industry' (Murray 2010).

20 For more on this idea, see Booth (2011a: 33–5).

4 Ethiopia

1 World Bank, World Development Indicators, www.google.com/publicdata. In PPP terms this was calculated at $1,074 (Various Authors 2011d).

2 Falling to 1.5 percent per capita growth, given high population growth. Mulatu Wubneh (1991) has a figure of 4.4 percent per annum for the period 1960–70.

3 Also sometimes spelled 'Derg'.

4 The EPRDF is a coalition of four ethnic-based fronts, among which the Tigrayan TPLF is the most influential.

5 The plan envisages a doubling of agricultural output, an increase in per capita GDP from $400 to $700, 2,000 kilometers of new railway line, a quadrupling of electricity generation, a quadrupling of mobile phone density, a tripling in the length of the road

network, and so on (Various Authors 2011e: 13).

6 More insight into the economic theories of the regime is provided in Meles Zenawi (2011: 140–74).

7 The Economist Intelligence Unit (2008a: 31) claims that 'the regions remain politically subservient to – and financially dependent on – the central government'.

8 See grandmillenniumdam.net.

9 For a dissenting view, see Hagmann (2006: 605–12). And Abbink's reply (Abbink 2006b).

10 Getu cites higher figures (Getu 2010: 240).

11 Although it is perhaps less than clear that this kind of clean sheet applies to endowment companies in some other parts of the country, where there is less focus on adding productive value or manufacturing capability than on extracting rent from the trade of commodities such as coffee and the mild narcotic khat (*Catha edulis*).

12 It is also worth noting that we have found no credible evidence that EFFORT profits feed back into the ruling party corporately, as they do in Rwanda.

13 At the time of research there were about 16.85 birr to the US dollar.

14 *The Economist* cites figures of exports of leather and leather products increasing from $44 million in 2004 to $75 million in 2005/06 (Economist Intelligence Unit 2008a: 34).

5 Rwanda

1 It costs $3,275 to ship a container from Rwanda, compared to the African average of $1,960 (Economist Intelligence Unit 2011c). In much of Africa low person–land ratios have historically been considered a problem, but in Rwanda, the reverse is true.

2 Interview with Rwandan manufacturer, Kigali, March 2009; interview

with Rwandan printing company, Kigali, November 2010.

3 In November 2011, *The Economist*'s correspondent alluded to 'the growing number of Tutsis who used to support the party but now consider it to be corrupt and nepotistic. Worryingly for the President, these include a number of senior officers in the armed forces, some of whom have gone into exile' (Economist Intelligence Unit 2011c). The regime's counter-charge is that it is precisely these disaffected elements who are corrupt, and this seems plausible. However, as always in Rwanda, the truth is difficult to discern.

4 Different aspects of this story are well treated, with a bias toward human rights concerns, in Straus and Waldorf (2011).

5 Interviews with Rwandan government minister, permanent secretary, and high-ranking security official, Kigali, December 2007 and March 2009.

6 A good flavor of the way government functions in Rwanda and why is conveyed in a very readable form in Kinzer (2008).

7 Inspired by the oaths declared by warriors at the king's court in precolonial times.

8 For further discussion of this point, see reports from the Africa Power and Politics Programme's local governance research (Chambers 2012; Chambers and Golooba-Mutebi 2012).

9 Until recently, the firm's website rather confusingly named three individuals as 'shareholders'. However, the legal position is that the three are RPF members with significant business experience who act as trustees on behalf of the party. Currently, the website states that CVL 'is wholly owned by Rwandan business people who pooled resources together to meet challenges of economic recovery and take advantage of growth opportunities in a virgin environment'. See crystalventuresltd.com/index.php. Both formulas reflect the sensitivity surrounding the idea of a governing political party being a substantial private entrepreneur, not the real situation (interviews, senior journalist; CVL executive; government minister, and senior government figure, Kigali, February 20 and November 8, 2010, 17 February and April 22, 2011).

10 Interviews with high-ranking executives, Crystal Ventures, Kigali, March and November 2010.

11 Ibid.

12 Interviews with high-ranking executives, Crystal Ventures, March 2009 and November 2010; interview with ICT firm, March 2009; www.engineering-news.co.za, accessed Feburary 25, 2011; www.newtimes.co.rw, accessed February 26, 2011.

13 www.iol.co.za/business/companies, accessed October 7, 2011.

14 Today, the MTN operation is invariably one of the top two taxpayers in Rwanda. It employs 690 people directly, only two of whom are expatriates. Indirect employment, including dealerships and security guards, is estimated at over five thousand. Interview with information technology consultant, March 2009.

15 Interviews with high-ranking executives, Crystal Ventures, Kigali, March and November 2010.

16 Inyange Industries, Intersec Security, Bourbon Coffee, NPD-COTRACO, Mutara Enterprises, Graphic Print Solutions, Real Contractors, CVL Developers, Media Systems Group, Ruliba Clays and East African Granite Industries. The last two firms are controlled through a joint venture with the Rwanda Social Security Board called Building Materials Industries Ltd.

17 Extract from CVL 2009 accounts provided by the company's chief executive. The same source gives group

employment as over five thousand, of which 3,500 are classified as permanent.

18 Calculated from NISR (2011) and RRA (2010).

19 Interview with Horizon Group executive, Kigali, November 2010.

20 www.rig.co.rw.

21 Interview with government minister, December 2007.

22 See www.rig.co.rw.

23 Interview with investment group executive, Kigali, March 2010.

24 Interviews, 2007–10.

25 Ibid.

26 Interview with horticultural association member, Kigali, March 2010; interview with government minister, Kigali, November 2010.

27 Interviews with horticultural association member and horticultural association office-holder, Kigali, March 2010.

28 Interview with Rwanda Development Board official, Kigali, March 2010.

29 Ibid.

30 Interview with horticultural association member, Kigali, March 2010; interview with government minister, Kigali, November 2010.

31 Interview with Rwanda Development Board official, Kigali, March 2010.

32 Interviews with horticultural association member and horticultural investor, Kigali, March 2010.

33 Ibid.

34 Interview with Rwanda Development Board official, Kigali, March 2010.

35 Interview with government minister, November 2010.

36 Interview with horticultural association member, Kigali, March 2010.

6 Conclusion

1 In successful developmental states all three of these rent centralization functions are likely to be present. However, state by state, some may be more prominent than others.

2 As in Chapter 1, this paragraph draws heavily on Khan. See Khan (2000a, 2000b).

3 Note that properly comparable figures are not yet available for 2011. Note also that UNDP gives significantly higher figures for income poverty in Tanzania than other sources. However, sources are agreed that poverty reduction in Tanzania has been negligible.

4 Statistics from the UNDP confirm the impression that Rwanda and Ethiopia are performing better in terms of human development than Ghana and Tanzania. Between 2000 and 2010, the human development index rose by 39 percent in Rwanda, 33 percent in Ethiopia, 28 percent in Tanzania, and 20 percent in Ghana. See hdrstats.undp. org/en/countries/profiles/.

5 Perhaps the closest example in Tanzania is Meremeta, a gold mining company run by the army, that acted as little more than a front for channeling funds to CCM. See Cooksey (2011a).

6 We hope that this finding does not prove to be undermined by the recent appointment of Meles Zenawi's wife as CEO of EFFORT.

7 Angola may represent an alternative subtype (Sogge 2009).

8 In this sense Ghana comes closer than our other cases to the successful Southeast Asian model of putting agriculture first.

9 Clearly it was not completely decentralized: Thailand, for example, has been described as a case of 'hard budget clientelism'. See Doner and Ramsay (2000: 151–5).

10 Although it is notable that Vietnam nevertheless has a strong vocational education system (Van Arkadie and Dinh 2004).

BIBLIOGRAPHY

Aalen, L. and K. Tronvoll (2009) 'The end of democracy? Curtailing civil and political rights in Ethiopia', *Review of African Political Economy*, 120: 193–207.

Aaron Tesfaye (2002) *Political Power and Ethnic Federalism: The struggle for democracy in Ethiopia*, Lanham, MD: University Press of America.

Abbink, J. (2006a) 'Discomfiture of democracy? The 2005 election crisis in Ethiopia and its aftermath', *African Affairs*, 105(419): 173–200.

— (2006b) 'Interpreting Ethiopian elections in their context – a reply to Tobias Hagmann', *African Affairs*, 105(421): 613–20.

Abdallah, N. (2010) 'Inside Ghana's collapsing textile industry', inwent-iij-lab.org/Weblog/2010/06/29/inside-ghana's-collapsing-textile-industry/.

Abdel-Latif, A. and H. Schmitz (2009) 'State–business relations and investment in Egypt', Research Report, 2009(61) Brighton: Center for the Future State, Institute of Development Studies, University of Sussex.

Access Capital (2010a) 'Ethiopia's export performance', Addis Ababa: Access Capital.

— (2010b) 'The Ethiopia macroeconomic handbook 2010. Investing in Ethiopia', Addis Ababa: Access Capital.

Adadevoh, D. (2008) 'Ayensu starch factory revived', *Ghanaian Times*, www.ModernGhana.com.

Addis Fortune Newspaper (2011) 'Development bank to offer citizens govt bonds', January 30, www.addisfortune.com/Development%20Bank%20to%20Offer%20Citizens%20Gov't%20Bonds.htm, accessed February 2011.

Ajulu, R. (1998) 'Kenya's democracy experiment: the 1997 elections', *Review of African Political Economy*, 25(76): 275–85.

Akindes, F. (2004) 'The roots of the military-political crises in Côte d'Ivoire', Research report no. 128, Uppsala: Nordic Africa Institute.

Alden, C. (2007) *China in Africa*, London: Zed Books.

Alemayehu Dereje (1997) *The Crisis of Capitalist Development in Africa: The case of Côte d'Ivoire*, Hamburg: Bremer Afrika Studien.

Alemayehu Geda (2005) 'Explaining African growth performance: the case of Ethiopia', Working paper, Nairobi: African Economic Research Consortium.

Allen, C. (1995) 'Understanding African politics', *Review of African Political Economy*, 65: 301–20.

Altenburg, T. (2010) 'Industrial policy in Ethiopia', Discussion Paper 2/2010, Bonn: German Development Institute.

— (2011) 'Can industrial policy work under neopatrimonial rule?', Working Paper no. 2011/41, Helsinki: UNU-WIDER.

Amoako, K. Y. (2011) 'Transforming Africa – start now, we can't wait', *African Business*, July, pp. 24–7.

Anders, G. (2006) 'Like chameleons: civil servants and corruption in Malawi', *Le Bulletin de l'APAD*, 23/24.

Anonymous (2011) 'Ghana: Parliament

approves Petroleum Management Bill', www.loc.gov/lawweb/servlet/lloc_news?disp3_l205402559_text.

Anyang' Nyong'o, P. (1989) 'State and society in Kenya: the disintegration of the nationalist coalitions and the rise of presidential authoritarianism 1963–78', *African Affairs*, 88(351): 229–51.

Arnold, M. and W. Wallis (2010) 'Ghana and Kosmos sign truce agreement', *Financial Times*, December 22.

Asche, H. and M. Fleischer (2011) 'Modernizing Rwanda: information and communication technologies as driver for economic growth', *e-ULPA*, 02.

Assefa Fiseha (2010) *Federalism and the Accommodation of Diversity in Ethiopia. A comparative study*, Addis Ababa: Eclipse Printing Press.

Austin, G. (1996) 'National poverty and the "Vampire State" in Ghana: a review article', *Journal of International Development*, 8(4) 553–73.

— (2005) *Labour, Land and Capital in Ghana: From slavery to free labour in Asante, 1807–1956*, Rochester, NY: University of Rochester Press.

Bahru Zewde (1991) *A Modern History of Ethiopia, 1855–1974*, London: James Currey.

Bakary, T. (1984) 'Elite transformation and political succession', in I. William Zartmann and C. Delgado (eds), *The Political Economy of Côte d'Ivoire*, New York: Praeger, pp. 21–55.

Baker, C. (2001) *Revolt of the Ministers: The Malawi Cabinet Crisis, 1964–65*, London: I. B. Tauris.

Bank of Ghana (2011a) 'Quarterly bulletin, January–March 2011', Accra: Bank of Ghana.

— (2011b) 'Statistical bulletin, June 2011', Accra: Bank of Ghana.

Barkan, J. (1994) 'Divergence and convergence in Kenya and Tanzania: pressures for reform', in J. Barkan (ed.), *Beyond Capitalism Vs Socialism in Kenya and Tanzania*, Boulder, CO: Lynne Rienner, pp. 1–46.

Bates, R. (1981) *Markets and States in Tropical Africa: The political basis of agricultural policies*, Berkeley: University of California Press.

— (1988) 'Governments and agricultural markets in Africa', in R. Bates (ed.), *Toward a Political Economy of Development: A rational choice perspective*, Berkeley: University of California Press, pp. 331–58.

— (1989) *Beyond the Miracle of the Market: The political economy of agrarian development in Kenya*, Cambridge: Cambridge University Press.

Berg, E. J. (1971) 'Structural transformation versus gradualism: recent economic development in Ghana and the Côte d'Ivoire', in P. Foster and A. R. Zolberg (eds), *Ghana and the Côte d'Ivoire: Perspectives on modernization*, Chicago, IL, and London: University of Chicago Press, pp. 185–230.

Berger, M. T. (1997) 'Old state and new empire in Indonesia: debating the rise and decline of Suharto's New Order', *Third World Quarterly*, 18(2): 321–61.

Berhanu Abegaz (2011) 'Political parties in business', Working Paper no. 113, Williamsburg, VA: College of William and Mary.

Berman, B. (1997) 'Nationalism, ethnicity and modernity: the paradox of Mau Mau', in R. R. Grinker and C. B. Steiner (eds), *Perspectives on Africa: A reader in culture, history and representation*, Oxford: Blackwell, pp. 653–71.

— (1998) 'Ethnicity, patronage and the African state', *African Affairs*, 97(389): 305–41.

Berman, B. and J. Lonsdale (1992) *Unhappy Valley: Conflict in Kenya* and Africa, Book Two: *Violence and Ethnicity*, London: James Currey.

Bigsten, A. and A. Danielson (2001) 'Tanzania: is the ugly duckling finally growing up?', Research report no. 120, Uppsala: Nordic African Institute.

Booth, D. (2011a) 'Getting governance right for development in Africa: no time for complacency', *Commonwealth Good Governance*, London: Commonwealth Secretariat, pp. 33–5.

— (2011b) 'Governance for development in Africa: building on what works', Policy Brief 01, London: Africa Power and Politics Programme.

— (2012) 'Working with the grain and swimming against the tide: barriers to uptake of research findings on governance and public services in low-income Africa', *Public Management Review*, forthcoming.

Booth, D. and F. Golooba-Mutebi (2009) 'Aiding economic growth in Africa: the political economy of roads reform in Uganda', Working Paper 307, London: Overseas Development Institute.

— (2012a) 'Developmental patrimonialism? The case of Rwanda', *African Affairs*, 111(444): 379–403.

— (2012b) 'Policy for agriculture and horticulture in Rwanda: a different political economy?', Working Paper, London and Brighton: Future Agricultures Consortium/Africa Power and Politics Programme.

Bratton, M. and N. Van de Walle (1997) *Democratic Experiments in Africa*, Cambridge: Cambridge University Press.

Breisinger, C. and X. Diao (2008) 'Economic transformation in theory and practice: what are the messages for Africa?', Working Paper no. 10, Washington, DC: Regional Strategic Analysis and Knowledge Support System.

Broemmelmeier, M., T. Gerster and J. Spatz (2007) 'Driving business environment reforms through private sector development strategies – the cases of Ghana and Namibia', Paper presented at the Africa Regional Consultative Conference 'Creating better business environments for enterprise development – African and global lessons for more effective donor practices', Accra, November 5–7.

Bryceson, D. F. (1990) *Food Insecurity and the Social Division of Labour in Tanzania, 1919–85*, London: Macmillan.

Buur, L. and L. Whitfield (2011) 'Engaging in productive sector development: comparisons between Mozambique and Ghana', Working Paper 2011: 22, Copenhagen: Danish Institute for International Studies.

Callaghy, T. (1988) 'The state and development of capitalism in Africa', in N. Chazan and D. Rothchild (eds), *The Precarious Balance: State and society in Africa*, Boulder, CO: Westview Press, pp. 67–99.

Cammack, D. (1998) 'Freedom of expression and communication in Malawi', *ARTICLE 19*.

— (2000) 'At the crossroads: freedom of expression in Malawi, 1999', *ARTICLE 19*.

— (2011) 'Malawi's political settlement in crisis, 2011', Background Paper 04, London: Africa Power and Politics Programme.

Cammack, D. and T. Kelsall (2011) 'Neo-patrimonialism, institutions and economic growth: the case of Malawi 1964–2009', *IDS Bulletin*, 42(2): 88–96.

Cammack, D., T. Kelsall and D. Booth (2010) 'Developmental patrimonialism? The case of Malawi', Working Paper 12, London: Africa Power and Politics Programme.

Campbell, B. (1987) 'The state and

capitalist development in the Côte d'Ivoire', in P. M. Lubeck (ed.), *The African Bourgeoisie: Capitalist development in Nigeria, Kenya, and the Côte d'Ivoire*, Boulder, CO: Lynne Rienner.

Campbell, H. and H. Stein (eds) (1992) *Tanzania and the IMF: The Dynamics of Liberalization*, Boulder, CO: Westview Press.

Chabal, P. and J.-P. Daloz (1999) *Africa Works: Disorder as political instrument*, Oxford: James Currey.

Chambers, V. (2012) 'Improving maternal health when resources are limited: safe motherhood in rural Rwanda', Policy Brief 05, London: Africa Power and Politics Programme.

Chambers, V. and F. Golooba-Mutebi (2012) 'Is the bride too beautiful? Safe motherhood in rural Rwanda', Research Report 04, London: Africa Power and Politics Programme.

Chang, H.-J. (2002) *Kicking Away the Ladder: Development strategy in historical perspective*, London: Anthem Press.

— (2010) 'How to "do" a developmental state: political, organisational and human resource requirements for the developmental state', in Omano Edigheji (ed.), *Constructing a Democratic Developmental State in South Africa*, Cape Town: HSRC Press, pp. 82–97.

Chanock, M. (1977) 'Agricultural change and continuity in Malawi', in R. Palmer and N. Parsons (eds), *The Roots of Rural Poverty in Central and Southern Africa*, London: Heinemann, pp. 396–410.

Chipeta, C. and M. Mkandawire (2008) 'Man-made opportunities and growth in Malawi', in B. J. Ndulu et al. (eds), *The Political Economy of Economic Growth in Africa 1960–2000*, vol. 2: *Country Case Studies*, Cambridge: Cambridge University Press, pp. 143–65.

Clapham, C. (1976) *Liberia and Sierra Leone: An essay in comparative politics*, Cambridge: Cambridge University Press.

— (1988) *Transformation and Continuity in Revolutionary Ethiopia*, Cambridge: Cambridge University Press.

— (2009) 'Post-war Ethiopia: the trajectories of crisis', *Review of African Political Economy*, 120: 181–92.

Clark, P. and Z. D. Kaufman (eds) (2008) *After Genocide: Transitional justice, post-conflict reconstruction and reconciliation in Rwanda and beyond*, London: Hurst.

Clay, J. and B. Holcomb (1986) *Politics and the Ethiopian Famine, 1984–85*, Cambridge: Cultural Survival.

Confederation of Tanzania Industries (2011) 'Challenges of unreliable electricity supply to manufacturers in Tanzania. A policy research paper submitted to energy sector stakeholders in advocacy for ensured [sic] reliable electricity supply to Tanzanian manufacturers', Dar es Salaam: CTI.

Cooksey, B. (2002) 'The power and the vainglory: anatomy of a Malaysian IPP in Tanzania', in K. S. Jomo (ed.), *Ugly Malaysians? South–South investment abused?*, Durban: Centre for Black Research, pp. 47–67.

— (2011a) 'The investment and business environment for gold exploration and mining in Tanzania', Background Paper 03, London: Africa Power and Politics Programme.

— (2011b) 'Public goods, rents and business in Tanzania', Background Paper 01, London: Africa Power and Politics Programme.

— (2011c) 'The investment and business environment for export horticulture in northern Tanzania', Background Paper 02, London: Africa Power and Politics Programme.

Cooksey, B. and T. Kelsall (2011) 'The

political economy of the investment climate in Tanzania', Research Report 01, London: Africa Power and Politics Programme.

Corporate Guides International Ltd (2010) 'Corporate Tanzania: the business, trade and investment guide 2010/2011', Cologne: Corporate Guides International Ltd.

Coughlin, P. (1990) 'Moving to the next phase?', in R. C. Riddell (ed.), *Manufacturing Africa: Performance and prospects in seven countries*, London: James Currey, pp. 242–55.

Coulson, A. (1982) *Tanzania: A political economy*, Oxford: Clarendon Press.

Crook, R. (1989) 'Patrimonialism, administrative effectiveness and economic development in Côte d'Ivoire', *African Affairs*, 88(351): 205–28.

— (1990a) 'State, society and political institutions in Côte d'Ivoire and Ghana', in J. Manor (ed.), *Rethinking Third World Politics*, Harlow: Longman, pp. 213–41.

— (1990b) 'Politics, the cocoa crisis, and administration in Côte d'Ivoire', *Journal of Modern African Studies*, 28(4): 649–69.

— (2010) 'Rethinking civil service reform in Africa: "islands of effectiveness" and organisational commitment', *Commonwealth and Comparative Politics*, 48(4): 479–504.

Crouch, H. (1979) 'Patrimonialism and military rule in Indonesia', *World Politics*, 31(4): 571–87.

Danish Ministry of Foreign Affairs/ Danida (2009) 'Ghana: support to Private Sector Development Phase II, SPSDII, 2010–2014. Programme Support Document', www.ambaccra. um.dk/NR/rdonlyres/E46CDF86- 09F4-4720-85BA-EA5068B3B690/0/ GhanaSPSDIIProgrammeSupport DocumentGovernmentAgreement. pdf.

Department for International Development (2011) 'Summary of DfID's work in Tanzania 2011–2015', London: DfID.

Desalegn Rahmato (2011) *Land to Investors: Large Scale Land Transfers in Ethiopia*, Addis Ababa: Forum for Social Studies.

Doner, R. F. and A. Ramsay (2000) 'Rent-seeking and economic development in Thailand', in M. Khan and K. S. Jomo (eds), *Rents, Rent-seeking and Economic Development: Theory and evidence in Asia*, Cambridge: Cambridge University Press, pp. 145–81.

Donham, D. and W. James (eds) (1986) *The Southern Marches of Imperial Ethiopia*, Cambridge: Cambridge University Press.

Dowling, M. and Y. Chin-Fang (2008) 'Indonesian economic development: mirage or miracle?', *Journal of Asian Economics*, 19: 474–85.

Doya, D. M. (2011) 'Kamal Group of India plans to invest $213 million in Tanzanian steel mill. May 26, 2011', www. bloomberg.com/news/2011-05-26/ kamal-group-of-india-plans-to-invest- 213-million-in-tanzanian-steel-mill. html, accessed September 7, 2011.

Duval Smith, A. (2011) 'Kagame puts down marker for third term', *Independent*, December 13.

Economist (2000) 'The hopeless continent', *The Economist*, May 13.

— (2011) 'The lion kings? Africa is now one of the world's fastest growing regions', *The Economist*, January 6.

Economist Intelligence Unit (2008a) 'Ethiopia country profile', London: Economist Intelligence Unit.

— (2008b) 'Tanzania country profile', London: Economist Intelligence Unit.

— (2008c) 'Kenya country report October 2008', London: Economist Intelligence Unit.

— (2009) 'Kenya country report October 2009', London: Economist Intelligence Unit.

— (2011a) 'Ethiopia country report

November 2011', London: Economist Intelligence Unit.

— (2011b) 'Ghana country report November 2011', London: Economist Intelligence Unit.

— (2011c) 'Rwanda country report November 2011', London: Economist Intelligence Unit.

— (2011d) 'Tanzania country report November 2011', London: Economist Intelligence Unit.

EFFORT (2010) *EFFORT: From Where to Where?*, Unpublished report, Office of the Investment Centre, Mekelle, Ethiopia, April.

Ellis, F. (1983) 'Agricultural marketing and peasant–state transfers in Tanzania', *Journal of Peasant Studies*, 10(4): 214–42.

Englund, H. (2001) 'The culture of chameleon politics', in H. Englund (ed.), *A Democracy of Chameleons: Politics and culture in Malawi*, Uppsala: Nordic African Institute.

EPZA (2010) 'New companies receive EPZA license', www.epza.co.tz/Eight-New-Companies.html, accessed August 31, 2011.

Eshetu Chole (1994) 'Reflections on underdevelopment: problems and prospects', in A. Zegeye and S.Pausewang (eds), *Ethiopia in Change: Peasantry, nationalism, and democracy*, London: British Academic Press, pp. 95–118.

ESRF (1999) 'Quarterly economic review. Volume 2, Issue 2, April–June', Dar es Salaam: Economic and Social Research Foundation.

Evans, P. (1989) 'Predatory, developmental, and other apparatuses: a comparative political economy perspective on the Third World state', *Sociological Forum*, 4(4): 561–87.

— (1995) *Embedded Autonomy: States and industrial transformation*, Princeton, NJ: Princeton University Press.

Felix, F. (2011) 'TZ-China in Shs 4tr Mchuchuma talks. Jamii Forums. 17 January 2011', www.jamiiforums.com.

Fenkenberger, T. et al. (2003) 'Livelihood erosion through time: macro and micro factors that influenced livelihood trends in Malawi over the past 30 years', Lilongwe: CAR.

Fjelstad, O.-H. (2003) 'Fighting fiscal corruption: lessons from the Tanzania Revenue Authority', *Public Administration and Development*, 23: 165–75.

Forrest, T. (1993) *Politics and Economic Development in Nigeria*, Boulder, CO: Westview Press.

Freedom House (2012) 'Freedom in the world 2012: the Arab uprisings and their global repercussions', www.freedomhouse.org/sites/default/files/inline_images/Table%20of%20Independent%20Countries%2C%20FIW%202012%20draft.pdf.

G&N Consultants (2008) 'A survey report on the status of horticulture in Rwanda' Kigali: Rwanda Horticulture Development Agency.

Gainsborough, M. (2002) 'Beneath the veneer of reform: the politics of economic liberalisation in Vietnam', *Communist and Post-communist Studies*, (35): 353–68.

— (2003) 'Corruption and the politics of economic decentralisation in Vietnam', *Journal of Contemporary Asia*, 33(1): 69–84.

Gebre Yntiso (2009) 'Why did resettlement fail? Lessons from Metekel', in A. Pankhurst and F. Piguet (eds), *Moving People in Ethiopia: Development, displacement and the state*, Woodbridge: James Currey, pp. 119–29.

Gebreeyesus, M. and M. Lizuka (2010) 'Experimentation and coordination as industrial policy: examples from Ethiopia and Chile', *UNU-WIDER Newsletter*, September, Helsinki: UNU-WIDER.

Gebru Tareke (2009) *The Ethiopian Revolution: War in the Horn of Africa*, New Haven, CT: Yale University Press.

Gerschenkron, A. (1965) *Economic Backwardness in Historical Perspective: A book of essays*, London: Praeger.

Getu, M. (2010) 'Ethiopian floriculture and its impact on the environment', *Mizan Law Review*, 3(2): 240–71.

Ghana Investment Promotion Centre (n.d.) 'President's Special Initiatives (PSIs)', www.gipcghana.com.

Ghana National Commission for UNESCO (n.d.) 'Manufacturing: struggling to survive', www.natcomreport.com/ghana/livre/manufacturing.pdf.

Gibbon, P. (ed.) (1995) *Liberalised Development in Tanzania*, Uppsala: Nordic African Institute.

Gibbon, P., K. J. Havnevik and K. Hermele (1993) *A Blighted Harvest: The World Bank and African agriculture in the 1980s*, Oxford: James Currey.

Global Integrity Report (2007) 'Malawi: corruption timeline', report.globalintegrity.org/Malawi/2007/timeline.

Gökgür, N. (2011) 'Formulating a broad-based private sector development strategy for the Ministry of Trade and Industry, Rwanda: Inception Report', Kigali: submitted to MINICOM.

Goldsworthy, D. (1982) *Tom Mboya: The man Kenya wanted to forget*, London: Heinemann Educational.

Golooba-Mutebi, F. (2008) 'Collapse, war and reconstruction in Rwanda: an analytical narrative on state-making', Working Paper 28.2, London: Crisis States Research Centre, London School of Economics.

Gottesman, E. (2004) *Cambodia after the Khmer Rouge: Inside the politics of nation building*, Chiang Mai: Silkworm Books.

Government of Ghana Private Sector Development Strategy (2010) 'Final performance assessment and programme completion report, December 2010', Accra: Government of Ghana Private Sector Development Strategy.

Government of Malawi (2006) 'Malawi Development and Growth Strategy', Lilongwe: Government of Malawi.

Government of Rwanda (2000) 'Rwanda Vision 2020', Kigali: Ministry of Finance and Economic Planning.

— (2007) *Economic Development and Poverty Reduction Strategy, 2008–2012*, Kigali: Republic of Rwanda.

Gray, H. (2012) 'Tanzania and Vietnam: a comparative economy in political transition', PhD thesis, School of Oriental and African Studies, University of London.

Grindle, M. (2004) 'Good enough governance: poverty reduction and reform in developing countries', *Governance: An International Journal of Policy, Administration, and Institutions*, 17(4): 525–48.

Groum Abate (2011) 'Government will get 11 bln a year from sale of bonds to banks', *Capital*, 11 April.

Gyimah-Boadi, E. (2009) 'State funding of political parties in Ghana', *Critical Perspectives*, 24, Accra: Centre for Democratic Development.

Hadiz, V. R. and R. Robison (2005) 'Neo-liberal reforms and illiberal consolidations', *Journal of Development Studies*, 41(2): 220–41.

Hagmann, T. (2006) 'Ethiopian political culture strikes back: a rejoinder to J. Abbink', *African Affairs*, 105(421): 605–12.

HakiElimu and Policy Forum (2010) 'Understanding the budget process in Tanzania. A civil society guide', Dar es Salaam: HakiElimu and Policy Forum.

Hall, D. G. E. (1981) *A History of South-East Asia*, 4th edn, Basingstoke: Palgrave Macmillan.

Handley, A. (2008) *Business and the State in Africa: Economic policy making in the neo-liberal era*, Cambridge: Cambridge University Press.

Harrigan, J. (2001) *From Dictatorship to Democracy: Economic policy in Malawi, 1964–2000*, Aldershot: Ashgate.

Hart, E. and E. Gyimah-Boadi (2000) 'Business associations in Ghana's economic and political transition', *Critical Perspectives*, 3, Accra: Centre for Democratic Development.

Havnevik, K. J. (1993) *Tanzania: The limits to development from above*, Uppsala: Scandinavian Institute of African Studies.

Henley, D. (2010a) 'Three principles of successful development strategy: outreach, urgency, expediency', Paper prepared for the 3rd plenary Tracking Development Conference, Kuala Lumpur.

— (2010b) 'A rare case of rural bias in Africa? Kenyan development strategy in the Malaysian mirror', Paper presented to the 3rd plenary Tracking Development Conference, Kuala Lumpur.

Hesselbein, G. (2011) 'Patterns of resource mobilisation and the underlying elite bargain: drivers of state stability or state fragility', Working Paper no. 88, London: London School of Economics, Destin.

Heyer, J. (1981) 'Agricultural development policy in Kenya from the colonial period to 1975', in J. Heyer, P. Roberts and G. Williams (eds), *Rural Development in Tropical Africa*, Basingstoke: Macmillan, pp. 90–119.

Holloway, J. (2000) *All Poor Together*, Privately published MS.

Holm, J. D. (1988) 'Botswana: a paternalistic democracy', in L. Diamond, J. J. Linz and S. M. Lipset (eds), *Democracy in Developing Countries*, vol. 2: *Africa*, Boulder, CO: Lynne Rienner.

Hughes, C. and T. Conway (2003) 'Understanding pro-poor political change:

the policy process – Cambodia', 2nd draft, August, London: Overseas Development Institute.

Human Rights Watch (2011) 'Submission to the International Development Committee, May 2011: Working effectively in fragile and conflict-affected states – DRC, Rwanda and Burundi', London: Human Rights Watch.

Hyden, G. (1983) *No Shortcuts to Progress: African development management in perspective*, London: Heinemann.

International Monetary Fund (1998) 'Public Information Notice 88/98', December 30.

— (2003) 'Malawi – letter of intent', September 19, Lilongwe.

Iyob, R. (1995) *The Eritrean Struggle for Independence: Domination, resistance, nationalism, 1941–1993*, Cambridge: Cambridge University Press.

Jackson, R. H. and C. G. Rosberg (1982) *Personal Rule in Black Africa: Prince, autocrat, prophet, tyrant*, Berkeley: University of California Press.

Jeffries, R. (1996) 'Ghana's PNDC regime: a provisional assessment', *Africa*, 66(2): 288–99.

Jerven, M. (2010) 'The relativity of poverty and income: how reliable are African economic statistics?', *African Affairs*, 109(434): 77–96.

Johnson, C. (1982) *MITI and the Japanese Miracle: The growth of industrial policy, 1925–1975*, Stanford, CA: Stanford University Press.

Kalberg, S. (1994) *Max Weber's Comparative Historical Sociology*, Cambridge: Polity Press.

Kaluwa, B. M. et al. (1992) *The Structural Adjustment Programme in Malawi: A case for successful adjustment?*, Harare: SAPES Books.

Kamndaya, S. (2011) 'Manufactured exports rise by 84pc on high demand', *The Citizen*, June 29.

Kamukama, D. (1997) *Rwanda Conflict: Its*

roots and regional implications, 2nd edn, Kampala: Fountain Publishers.

Kelsall, T. (2002) 'Shop windows and smoke-filled rooms: governance and the re-politicisation of Tanzania', *Journal of Modern African Studies*, 40(4): 597–620.

— (2003) 'Governance, democracy and recent political struggles in Tanzania', *Commonwealth and Comparative Politics*, 41(2): 55–82.

— (2007) 'The Presidential and Parliamentary elections in the United Republic of Tanzania, October and December 2005', *Electoral Studies*, 26(2): 525–9.

— (2011) 'Rethinking the relationship between neo-patrimonialism and economic development in Africa', *IDS Bulletin*, 42(2): 76–87.

Kelsall, T. et al. (2010) 'Developmental patrimonialism? Questioning the orthodoxy on political governance and economic progress in Africa', Working Paper 9, London: Africa Power and Politics Programme.

Khan, M. (1996) 'The efficiency implications of corruption', *Journal of International Development*, 8(5): 683–96.

— (2000a) 'Rents, efficiency and growth', in M. Khan and K. S. Jomo (eds), *Rents, Rent-seeking and Economic Development: Theory and Evidence in Asia*, Cambridge: Cambridge University Press, pp. 21–69.

— (2000b) 'Rent-seeking as process', in M. Khan and K. S. Jomo (eds), *Rents, Rent-seeking and Economic Development: Theory and evidence in Asia*, Cambridge: Cambridge University Press, pp. 70–144.

— (2005) 'Markets, states and democracy: patron–client networks and the case for democracy in developing countries', *Democratization*, 12(5): 704–24.

— (2007) 'Governance, economic growth and development since the 1960s', in J. A. Ocampo, K. S. Jomo and R. Vos (eds), *Growth Divergences: Explaining differences in economic performance*, London: Zed Books/United Nations, pp. 285–323.

— (2010) 'Political settlements and the governance of growth-enhancing institutions', Draft paper, Research Paper Series on 'Growth-Enhancing Governance', London: SOAS, University of London.

— (2011a) 'Governance and growth challenges for Africa', in A. Noman et al. (eds), *Good Growth and Governance in Africa: Rethinking development strategies*, Oxford: Oxford University Press, pp. 114–39.

— (2011b) 'Governance and growth: history, ideology, and methods of proof', in A. Noman et al. (eds), *Good Growth and Governance in Africa: Rethinking development strategies*, Oxford: Oxford University Press, pp. 51–79.

Khan, M. and H. Gray (2006) 'State weakness in developing countries and strategies of institutional reform – operational implications for anti-corruption policy and a case-study of Tanzania', Report commissioned by the UK Department for International Development, London: SOAS.

Khembo, N. S. (2004) 'Political parties in Malawi: from factions to splits, coalitions and alliances', in M. Ott et al. (eds), *The Power of the Vote: Malawi's 2004 Parliamentary and presidential elections*, Zomba: Kachere.

Killick, T. (2005) 'The politics of Ghana's budgetary system', CDD/ODI Policy Brief no. 2, London and Accra: ODI/CDD.

— (2010) *Development Economics in Action: A study of economic policies in Ghana*, Abingdon: Routledge.

Kinzer, S. (2008) *A Thousand Hills: Rwanda's rebirth and the man who dreamed*, Oboken, NJ: Wiley.

Krueger, A. O. (1974) 'The political economy of the rent-seeking society', *American Economic Review*, 64(3): 291–303.

Le Billon, P. (2000) 'The political ecology of transition in Cambodia 1989–1999: war, peace, and forest exploitation', *Development and Change*, 31: 785–805.

Lefort, R. (2010) 'Powers – mengist – and peasants in rural Ethiopia: the post-2005 interlude', *Journal of Modern African Studies*, 48(3): 435–60.

Leo, C. (1984) *Land and Class in Kenya*, Toronto: University of Toronto Press.

Leonard, D. K. (1991) *African Successes: Four public managers of Kenyan rural development*, Berkeley: University of California Press.

Lewis, P. M. (2007) *Growing Apart: Oil, politics, and economic change in Indonesia and Nigeria*, Ann Arbor: University of Michigan Press.

Leys, C. (1975) *Underdevelopment in Kenya: The political economy of neo-colonialism*, Berkeley and Los Angeles: University of California Press.

— (1996) 'Rational choice or Hobson's choice? The "new political economy" as development theory', in C. Leys (ed.), *The Rise and Fall of Development Theory*, Oxford: James Currey, pp. 80–106.

Lin, J. Y. (2011a) 'Transformation without tears', *African Business*, July, pp. 13–16.

— (2011b) 'New structural economics: a framework for rethinking development', *World Bank Research Observer*, Oxford: Oxford University Press on behalf of IBRD.

Lindberg, S. I. (2009) 'Member of the Parliament of Ghana: a hybrid institution with mixed effects', Working Paper 02, London: Africa Power and Politics Programme.

MacDougall, C. (2011) 'Ghana launches industrial policy to avoid Nigerian kind of oil curse', *Africa Undisguised*, www.africaundisguised.com/newsportal/story/ghana-launches-industrial-policy-avoid-nigerian-kind-oil-curse, accessed October 4, 2011.

MacGaffey, J. (1987) *Entrepreneurs and Parasites: The struggle for indigenous capitalism in Zaire*, Cambridge: Cambridge University Press.

MacIntyre, A. (2000) 'Funny money: fiscal policy, rent-seeking and economic performance in Indonesia', in M. Khan and K. S. Jomo (eds), *Rents, Rent-seeking and Economic Development: Theory and evidence from Asia*, Cambridge: Cambridge University Press, pp. 248–73.

Maliyamkono, T. L. and M. S. D. Bagachwa (1990) *The Second Economy in Tanzania*, London: James Currey.

Markakis, J. (1974) *Ethiopia: Anatomy of a traditional polity*, Oxford: Clarendon Press.

— (1987) *National and Class Conflict in the Horn of Africa*, Cambridge: Cambridge University Press.

Mbelle, A. V. Y. (2007) 'Macroeconomic policies and poverty reduction initiatives in Tanzania: what needs to be done?', Paper presented at the ESRF Policy Dialogue Seminar, Dar es Salaam: Economic and Social Research Foundation.

McCaskie, T. M. (2008) 'The United States, Ghana and oil: global and local perspectives', *African Affairs*, 107(428): 313–32.

McKinsey Global Institute (2010) 'Lions on the move: the progress and potential of African economies', Seoul, San Francisco, London and Washington: McKinsey and Co.

Médard, J.-F. (1982) 'The underdeveloped state in Tropical Africa: political clientelism or neo-patrimonialism', in C. Clapham (ed.), *Private Patronage and Public Power: Political clientelism in the modern state*, London: Pinter, pp. 162–92.

— (1991) 'The historial trajectories of the Ivorian and Kenyan states', in J. Manor (ed.), *Rethinking Third World Politics*, Harlow: Longman, pp. 185–212.

Meles Zenawi (2011) 'States and markets: neoliberal limitations and the case for a developmental state', in A. Noman et al. (eds), *Good Growth and Governance in Africa: Rethinking development strategies*, Oxford: Oxford University Press, pp. 140–74.

Mhone, G. C. Z. (ed.) (1992) *Malawi at the Crossroads: The postcolonial political economy*, Harare: SAPES Books.

Migdal, J. S. (1988) *Strong Societies and Weak States: State–society relations and state capabilities in the Third World*, Princeton, NJ: Princeton University Press.

MINECOFIN (2011) 'Budget Speech, Financial Year 2011/12', Kigali: Ministry of Finance and Economic Planning.

MINICOM (2011) 'Rwanda National Export Strategy (NES)', Kigali: Ministry of Trade and Industry.

MINIRENA (2008) 'Mineral status of Rwanda', Kigali: Ministry of Natural Resources.

— (2009) 'A revised Rwandan mining policy: transforming Rwanda's mining industry', Kigali: Ministry of Natural Resources.

Mitchell, A. (2011) 'Africa is open for business', Speech to the London School of Business, July 11, 2011, webarchive.nationalarchives.gov. uk/+/http://www.dfid.gov.uk/news/ speeches-and-articles/2011/andrew-mitchell-on-why-trade-and-business-is-booming-in-africa/.

Mkandawire, T. (2011) 'Institutional monocropping and monotasking in Africa', in A. Noman et al. (eds), *Good Growth and Governance in Africa: Rethinking development strategies*, Oxford: Oxford University Press, pp. 80–113.

Moore, M. (1993) 'Good government?', *IDS Bulletin*, 24(1): 1–6.

Moore, M. and H. Schmitz (2008) 'Idealism, realism and the investment climate in developing countries', Working Paper 307, Brighton: Centre for the Future State, Institute of Development Studies, University of Sussex.

Mtewa, M. (1986) *Malawi: Democratic theory and public policy*, Cambridge, MA: Schenkman Books.

Mulatu Wubneh (1991) 'Ethiopia: Library of Congress country study. Chapter 3 – growth and structure of the economy', Library of Congress, lcweb2.loc. gov/frd/cs/ettoc.html#et0088.

Murangwa, Y. (2012) 'EDPRS2, EICV3 and DHS4 joint launch: key statistics highlights, 7 February 2012', Kigali: National Institute of Statistics of Rwanda.

Murray, C. (2010) 'Blog archive. The UK and corruption in Ghana', www. craigmurray.org.uk/.

Mustapha, R. (2002) 'States, predation and violence: reconceptualizing political action and political community in Africa', Paper delivered at the Council for the Development of Social Science Research in Africa (CODESRIA) 10th General Assembly on the theme 'Africa in the New Millennium', Kampala.

Mwaigomole, E. A. (2009) 'Industrial manufacturing and trade development in Tanzania', *Journal of International Cooperation Studies*, 16(3): 23–49.

Mwega, F. M. and N. S. Ndung'u (2008) 'Explaining African growth performance: the case of Kenya', in B. J. Ndulu et al. (eds), *The Political Economy of Economic Growth in Africa 1960–2000*, vol. 2: *Country Case Studies*, Oxford: Oxford University Press, pp. 325–68.

National Development Corporation

(n.d.) 'Mtwara Development Corridor. Regional development initiatives', www.metier.co.mz/b/pr_Mtwara.pdf.

Ndulu, B. J. and S. A. O'Connell (n.d.) 'Policy plus: African growth performance 1960–2000', www.swarthmore.edu/SocSci/soconne1/documents/Chap1_BNSOC.pdf.

NISR (2011) 'Gross domestic product and its structure by activity', Kigali: National Institute of Statistics of Rwanda.

Noman, A. and J. E. Stiglitz (2011) 'Strategies for African development', in A. Noman et al. (eds), *Good Growth and Governance in Africa: Rethinking development strategies*, Oxford: Oxford University Press, pp. 3–50.

Noman, A. et al. (eds) (2011) *Good Growth and Governance in Africa: Rethinking development strategies*, Oxford: Oxford University Press.

North, D. C., J. J. Wallis and B. R. Weingast (2006) 'A conceptual framework for interpreting recorded human history', Working Paper 12,795, Cambridge, MA: National Bureau of Economic Research.

North, D. C. et al. (2007) 'Limited access orders in the developing world: a new approach to the problems of development', Washington, DC: Country Relations Division, Independent Evaluation Group, World Bank.

Nugent, P. (2001) 'Winners, losers and also rans: money, moral authority and voting patterns in the Ghana 2000 election', *African Affairs*, 100(400): 405–28.

Nyerere, J. K. (1962) 'Ujamaa – the basis of African socialism', in J. K. Nyerere (ed.), *Freedom and Unity: A collection from writings and speeches 1952–62*, Dar es Salaam: Oxford University Press.

Oakland Institute (2011) *Understanding Land Investment Deals in Africa: Ethiopia Country Report*, www.oakland institute.org/sites/oaklandinstitute.org/files/OI_Ethiopa_Land_Investment_report.pdf.

Olson, M. (1993) 'Dictatorship, democracy and development', *American Political Science Review*, 87(3): 567–76.

Olukoshi, A. (2002) 'Governing the African development process: the challenge of the New Partnership for Africa's Development', Occasional paper, Copenhagen: Centre for African Studies.

— (2003) 'The elusive Prince of Denmark: structural adjustment and the crisis of governance in Africa', in P. T. Mkandawire and C. C. Soludo (eds), *African Voices on Structural Adjustment: A companion to Our Continent, Our Future*, Trenton, NJ: CODESRIA with the International Development Research Center and Africa World Press Inc., pp. 229–74.

— (2011) 'Democratic governance and accountability in Africa. In search of a workable framework', Discussion Paper 64, Uppsala: Nordic Africa Institute.

Opoku, D. K. (2010) *The Politics of Government–Business Relations in Ghana, 1982–2008*, Basingstoke: Palgrave Macmillan.

Otchere-Darko, A. (2011) '"The Deal": housing agreement between Government of Ghana and STX Korea', danquahinstitute.org/docs/TheDeal.pdf.

Overseas Development Institute (2011) 'Mapping progress: evidence for a new development outlook', London: Overseas Development Institute.

Owen, N. G. (1999) 'Economic and social change', in N. Tarling (ed.), *The Cambridge History of Southeast Asia*, vol. 4: *From World War II to the Present*, Cambridge: Cambridge University Press, pp. 139–200.

Painter, M. (2005) 'The politics of state sector reforms in Vietnam: contested agendas and uncertain trajectories', *Journal of Development Studies*, 41(2): 261–83.

Pankhurst, A. and F. Piguet (eds) (2009) *Moving People in Ethiopia: Development, displacement and the state*, Woodbridge: James Currey.

Parliamentary Select Committee (2008) 'Richmond Report', Unofficial English translation, mimeo, Dar es Salaam.

Paul, J. C. N. and C. S. Clapham (1967) *Ethiopian Constitutional Development: A sourcebook*, Addis Ababa: Faculty of Law, Haile Selassie I University.

Peterson, S. B. (2011) 'Plateaus not summits: reforming public financial management in Africa', *Public Administration and Development*, 31(3): 205–13.

Pitcher, A., M. H. Moran and M. Johnston (2009) 'Rethinking patrimonialism and neo-patrimonialism in Africa', *African Studies Review*, 52(1): 125–56.

Policy Forum (2009) 'Reducing poverty through Kilimo Kwanza: what can we learn from the East?', Media Brief 1.09, Dar es Salaam: Policy Forum.

— (2010) 'Growth in Tanzania: is it reducing poverty?', www.policyforum-tz.org/files/GrowthTanzania.pdf.

Pottier, J. (2002) *Re-imagining Rwanda: Conflict, survival and disinformation in the late twentieth century*, Cambridge: Cambridge University Press.

Pratt, C. (1972) 'The Cabinet and presidential leadership in Tanzania, 1960–66', in L. Cliffe and J. S. Saul (eds), *Socialism in Tanzania: An interdisciplinary reader*, vol. 1, Nairobi: East African Publishing House.

— (1976) *The Critical Phase in Tanzania 1945–1968: Nyerere and the emergence of a socialist strategy*, Cambridge: Cambridge University Press.

Press Corporation (2009) 'Circular to Press Corporation shareholders', 27 June, www.presscorp.com/

upload/dl/PCL_Rights_Offer_Issue/ PRESS_CORP_COMBINED.pdf.

Private Sector Federation (2011) 'Disinvestments and investor aftercare in Rwanda: assessment report', Kigali: PSF.

Prunier, G. (1999) *The Rwanda Crisis: History of a genocide*, 2nd edn, Kampala: Fountain Publishers.

— (2009) *From Genocide to Continental War: The 'Congolese' conflict and the crisis of contemporary Africa*, London: Hurst.

Pryor, F. L. (1990) *Malawi and Madagascar: The political economy of poverty, equity, and growth*, Oxford: Oxford University Press.

Radelet, S. (2010) *Emerging Africa: How 17 countries are leading the way*, Washington, DC: Center for Global Development.

Raikes, P. L. (1986) 'Eating the carrot and wielding the stick: the agricultural sector in Tanzania', in J. Boesen et al. (eds), *Tanzania: Crisis and struggle for survival*, Uppsala: Nordic Africa Institute.

Rapley, J. (1993) *Ivoirien Capitalism: African entrepreneurs in Côte d'Ivoire*, Boulder, CO: Lynne Rienner.

Rathbone, R. (1973) 'Businessmen in politics: party struggle in Ghana, 1949–57', *Journal of Development Studies*, 1: 391–401.

— (1978) 'Ghana', in J. Dunn (ed.), *West African States: Failure and promise*, Cambridge: Cambridge University Press, pp. 22–35.

RDB/RHODA (2010) 'Investment opportunities in Rwanda's horticulture sector', Kigali: Rwanda Development Board and Rwanda Horticulture Development Authority.

Reno, W. (1995) *Corruption and State Politics in Sierra Leone*, Cambridge: Cambridge University Press.

Republic of Ghana (2010) 'The Coordinated Programme of Economic and Social Development Policies, 2010–2016. An agenda for shared growth and accelerated development for a better Ghana', Accra: Republic of Ghana.

— (2011) 'Industrial Sector Support Programme (ISSP) 2011–2015', Accra: Ministry of Trade and Industry.

Reyntjens, F. (2009) *The Great African War: Congo and regional geopolitics, 1996–2006*, Cambridge: Cambridge University Press.

Riboud, M. (1987) 'The Côte d'Ivoire: 1960–1985', San Francisco, CA: Institute for Contemporary Studies.

Riddell, R. C. (1990) 'Côte d'Ivoire', in R. C. Riddell (ed.), *Manufacturing Africa*, London: James Currey, pp. 152–89.

Rimmer, D. (1992) *Staying Poor: Ghana's political economy, 1950–1990*, New York: Pergamon Press for the World Bank.

Rock, M. T. (1999) 'Reassessing the effectiveness of industrial policy in Indonesia: can the neoliberals be wrong?', *World Development*, 27(4): 691–704.

Rodrik, D. (2003) 'Growth strategies', Draft chapter for *Handbook of Economic Growth*, info.worldbank.org/etools/docs/library/110117/growth.pdf.

— (2004) 'Industrial policy for the twenty-first century', Paper prepared for UNIDO, mimeo, Cambridge, MA.

RRA (2010) 'Annual activity report for 2009/10', Kigali: Rwanda Revenue Authority.

Rwanda (2003) 'Constitution of the Republic of Rwanda', Kigali: Government of Rwanda.

Samatar, A. I. (1999) *An African Miracle: State and class leadership and colonial legacy in Botswana development*, Portsmouth, NH: Heinemann.

Sandbrook, R. (1985) *The Politics of Africa's Economic Stagnation*, Cambridge: Cambridge University Press.

Sandbrook, R. and J. Oelbaum (1999) 'Reforming the political kingdom: governance and development in Ghana's Fourth Republic', *Critical Perspectives*, Accra: Centre for Democracy and Development.

Schaefer, C. (2011) 'Ethiopia's transformation: authoritarianism and economic development in *Rewriting the Rulebook: The New Politics of African Development*', *World Politics Review*, Feature Report, July, pp. 14–20.

Schatzberg, M. (1988) *The Dialectics of Oppression in Zaire*, Bloomington: Indiana University Press.

— (2002) *Political Legitimacy in Middle Africa: Father, family, food*, Bloomington: Indiana University Press.

Sen, K. and D. W. te Velde (2011) 'State–business relations, investment climate reform, and economic growth in sub-Saharan Africa', in A. Noman et al. (eds), *Good Growth and Governance in Africa: Rethinking development strategies*, Oxford: Oxford University Press, pp. 303–22.

Shao, J. (1986) 'The villagisation programme and the disruption of the ecological balance in Tanzania', *Canadian Journal of African Studies*, 20(2): 219–39.

Sharpley, J. and S. Lewis (1990) 'Kenya', in R. C. Riddell (ed.), *Manufacturing Africa: Performance and prospects in seven African countries*, London: James Currey, pp. 206–41.

Short, P. (1974) *Banda*, London: Routledge and Kegan Paul.

Sogge, D. (2009) 'Angola: "failed" yet "successful"', FRIDE Working Paper 81, Madrid: Fundación para Las Relaciones Internacionales y el Diálogo Exterior.

Southall, R. (2009) 'Scrambling for Africa? Continuities and discontinuities with formal imperialism', in R. Southall and H. Melber (eds), *A New Scramble for Africa? Imperial-*

ism, investment and development, Scottsville: University of KwaZulu-Natal Press, pp. 1–34.

Spear, T. (1997) *Mountain Farmers: Moral economies of land and agricultural development in Arusha and Meru*, Oxford: James Currey.

Spencer, D. (2008) 'Is the medium size the next growth phase in the mineral sector in Tanzania?', Discussion Paper draft 4, mimeo, Dar es Salaam.

Stein, H. (2011) 'Africa, industrial policy, and export processing zones: lessons from Asia', in A. Noman et al. (eds), *Good Growth and Governance in Africa: Rethinking development strategies*, Oxford: Oxford University Press, pp. 322–44.

Sterkenburg, J. J. and B. Thoden van Velzen (1973) 'The party supreme', in L. Cliffe and J. S. Saul (eds), *Socialism in Tanzania: An interdisciplinary reader*, vol. 1, Dar es Salaam: East African Publishing House.

Straus, S. and L. Waldorf (eds) (2011) *Remaking Rwanda: State building and human rights after mass violence*, Madison: University of Wisconsin Press.

Svendsen, K. E. (1986) 'The creation of macro-economic imbalances and a structural crisis', in J. Boesen, K. Havnevik and R. Odgaard (eds), *Tanzania – crisis and struggle for survival*, Uppsala: Nordic Africa Institute.

Swainson, N. (1987) 'Indigenous capitalism in postcolonial Kenya', in P. M. Lubeck (ed.), *The African Bourgeoisie: Capitalist development in Kenya, Nigeria and the Côte d'Ivoire*, Boulder, CO: Lynne Rienner, pp. 137–66.

Tamarkin, M. (1978) 'The roots of political stability in Kenya', *African Affairs*, 77(308): 297–320.

Tangri, R. (1999) *The Politics of Patronage in Africa: Parastatals, privatization and private enterprise*, Trenton, NJ: Africa World Press.

Tanzania Horticulture Association (2009) 'Narrative report year 2008–9', Arusha: TAHA.

Tarimo, J. (2008) 'Karamagi in hot soup over TICTS contract approval claims', *Guardian* (Dar es Salaam), 26 April.

Taylor, R. H. (2009) *The State in Myanmar*, London: Hurst.

Tekeste Nagash (1997) *Eritrea and Ethiopa: The federal experience*, Uppsala: Nordic Africa Institute.

Tettehfio, L. A. (2009) 'The role of the indigenous Ghanaian textile industry in relation to the President's Special Initiative (PSI) on textiles and garments', Kwame Nkrumah University of Science and Technology.

Therkilsden, O. (2005) 'Understanding public management through neopatrimonialism: a paradigm for all seasons?', in U. Engel and G. Rye Olsen (eds), *The African Exception*, Aldershot: Ashgate, pp. 53–68.

— (2011) 'Policy making and implementation in agriculture: Tanzania's push for irrigated rice', Working Paper 2011: 26, Copenhagen: Danish Institute for International Studies.

Thomas, S. (1975) 'Economic development in Malawi since Independence', *Journal of Southern African Studies*, 2(1): 30–51.

Throup, D. and C. Hornsby (1998) *Multiparty Politics in Kenya*, Oxford: James Currey.

Tripp, A. M. (1997) *Changing the Rules: The politics of liberalisation and the informal economy in Tanzania*, Berkeley and London: University of California Press.

Tronvoll, K. (2008) 'Briefing: the 2008 Ethiopian local elections: the return of electoral authoritarianism', *African Affairs*, 108(430): 111–20.

Tuinder, B. A. den (1978) *Côte d'Ivoire: The challenge of success*, Baltimore, MD, and London: Johns Hopkins University Press for the World Bank.

Un, K. (2005) 'Patronage politics and hybrid democracy: political change in Cambodia, 1993–2003', *Asian Perspective*, 29(2): 203–30.

— (2010) 'Rural road infrastructures and investment: lessons from Uganda and Cambodia', Paper presented to the Tracking Development 3rd Plenary Conference, Kuala Lumpur.

UN Panel (2002) Final Report of the Panel of Experts on the Illegal Exploitation of Natural Resources and Other Forms of Wealth of the Democratic Republic of the Congo, Online text, United Nations Security Council.

UNDP (2012) International Human Development Indicators, hdr.undp.org/en/statistics/, accessed March 16, 2012.

UNIDO (n.d.) 'Tanzania: country brief', www.unido.org/index.php?id=5028.

United Nations (2011) 'MDG Monitor. Tracking the Millennium Development Goals. Rwanda', www.mdgmonitor.org/country_progress.cfm?c=RWA&cd=646., accessed December 7, 2011.

United Nations Economic Commission for Africa (2011) 'Governing development in Africa: the role of the state in economic transformation', Addis Ababa: United Nations Economic Commission for Africa.

United Republic of Tanzania (2005) 'National Strategy for Growth and Reduction of Poverty', Dar es Salaam: Vice President's Office.

Uvin, P. (1998) *Aiding Violence: The development enterprise in Rwanda*, West Hartford, CT: Kumarian Press.

Vail, L. (1976) 'The making of an imperial slum: Nyasaland and its railways, 1895–1935', *Journal of African History*, 16(1): 89–112.

— (1977) 'Railway development and colonial underdevelopment: the Nyasaland case', in R. Palmer and N. Parsons (eds), *The Roots of Rural Poverty in Central and Southern Africa*, London: Heinemann.

Van Arkadie, B. and D. D. Dinh (2004) 'Economic reform in Tanzania and Vietnam: a comparative commentary', Working Paper Number 706, William Davidson Institute at the University of Michigan Business School.

Van de Walle, N. (2001) *African Economies and the Politics of Permanent Crisis*, Cambridge: Cambridge University Press.

— (2007) 'Meet the new boss, same as the old boss? The evolution of political clientelism in Africa', in H. Kitschelt and S. I. Wilkinson (eds), *Patrons, Clients, and Policies: Patterns of democratic accountability and political competition*, Cambridge: Cambridge University Press, pp. 50–67.

Van Dijk, M. and A. Szirmai (2006) 'Industrial policy and technology diffusion: evidence from paper making machinery in Indonesia', *World Development*, 34(12): 2137–52.

Van Donge, J. K. (2002) 'The fate of an African "chaebol": Malawi's Press Corporation after democratization', *Journal of Modern African Studies*, 40(4): 651–81.

Van Donge, J. K., D. Henley and P. M. Lewis (2012) 'Tracking development in Southeast Asia and sub-Saharan Africa: the primacy of policy', *Development Policy Review*, 30(s1): s5–s24.

Various Authors (2007) 'Ethiopia', in I. Frame (ed.), *Africa South of the Sahara*, 36th edn, London and New York: Routledge.

— (2011a) 'Rwanda 2011', African Development Bank, Organisation for Economic Co-operation and Development, United Nations Development Programme, United Nations Economic Commission for Africa.

— (2011b) 'Tanzania 2011', African Development Bank, Organisation for Economic Co-operation and Development, United Nations Development Programme, United Nations Economic Commission for Africa.

— (2011c) 'Ghana 2011', African Development Bank, Organisation for Economic Co-operation and Development, United Nations Development Programme, United Nations Economic Commission for Africa.

— (2011d) 'African economic outlook 2011', African Development Bank, Organisation for Economic Co-operation and Development, United Nations Development Programme, United Nations Economic Commission for Africa.

— (2011e) 'Ethiopia 2011', African Development Bank, Organisation for Economic Co-operation and Development, United Nations Development Programme, United Nations Economic Commission for Africa.

Vaughan, S. (2006) 'Responses to ethnic federalism in Ethiopia's Southern region', in D. Turton (ed.), *Ethnic Federalism: The Ethiopian experience in comparative perspective*, Oxford: James Currey, pp. 181–207.

— (2011) 'Ethnic and civic nationalist narratives in Ethiopia', in T. Harrison and S. Drakulik (eds), *Against Orthodoxy: Studies in nationalism*, Vancouver: University of British Columbia Press, pp. 154–82.

Vaughan, S. and M. Gebremichael (2011) 'Rethinking business and politics in Ethiopia: the role of EFFORT, the Endowment Fund for the Rehabilitation of Tigray', Research Report 02, London: Africa Power and Politics Programme.

Vaughan, S. and K. Tronvoll (2003) 'The culture of power in contemporary Ethiopian life', Sida Studies no. 10, Stockholm: Sida.

Wade, R. (1990) *Governing the Market: Economic theory and the role of government in East Asian industrialization*, Princeton, NJ, and Oxford: Princeton University Press.

Weber, M. (1947) *The Theory of Social and Economic Organization*, trans. A. R. Henderson and T. Parsons, London: William Hodge and Co.

Whitfield, L. (2009) '"Change for a better Ghana": party competition, institutionalization and alternation in Ghana's 2008 elections', *African Affairs*, 108(433): 621–42.

— (2010) 'Developing technological capabilities in agro-industry: Ghana's experience with fresh pineapple exports in comparative perspective', Working Paper 2010: 28, Copenhagen: Danish Institute for International Studies.

— (2011a) 'How countries become rich and reduce poverty: a review of heterodox explanations of economic development', Working Paper 2011: 13, Copenhagen: Danish Institute for International Studies.

— (2011b) 'Competitive clientelism, easy financing and weak capitalists: the contemporary political settlement in Ghana', Working Paper 2011: 27, Copenhagen: Danish Institute for International Studies.

— (2011c) 'Growth with transformation: economic impacts of Ghana's political settlement', Working Paper 2011: 28, Copenhagen: Danish Institute for International Studies.

Whitfield, L. and O. Therkilsden (2011) 'What drives states to support the development of productive sectors? Strategies ruling elites pursue for political survival and their policy implications', Working Paper 2011: 15, Copenhagen: Danish Institute for International Studies.

Widner, J. A. (1992) *The Rise of a Party-State in Kenya: From 'Harambee!' to 'Nyayo!'*, Berkeley: University of California Press.

Wiggins, S. and H. Leturque (2011) 'Ghana's sustained agricultural growth: putting underused resources to work', London: Overseas Development Institute.

Williams, D. and T. Young (1994) 'Governance, the World Bank, and liberal theory', *Political Studies*, XLII: 84–100.

Williams, D. T. (1978) *Malawi: The politics of despair*, Ithaca, NY: Cornell University Press.

Williams, Gareth et al. (2009) 'Politics and growth', *Development Policy Review*, 27(1): 3–29.

Williams, Gavin (1994) 'Why structural adjustment is necessary and why it doesn't work', *Review of African Political Economy*, 60: 214–25.

Wolde-Selassie Abbute (2009) 'Social impact of resettlement in the Beles Valley', in A. Pankhurst and F. Piguet (eds), *Moving People in Ethiopia: Development, displacement and the state*, Woodbridge: James Currey, pp. 130–7.

World Bank (1981) 'Accelerated development in sub-Saharan Africa: an agenda for action', Washington, DC: World Bank.

— (1992) 'Governance and development', Washington, DC: World Bank.

— (2004) *World Development Report 2005: A better investment climate for everyone*, Washington, DC, and New York: World Bank and Oxford University Press.

— (2005) 'Tanzania: diagnostic trade integration study, Volume 1', Washington, DC: World Bank Africa Region.

— (2009a) *World Development Report 2010: Development and climate change*, Washington, DC: World Bank.

— (2009b) 'Toward the competitive frontier: strategies for improving Ethiopia's investment climate', Report 48472-ET, Washington, DC: World Bank.

— (2011a) 'Africa's future: and the World Bank's support to it', Washington, DC: World Bank.

— (2011b) 'Africa's pulse: an analysis of the issues shaping Africa's economic future', vol. 3, Washington, DC: World Bank.

World Bank and International Finance Corporation (2010) 'Doing Business 2011: making a difference for entrepreneurs', Washington, DC: World Bank and International Finance Corporation.

— (2011) 'Doing Business 2012: doing business in a more transparent world', Washington, DC: World Bank and International Finance Corporation.

Wrong, M. (2009) *It's Our Turn to Eat: The story of a Kenyan whistleblower*, London: Fourth Estate.

Zewde, B. (2009) 'The history of the red terror', in K. Tronvoll, C. Schaefer and Girmachew Alemu Aneme (eds), *The Ethiopian Red Terror Trials*, Woodbridge: James Currey, pp. 17–32.

Zolberg, A. (1966) *Creating Political Order: The party states of West Africa*, Chicago, IL: Chicago University Press.

INDEX